Suppose:

The entire population of the world were sterilized by bad planning.

A man were transformed into a dinosaur.

You were dosed with nerve gas.

You were fifteen and decided to sell your brain to the fat gringo.

Imagine:

If you wanted to communicate, the only sane thing to do was lie.

Madame kept killing her and otherwise punishing her.

All right, the intelligent cats got rid of the rats. Now think about intelligent cats.

Time bubbles kept forming. Bringing all sorts of things. All sorts.

Dream:

You're a simple backwoods priest on Mars . . . and then they promote you, big-time.

She grasps his shoulders and lifts until he sits up. "The resurrection will leave you weak and dizzy for a few moments," she says.

He is a wounded soldier. She is a cloned little girl. They form an unbreakable bond.

The strange, tattered woman moves north constantly, searching for those who have done great wrong.

These . . . and more . . . are the wonders in this volume.

Enjoy!

What has been said about the
L. RON HUBBARD
PRESENTS
WRITERS OF THE FUTURE
ANTHOLOGIES

"This has become a major tributary to the new blood in fantastic fiction."

GREGORY BENFORD

"From cutting-edge high tech to evocative fantasy, this book's got it all—it's lots of fun and I love the chance to see what tomorrow's stars are doing today."

TIM POWERS

"I recommend the Writers of the Future Contest at every writers' workshop I participate in."

FREDERIK POHL

". . . an exceedingly solid collection, including SF, fantasy and horror . . ."

CHICAGO SUN TIMES

"A first-rate collection of stories and illustrations."

BOOKLIST

"It is rare to find this consistency of excellence in any series of science fiction and fantasy stories. The well-deserved reputation of L. Ron Hubbard's Writers of the Future has proven itself once again."

STEPHEN V. WHALEY
PROFESSOR ENGLISH & FOREIGN LANGUAGES
CALIFORNIA POLYTECHNICAL UNIVERSITY, POMONA

SPECIAL OFFER FOR SCHOOLS AND WRITING GROUPS

The eighteen prize-winning stories in this volume, all of them selected by a panel of top professionals in the field of speculative fiction, exemplify the standards that a new writer must meet if he expects to see his work published and achieve professional success.

These stories, augmented by "how to write" articles by some of the top writers of science fiction, fantasy and horror, make this anthology virtually a textbook for use in the classroom and an invaluable resource for students, teachers and workshop instructors in the field of writing.

The materials contained in this and previous volumes have been used with outstanding results in writing courses and workshops held on college and university campuses throughout the United States— from Harvard, Duke and Rutgers to George Washington, Brigham Young and Pepperdine.

To assist and encourage creative writing programs, the **L. Ron Hubbard Presents Writers of the Future** anthologies are available at special quantity discounts when purchased in bulk by schools, universities, workshops and other related groups.

For more information, write

Specialty Sales Department
Bridge Publications, Inc.
4751 Fountain Avenue
Los Angeles, CA 90029
or call toll-free (800) 722-1733
Internet address: www.bridgepub.com
E-mail address: info@bridgepub.com

L. RON HUBBARD

PRESENTS

WRITERS

OF THE

FUTURE

VOLUME
XVII

L. RON HUBBARD

PRESENTS

WRITERS

OF THE

FUTURE

VOLUME XVII

The Year's 18 Best Tales from the
Writers of the Future®
International Writers' Program
Illustrated by the Winners in the
Illustrators of the Future®
International Illustrators' Program

With Essays on Writing and Illustration by
L. Ron Hubbard • Roger Zelazny •
Sergey Poyarkov

Edited by Algis Budrys

Bridge Publications, Inc.

Boos and Taboos by L. Ron Hubbard: © 1992 L. Ron Hubbard Library
Black Box: © 2001 Janet Barron
A Familiar Solution: © 2001 Marguerite Devers Green
The Plague: © 2001 A. C. Bray
El Presidente Munsie: © 2001 Tony Daley
Time out of Mind: © 2001 Everett S. Jacobs
Brother Jubal in the Womb of Silence: © 2001 Tim Myers
The Sharp End: © 2001 Kelly David McCullough
The Writer's Life and Uniqueness: © 1985 Roger Zelazny
Lucretia's Nose: © 2001 Philip Lees
Dreams and Bones: © 2001 Eric M. Witchey
Marketplace of Souls: © 2001 David Lowe
Interrupt Vector: © 2001 Robert B. Schofield
Getting "Lucky": © 2001 Sergey Poyarkov
Ten Gallons a Whore: © 2001 Anna D. Allen
Magpie: © 2001 Meredith Simmons
God Loves the Infantry: © 2001 Greg Siewert
Hello and Goodbye: © 2001 Michele Letica
T.E.A. and Koumiss: © 2001 Steven C. Raine
An Idiot Rode to Majra: © 2001 J. Simon
Life Eternal: © 2001 Bob Johnston

Illustration on page   9 © 2001 Barry Cote
Illustration on page   28 © 2001 Dwayne Harris
Illustration on page   39 © 2001 Lee White
Illustration on page   71 © 2001 Lee White
Illustration on page 100 © 2001 Andy B. Clarkson
Illustration on page 127 © 2001 Carlo Arellano
Illustration on page 153 © 2001 Dwayne Harris
Illustration on page 184 © 2001 Amanda Anderson Gannon
Illustration on page 196 © 2001 Yanko Yankov
Illustration on page 210 © 2001 Ane M. Galego
Illustration on page 223 © 2001 Andy B. Clarkson
Illustration on page 247 © 2001 Dwayne Harris
Illustration on page 273 © 2001 Amanda Anderson Gannon
Illustration on page 297 © 2001 Andy Justiniano
Illustration on page 348 © 2001 Amanda Anderson Gannon
Illustration on page 370 © 2001 Andy B. Clarkson
Illustration on page 399 © 2001 Dwayne Harris
Illustration on page 422 © 2001 Dwayne Harris

Cover Artwork: *Jupiter Station* © 1984 Frank Kelly Freas

ISBN 1-57318-222-2

Library of Congress Catalog Card Number: 84-73270
First Edition Paperback 10 9 8 7 6 5 4 3 2 1
Printed in the United States of America

CONTENTS

INTRODUCTION

Written by
Algis Budrys

Welcome to the latest in the *L. Ron Hubbard Presents Writers of the Future* series of anthologies. Publishing the stories by winning new writers in the past year, illustrated by the outstanding new talents in their field, this book, year after year, has brought you the very best new names, many of which will go on to establish themselves as important contributors to the SF genre.

Seventeen years have now gone by since we began this series of anthologies. In that time, some small things have changed and important things have not. Basically, there have been slight tweaks of the rules, mainly to clarify some points. But the contests have clung to their original conceptions: We accept entries from anyone, provided they have not been published more than three times with a short story or once with a novelette, or more than three black-and-white illustrations or more than one color-process painting. We do not, then or at any other time, charge entry fees or take any money from the entrants. Everything is funded through the L. Ron Hubbard Library, which is glad to do so.

Once accepted, the stories and illustrations are turned over to the Contest Administrator, all traces of the author are removed from the entry, and the anonymized entries are turned over to the Coordinating Judges, who begin the judging. Then the best batch of stories is sent to the celebrity judges, who pick the winners. First place earns $1,000 in the writers' contest, $750 for second, and $500 for third. The illustrators' contest wins $500 for all three places.

This process goes on every three months, so that in the writers' contest we have four first-place winners at the end of the year (which comes on September 30). Before the annual awards event, the four winners are judged again and a single winner is picked. Much the same happens in the illustrators' contest. The writer and the illustrator of the best story and illustration of the year are each given $4,000, as well as a truly impressive trophy. All writers and illustrators have already spent several days in Hollywood, staying in an elegant local hotel, studying the workshops intended to put additional polish on their talents, attending the rooftop dinner. Now, with the main awards presented, we have the unveiling of the latest book, and then a party like no other.

It's a truly magnificent event, and in the process life-long friendships are formed. Equally important, the writers and illustrators will meet many of the judges, as well as other industry opinion leaders.

This is precisely as L. Ron Hubbard envisioned in the early 1980s. All we have done since then is to see to it that the vision not only does not fade but flourishes. He was a remarkable individual, and although he passed from this life in 1986, he continues, in many senses of the word, to enrich the lives of artists—by which he meant writers as well as illustrators—all over the planet.

The L. Ron Hubbard Library is a strong force in SF as well as elsewhere, and the Writers of the Future program is one of its best examples. It gives beginning artists a leg up. It does not pretend to have created them—the raw talent is already there. What it does do is shortcut the years of trial and error required to make a professional. It passes on the hard-won essentials that L. Ron Hubbard acquired over his apprenticeship, and it thus saves any new artist a noteworthy amount of grief and frustration. We have heard from many of our writers and illustrators over the years that this is precisely what happens. They have sold well over two hundred novels and countless shorter works, and done a great many illustrations since winning the contests. The program is doing what it was intended to do.

You need convincing? Read the stories and look at the illustrations contained here. It's the latest batch, and in the years to come, you will recognize many of the names many times over.

BLACK BOX

Written by
Janet Barron

Illustrated by
Barry Cote

About the Author

Janet Barron works in London as a free
lance biomedical writer and editor. She ha
an honors degree in biochemistry and a doctorate in molecula
biology and, as Janet Stephenson, has a publication record i
hematological oncology. She has also worked as the managin
editor of Odyssey and as a contributing editor to Matrix, th
British Science Fiction Association's news publication, and t
other BSFA publications. Her news items can be found in Th
Lancet Oncology. She is a graduate of Clarion.

About the Illustrator

Barry Cote was born in Regina, Saskatchewan, in 1954 and has been painting for approximately thirty years. Barry's recent focus has been on large indoor and outdoor murals, and fine art paintings. His work hangs in the collections of many well-known Canadians. He recently moved to the Slocan Valley from Vancouver Island. He paints full time and gives a good deal of attention to his two-year-old daughter.

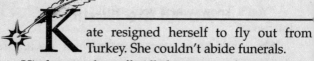**K**ate resigned herself to fly out from Turkey. She couldn't abide funerals.

Hiroku saw her off. All the way to the airport, he smiled in discomfort, but she chose to ignore it and retired behind her sunglasses. Heat baked the tarmac outside the car, sun glared from chrome and glass. She imagined fresh English coastal mist soft on her cheeks, and shut her eyes on an urgent need to be at Seacliffs now.

At Departures, Hiroku stopped short.

"I can cancel meeting Ozbek," he said. Unspoken, behind his eyes, lay the thought that she devalued her mother's death by going alone.

She shook her head like a dog shedding water, shedding anger that surfaced at the image of Hiroku, solemn in the churchyard. She only wanted to be alone. Couldn't he just leave it?

"Don't be soft," she told him. "We need the business." He took a step forward and she bridled. There were whole months when it quite escaped her why she'd married. "No, really, Hiro. After the funeral, all I have to do is check a few things, sign a few forms." Her flight was being called. "I don't even have to see Seacliffs if I don't feel like it. I could stay at the Red Lion."

Hiroku caught her arm.

"You should see it," he said. "Stay as long as you have to."

She shrugged.

"But, Kate? You will—" He changed whatever he had started to say. "Bring me something back."

She stared at him. Final call. What was he on about now?

"Something from the house? Like what?"

"You'll know when you see it." He stared at her. Intense.

She would know when she saw it.

Her hand clenched on her passport.

•••

At the graveside, as the vicar ended the service, cool air begrudgingly discharged a drizzle as oily as burning rubber.

Kate's eyes stung. No one else seemed to notice as they clumped, caps pulled down and head-scarves limp, into huddles of commiseration. Only two slender— Mum would have called them scrawny and fed them dumplings—teenage girls kept themselves aloof. Kate's skin felt clogged, and despite, or maybe because of, the glances of sympathy, she felt exposed and excluded. Now that she had no choice, she wished, perversely, that Hiroku were here. Failing that, she wished she had checked into the Lion and taken a shower, instead of dumping her bags at the house. The heavy key ring banged in her pocket, a nagging reminder of Hiroku's request. If that were a test, she had no conviction she would pass it.

Her craving to be here was now a desperate need to be gone, even back to the parching sun.

"Nothing changes here, y'know." Two light voices spoke in perfect synchrony, in a twang out of place among the soft fenland burrs. "But your Mum liked that, di'n't she?" The only way she could tell two people had spoken was that they were speaking from about ten feet apart. The two girls—identical twins—drifting up over tussocks of ryegrass, were a little older than she had first thought; maybe nineteen or twenty. They faced her, one to each side.

Kate half-smiled an inquiry. Two pairs of blue eyes under level brows stared solemnly back. They had the latest samurai hairstyle, their shaven fore-skulls glistening in the wet. There were probably Q implants under the shadowed skin.

"I'm Lyndie—"

"And I'm Lyndie." The identity of timbre, tone and split-second timing was nothing short of eerie. Kate blinked; definitely Q-kids. Why *did* kids want to do such things to themselves?

"Hey,

"there's

"our

"Mum," they told her, and Kate, who refused to cry at funerals, turned to see the District Nurse with an enormous hanky at her faded eyes. Mum had certainly sung Nurse Thingummy's praises, and Kate braced herself for effusive condolence. But, to her relief, she found the crowd was breaking up, taking leave. Mum seemed to have been well liked. It couldn't have been easy, making a new life for herself here after Dad had died, but Mum was formidably active well into her seventies.

She turned back to the Lyndies, but they, too, had gone. And she should make a move. The house was waiting.

Illustrated by Barry Cote

•••

Seacliffs was one of the rambling early Victorian piles so common on the Suffolk coastline.

Mum had picked it up dirt-cheap a dozen years back since nobody, even then, needed over a dozen rooms of decaying brick, exposed to the elements, miles from anywhere. Stubborn as ever, she had resisted Kate's offer to buy her a bungalow somewhere sensible. "This'll see me out," she had said, flinging out a well-fleshed arm to encompass the horizon. "And just look!"

A hundred years of erosion of the soft eastern cliffs had left the house perched in isolation, with heart-stopping views. The sea had been held safely at bay for sixty years now, but the ravages of wind and spray still scoured wood and crumbled mortar. Kate doubted the house would find a buyer. Still, Mum had loved it here.

A squall tossed the delicate leaves of a salt-stunted Japanese maple and whipped her hair about her ears as she got out of the hired car. Over the bay below, seagulls shrieked echoing cries. The sea was a foam-capped gray blue.

Inside the house, the kitchen range was laid ready to fire. As the first flames licked around the outside of news-paper twists, Kate listened to the house creak and shiver. Then, hands in coat pockets, she wandered into the front room where a bed, pushed against the big bureau, was made up with fresh sheets of candy-striped cotton. She set a match to the fire laid in the grate. For a year or so, Mum had taken to using only this floor. Then at the end she had died in a hospital. Kate wondered when anyone had last investigated the other stories or the attic.

She was going to make a start checking Mum's paperwork. But traveling and the draining, dulled emotion of the funeral caught up with her, and she lay down on the bedcovers, thinking, *five minutes and I'll take off my coat. Ten and I'll make a cup of tea. . . .*

Aching gull calls echoed against bare floorboards and, as if summoned, Kate's bare feet found grit underfoot. The endless corridor was drafty—cold, she was cold, so cold—and the hem of the nightdress slapping her calves was dark and wringing wet. Salt and iron tainted the air.

Then the shrieks were a baby's cries—of course they were, how could she have forgotten?—and as she paced, they wailed louder. But each time she pushed the doors open—so many doors—the cries cut off. She lifted dusty cushions, moved vases, opened drawers. Nothing. Then the cries would start again, distant, behind a wall, down a bend, up yet another, yet another, yet another flight of stairs.

She was in the attic. Clock, ticked. She listened. Clock, tocked. Nothing else.

Then, from a Moses basket in the corner under the eaves, muffled, joyous, a baby gurgled.

She took a step forward.

How could she have forgotten?

She was so happy; the room seemed flooded with golden light.

The gurgle repeated. Precisely. The self-same recorded gurgle.

Her happiness turned to rage and she dashed aside the ancient pram in her way. She threw down a dusty oil from its easel. She stamped on porcelain. She cracked pots. She reached the sound and tore aside old lace. There sat a box. And inside . . .

A pearly round face, almost featureless, stared blindly up at her. Plump, stylized baby limbs sat in a nest of red silk.

A Japanese Gosho doll.

The shock woke her before she screamed.

Her hands were still shaking as the kettle huffed its way to the boil. She thought of Goshos, of tekno-karakun. Of Okimi. It was like a scar cracking open.

Damn all tekno-karakun to hell and back. That thing was lurking in this house somewhere.

The doorbell rang.

She pursed her lips and stomped to the front door, flinging it wide. "Yes?"

The Lyndies stood there, arms full of Tupperware.

"Hiya,

"Kate,

"gedda

"loada

"this," they said, breezy, and were in the house, heading into the kitchen, as Kate drew breath to say, "That's very kind but I really don't . . ."

Kate followed them in and sat down at the oak table, still shaken. Remembering, despite herself. She had been fascinated by the tradition of making Gosho dolls to symbolize and celebrate the birth of a boy. When Okimi was born, she had immediately thought of buying one for Mum. She and Hiroku had been married and in Japan for three rosy, affluent years by then, and thought they would settle. Eight years, too many continents and several failed businesses ago. For five of those years, by hard-won training, she had not thought of Okimi, alive or dead.

The Lyndies were unpacking quiches and casseroles.

"The WI

"and our Mum

"sent these," they said.

Bemused, she offered them tea.

It wasn't just that they looked the same and dressed the same. Even identical twins who are trying to match each other can't manage it a hundred percent or all of the time. Yet here all the subtle variations were missing. These Lyndies were truly identical, completely in phase with each other.

"Why did you do it?" she asked, and blushed.

The twins took it in good part. Although they looked fleetingly disappointed as though she should have first asked what and how rather than why, they rallied with:

"Your

"mum

"didn't

"pull

"punches,

"neither." There was a pause for them to glance and smile at each other as though to a mirror.

Completing each other's sentences one word at a time was some parlor trick, but not so different from ordinary twins. Or certain couples, come to that. What was uncanny was how they matched expression for expression as they did it. Already Kate was treating the split into two bodies as irrelevant, hearing "Your Mum didn't pull punches, neither," said Lyndie. Two minds with just a single . . .

"Can you turn it off?" she asked.

Two heads shook, pityingly. "Why would we wunna?" asked Lyndie. "Half the poor sods in the world go looking for someone to unnerstand, to unnerstand them, and they got a snowball's chance in hell. We goddit in one." They sipped tea. Two throats swallowed. "You know about Q'plants, then? You gunna get one? You're a bit old, y'know. Who's your other half?"

"No one," said Kate, hastily. "Quantum identity doesn't appeal." She might have done it once, in another life. It was only the tiniest exchange of tissue from the temporal lobe.

They'd said that at birth was the best time to take the sample. In Tokyo . . . She could feel she'd gone white. The Lyndies looked gratified. They must have run out of rural biddies to shock.

"It wouldn't suit everyone," they admitted smugly, "but we like it. We're gunna find two other Q-twins to marry. If we wunna marry."

"But you still think separately?"

"We did at first. We got Q'd for our fourteenth, after Mum *made* us move from Balham," said the Lyndies, pouting. Kate got her navel pierced at that age. Mum hadn't been what you'd call keen. "It's like, after a while feeling the same, you think the same, innit?" They looked perfectly complacent and painfully young. "We were joint donors. She gave me hers," they told her, "and she gave me hers."

"What happens if . . ." But Kate had already remembered; the twins could be apart all they wanted and it wouldn't register. Once tissue was synchronized at the quantum level, when you split it, one remained identical to the other, no matter what distance separated them. From Tokyo to Seacliffs, for instance. She felt dizzy. Her mouth ran ahead of her brain. ". . . if one of you dies?"

The Lyndies plainly thought this was in rotten taste, but were prepared to humor her on the day of a funeral.

First a shrug that said, who, me, die?

"We'd miss each other," said Lyndie. "Like, anyone would."

"But it's not like—," said Lyndie, "not the end of the world."

With one accord, they exchanged a glance so casual it was more intimate than a caress, and got up to go.

• • •

The house pressed in on Kate after their rapid footsteps had crunched away down the drive. Her world, the world of zest and juice and possibilities, had ended when she found Okimi cold in his cot. She had carried on. She had never looked back. That was then and this is now. Two cliffs separated by a dry riverbed.

Kate hadn't bought an ordinary Gosho doll for her mum. She had done something worse: found the best present possible for a granny who couldn't get to see her grandchild. Nothing but the best for the granny of the best baby on the globe. She found her jaw was clenched to dam back tears. Shit. No wonder she had spent so much effort in forgetting.

As far as Kate knew, Mum had never activated her present. The dire news had arrived before the precious package that had taken tekno-karakun.co three months to customize. That package contained the closest a dozen merged technologies could get to an interacting facsimile of a real infant: neural net meshed with Q-implant of tissue from Okimi's neonate cortex.

Mum never threw anything away.

Bring me something back.

Like the tekno-karakun Gosho boybaby known as "Q-Okimi"?

• • •

Three weeks later, Kate had systematically searched the entire house except for the room where she slept. The house clearance firm was on hold. They could take stuff away once she'd finished the boxing and bagging herself. It had to be here somewhere.

Sometimes, some bit of junk would raise the ghost of a good memory, her carefree childhood or the early years with Hiroku. These she wouldn't pack up, but would hastily stick them under the bed and not look at them. From the moment she woke until each evening when the Lyndies turned up—usually bringing far too much food—she worked like an automaton, rapid, thorough, blank. Work gave the shape to her day. Best to keep busy. She rather thought, when she allowed herself to think, that until the college year started again, she was the Lyndies' holiday project.

The house clearance, which had started as her own project, swelled to push out her waking thoughts.

It *had* to be here somewhere.

In her dreams, she prowled cold corridors while a baby shrieked like a soul in hell. Unless she woke first, she would eventually find a box in the attic. She would tug loose the big blue ribbon, pull aside the lid, and there nestling in red silk . . .

At first, the nacreous moon-face of a Gosho. Under that clamshell glaze was nothing but solid wood. The idiot smile was paint, the pinpoint eyes only lacquer. She would wake as she raised it to dash it to the floor.

But one momentous night, the lid was pushed up from inside by something bigger than the doll, bigger as a four-month child is bigger than a newborn, squeezing triumphantly out of the box as though it were just an opening. Kate remembered that tuft of hair that refused to lie down at the crown. When he raised his head, his eyes were closed, but chubby fingers reached and her heart clenched.

He was warm and heavy in her arms. Here she would stay, but the strain of that need sent her up through the warm waters of sleep to breach on the chill surface that passed for a bright, dry September morning. The harder she tried to stay, the faster she woke. The more painful the loss on waking.

During the day, as each black refuse bag was filled and tied off, her fear and urgency increased.

He had to be here somewhere.

One more room to go.

Today would surely be the day she found him. Mum had lived in this one room for most of a year, and here the most cherished mementos would be. And what could be more cherished than Okimi? She went cold, flushed hot and chilled again.

When the Lyndies arrived that evening, she was in a state of restless disbelief. She knew she was being rude but she took their food, then ignored their glances and shut the door on them. The anticlimax was so intense, she couldn't eat and couldn't sit down.

She had been through the whole house. Nothing. He wasn't here. She couldn't *bear* it.

She sorted, re-sorted or just paced until midnight.

But Mum *never* threw anything away.

Maybe he had never got here. He must have got here.

She went to the mahogany bureau and pulled out files, letters, sheaves of paper. She knew only too well the date she was looking for.

She found the tekno-karakun delivery note with a rush of mingled vindication and betrayal.

So where was he?

She glared at the fragile creamy paper and then saw that the blue note under her hand, dated eight days after the parcel from Japan, was also a delivery note: *Acer palmatum aureum* from the local garden center.

Of course. That was exactly what Mum would have done. Kate could just imagine her mum deciding not to open the box at all, but to bury it. "Okimi is looking down from Heaven," she remembered Mum saying, when they visited much later that year. "Don't you feel it?" Mum and Hiro had exchanged glances of agreement, though Kate knew they were imagining quite different heavens. Kate didn't feel it at all. She wasn't sure she believed in Heaven. She believed in Hell.

Kate could see her mum pondering through aisles of budding saplings and finally selecting the delicate tree that is, with its coral bark, as beautiful in winter as in full foliage. A Japanese maple to mark a Japanese grave.

She drew back the curtains and let the moonlight flood in.

The breeze barely touched the serrated maple leaves, almost ready to fall as tattered autumn tears. Kate cupped her hands around her eyes, vision strained against the shade at its base. Dig. She had to dig there now.

She couldn't find a spade, although she knew she had seen one somewhere not so very long ago.

She ended up using a soup ladle and, when that was too slow, using her hands to scoop up the loosened earth.

The soil was light, pale and sandy. When she exposed the box—the crate—it was black. In her dreams, it had been white, and small as a shoebox.

Shivering convulsively, light tremors running the whole length of her body, she heaved it up, clutched it to her chest and lurched inside.

The fire was embers.

Her fingers were too numb to open the package, so she forced herself to slow down. To breathe deeply and evenly. To mend and rake the fire, to make over-sweetened tea. She cupped the hot mug in tingling fingers, nails broken and filled with grit. The box lay framed by the Kashmir hearthrug. In Japan, it occurred to her, they made shrines to surround their most precious dolls.

Now that it was time, she was terrified.

She wanted Hiroku.

Would he open the box?

Since the funeral, when she phoned him, they had not talked of Okimi or of Q-Okimi. That silence was eight years deep. But she had assumed that the tekno-karakun now loomed as large in his thoughts as it did in hers. Maybe not. She didn't know. Perhaps he was expecting some trinket or some snapshot, and if she brought him . . .

How much of their child lay in that box?

She took a knife and cut and prised. But when she finally got it open, inside that outer casing was another, a tough rubberized black pod.

Between the two was the instruction manual. *Please to read before awaking your Neuro-Baby.*

She flipped through, unable to concentrate on more than a half-sentence here and there. It was written with nightmarish cheer.

Granny, remember! Q-flows into Baby and from Baby, so keep Baby chuckling and Mom and Dad will see their little one smile!

Your Baby's happistate will be affected by handling . . . Granny's voice . . . input from Baby's Quantum-implant. . . .

Baby's lovabilities will grow with you. . . . You will want to update QBabyGro every four weeks. . . .

The many of interactive triggers include Baby's name . . .

She threw the booklet down.

Then she slipped the catches and laid aside the lid.

Okimi lay on his front in the rompers with the primrose-yellow ducks. She rolled him over as carefully as though he might crack. Hair floated in shining tufts at his temples. Pitch-dark lashes lay against waxy skin. Big for four months, he was going to be taller than his—

She picked him up. He lolled. The weight was subtly in the wrong places, and she instinctively tucked his head into the crook of her arm and settled him. Suddenly, he felt right.

This wasn't her baby, she reminded herself. This was a tekno-karakun.co gadget, and maybe it preserved a link to Okimi, to Okimi's last moments, and maybe it didn't. She tried to imagine Okimi looking down from some heaven, but it was beyond her. She rocked him. Get a grip, Kate, this is only a doll. Yet treacherous fingers still gently stroked his silken cap of hair.

"Okimi . . ." What was she doing?

"Okimi, . . ." she crooned. *The many of interactive triggers include Baby's name . . .*

"Wake up, Okimi."

His lashes quivered, and his face was suddenly not that of a baby deeply asleep, but one with eyes closed in mischievous glee. Okimi always wanted to be coaxed awake.

"Mummy's here, Okimi. Wake up, precious, and look at Mummy." He wriggled a little deeper into her arms.

"Mummy's here, Mummy's—" her throat swelled tight. A tear burnt down her cheek. It fell on his shoulder and turned a duck-rump yolk-yellow. "—sorry. I'm sorry, 'Kimi-mine."

She was so desperately sorry. They said that there was nothing she could have done. But that simply couldn't be true. There had to have been some way to change things. If she'd known he was at risk. If she had seen him roll onto his front. If she had been five minutes earlier. If. If. If. She hadn't. She had failed him and that was that. She tightened her grip. "I'm so, so sorry."

The skin around his eyes scrunched in distress and flushed vivid puce. Kate recognized it as preparatory to the howls that babies achieve with dedicated all-exclusive concentration and earpiercing volume. She joggled him lightly.

"Hey, hey, it's all right, it's okay. Hey, hey, Okimi." At her tone, he settled; the tantrum clouds blew over, the skin returned to a delicate waxen flush. Hiro always said it was miraculous and that Okimi never responded so well with him. "It's okay, it's okay." She kissed the warm forehead. "Hey, hey, Okimi."

Okimi opened his big beautiful almond eyes, and gave a burble of delight and trust. Total love.

Something loosened inside her.

Her knees went weak and she sat down suddenly on the bed. She could see herself reflected in the window, with an expression she hadn't seen in her mirror for years. Her face floated, softened, bright-eyed, luminous against the night. She smiled.

It *was* okay. His gaze had told her it was okay.

"Granny would have loved you," she told him, and for a second she sensed Mum nodding vigorously, "just as much as I do." His emphatic sputter agreed with her absolutely.

"What do we do now, 'Kimi-mine, hmmmm?"

But he had shut his eyes again. He smacked his lips once, snuggled happily and was still.

And never moved again. She held him all through the night and, sometimes, she wept.

At first light, she buried him under the maple and then drove away through the gentle patter of morning rain.

The trinkets under the bed were left untouched. The thing she was bringing back for Hiro was herself. She remembered his face as she left, the hidden fear that, once gone, she would never come back.

He wouldn't be disappointed.

A FAMILIAR SOLUTION

Written by
Marguerite Devers Green

Illustrated by
Dwayne Harris

About the Author

Marguerite Devers Green is the mother of two remarkable sons and the wife of a generous and dedicated teacher. Two beautiful daughters have just been adopted by Marguerite and her husband. She has at various times been an actress, a singer, a waitress, a sales clerk, a secretary, a nanny, a nurse's aide and a supervisor at the American Museum of Natural History. She has a B.A. from Penn State, and has studied writing at N.Y.U. and Muhlenberg College. This story marks her first fiction publication.

About the Illustrator

Dwayne Harris was born in 1968, and was raised on his family's farm in the beautiful Ozark Mountains of southern Missouri, where his natural surroundings made a lasting impression. And, in third grade, he won first place in a writing competition with a story titled "The Space Spiders."

After graduating from the University of Missouri in Columbia in 1992, he worked as a graphic artist for a number of companies, but his dream has always been to support himself as a freelance illustrator. In 1999, he began sending his work to anyone he thought might be willing to give him a chance. He also continued to send work to L. Ron Hubbard's Illustrators of the Future Contest, and now, having won a place, feels that his illustration career is on the right track. His Web page is www.dwayneharris.com.

Matilda looked down into the grave. Madame's casket would be in there soon, and people would arrive to fill the hole with dirt and dead flowers. Under the threat of witnessing their pointless reminiscences, Matilda rushed a bit.

It bothered her all the way home: *I used the gypsum salts*, she thought, *I'm sure I did*. Without the salts, Madame's spirit would stay tethered to the body in that filthy hole instead of entering the new host she had picked out. She would be like those bloodless, table-knocking spooks the tabloids wrote about. Madame would be livid. Matilda grew nervous just thinking about it. She shook it off and got into a cab.

Three times she changed her hair color, twirling first one auburn strand and then a yellow one. It was a bad habit, she knew, but at least she had stopped biting her fingernails. The last time Matilda had bitten her finger-nails, Madame had cut off her hands and hidden them so well that it took thirteen days to find them. And when they did turn up, they were so full of fungus that . . . Matilda made herself sit still until she arrived at the shop on Dorsey Street.

Quagmire was waiting, curled up in the storefront window, taking a bit of sun. His hoard of treasure—catnip leaves, some hibernating flies, a bit of shiny foil—had been tucked behind the curtains where he could play with them at his leisure. The moment Matilda walked in, his golden eyes were on her.

"Come then, we have a little time before she gets here," Matilda said. She set a saucer of fresh cream on the kitchen floor, but Quagmire didn't touch it.

"What's wrong with you?" she asked the cat. But she knew what the problem was. A few months back, Madame had become impatient with the familiar, and had punished him severely. "Don't worry, she has other things on her mind today. Madame isn't likely to concern herself with you."

Matilda ran her hand along the top of her latest acquisition, a fifteen-foot display case. Parchments & Polyps was a tiny but successful shop. An eclectic collection of the latest gadgets shared dust with ancient objects and documents of subtle purpose. A large aquarium now took up half the showcase. The fish that swam inside it were an especially fine illusion, self-sustaining for up to a week. Matilda thought of it as her safe-deposit box.

Parchments & Polyps, under one name or another, had always been her home. At one hundred and fifteen, Matilda, too, had changed her name and face more times than she could easily recall—most often due to sudden death brought on by Madame's temper.

Quagmire's anxious mewing amplified her own nervousness. "You're not even completely black, you little upstart. Why should I listen to you?"

"Little upstart," that was Madame's line. Sometimes Matilda felt that she was turning into Madame.

Quagmire nimbly lifted his left paw, studied the white spot that spoiled his otherwise perfect coat, and slowly tipped the cream onto the floor.

"Quagmire, you rotten little fiend. Lucky for you that Madame isn't here. Remember what she did the last time you threw a tantrum." Matilda was instantly sorry for her words.

Three months ago, Madame had snatched up the sleek mastiff, whose body Quagmire was using at the time, and she had ripped its flesh into little pieces. Quagmire's life force had barely escaped in time, and had managed to penetrate only the weakest of hosts—a stillborn kitten. Ah, well, at least it made a smaller target.

"Please, let's have a quiet afternoon. She won't be staying long." Quagmire began to lick the cream up off the floor. "Thank you. That's much better."

Quagmire sneezed and shook his head distastefully, but his demeanor told her she had won. Just then, a booming voice gave both of them a start.

"Matilda!"

"Keep out of sight," Matilda told the cat. "You'll be all right. Both of us will be. I only owe her eighty-five more years, and then we're free."

Matilda stared hard at the doorway, then around the room. Barely visible against the butter-colored walls, a figure floated. It had a face—a rather greenish face—and it did not look happy.

"Oh, no," Matilda said.

"You forgot the gypsum salts!" Madame's voice pounded the room until plaster grit and paint flakes dropped from the ceiling.

"I was sure I did that first."

"You obviously did not!"

Matilda emptied her pockets onto the counter, confirming that a foul-smelling hankie and some bits of aluminum foil were empty of their contents.

Illustrated by Dwayne Harris

"This bit," Matilda said, holding it up, "this bit right here had gypsum salts. I think. I'm pretty sure."

Madame's ghost approached. It bent and sniffed. *"Well, this is useless,"* it said. *"My smeller doesn't work. Could have been sugar lumps in there for all I know."*

"Sugar lumps?"

"You know what I mean. Look in your purse, it's probably in there."

"No, all I carry in there is a bit of ferrous sulfate. You never know when you just might need a little bit of ferrous sulfate. Once I started cramping at the knees—"

"Oh, shut up! Where do you keep it in the shop?"

"Well . . ." Matilda paused. She felt as if she'd swallowed something nasty.

"Well?"

"Well, over there, but . . ."

Madame's shadow wafted through the room and slid inside the tall display case that Matilda had indicated. Several brown jars with childproof caps made up six tidy rows on the top shelf, and one of these was labeled "Gypsum Salts." Beneath the bottle was a small red slip of paper that read "Time to Reorder."

"This is going to be empty, isn't it?" said the ghost.

"I'm afraid it is. But, you see, that's how I know I dumped it in the grave. I distinctly remember tapping the last bits into one of these pieces of foil, and now they're all empty. What else could have been done with it?"

"Shut up! Shut up! Just go to the apothecary and get some more. Or borrow some. Where is the nearest contact?"

"You were my nearest contact! The next one is too far away for this type of emergency. You—"

"Shut up, Matilda! I'm fading, can't you see? Just get some gypsum salts and make it fast. Bring them to my new body at the house in . . . Why don't you move?"

"I went to the apothecary yesterday, as soon as I got your message that the funeral would be today. You see, I knew that it was getting low . . ."

"Oh, Matilda, spit it out."

"They haven't got any. It's on back order."

The shriek that filled the eardrums of all Dorsey Street was so piercing that a couple of the neighborhood dogs would have to be put down to end their agony.

All this was watched with seeming disinterest by the kitten that was not completely black. Matilda reached to pet it, wondering how its little ears were faring, only to have her hand swatted away by the force of Madame's presence. The ghost levitated Quagmire and sent him flying across the shop. He hit the wall with a thump and slid unconscious to the floor.

"There was no cause for that!" Matilda gasped at her own impertinence. Madame was four hundred years her senior. Still, that didn't give her the right to torture someone else's familiar. Matilda walked across the room and lifted Quagmire's small, limp body. He was still alive, and Matilda performed the simplest of spells to keep him that way. Directly, his eyes blinked open and he nuzzled her.

A sound of breathing had begun to spread through the room before Matilda noticed, and Madame's ghost let out a panic-ridden howl. The phantom was dissolving. In another moment, it would be gone. Five hundred years of magic, released to the wind for lack of the proper medication.

Matilda knew it was a tragedy, and that it had come about through her own failing, but she was having a hard time feeling sorry. "Nasty old thing," she murmured involuntarily to the cat.

"Matilda, you ungrateful upstart," Madame's ghost rasped, *"if I go into oblivion because of you, I'll take you with me. I'll have you for my permanent companion."*

Belatedly, Matilda heard the sound of her own impending death. A gasp filled the air and gradually grew stronger. It was like hot wind against Matilda's face. No object stirred within the room, but Quagmire's fur was rippling. Quickly, she set him down and shouted one last word. "Run."

• • •

The first customer to arrive next morning found Matilda's body, its skin in shreds, bones shattered— some of them to powder. Against what was left of her shoulder slept an almost all-black kitten, making noises like a nightmare-tortured child. The customer, an elderly pediatrician, tried to pick up the cat, but it hissed and vanished.

The police were called at once, Matilda's corpse was soon taken away, and the door to the shop was locked. Uniformed officers stood guard, while their higher-ups tried to decipher any clues that might explain the shop-keeper's sudden demise.

Three days passed. Matilda's death was proclaimed an accident, thus saving the police department much embarrassment, expense, and paperwork. The news-papers declared it the result of having dangerous chemicals about.

A funeral procession of one, the local pastor, followed Matilda's inexpensive coffin to its final resting place. He said his hasty prayers while trying not to breathe, because vile smells emanated from the muddy grave. When he was done, three laborers picked up shovels to bury Matilda in her box. Within an hour, the graveyard was deserted.

•••

Back at the shop on Dorsey Street, Quagmire was dusting off the shelves with his black tail. He'd sweep, then lick himself, then sweep again. His activity seemed designed more to ease his boredom than to have any hygienic effect.

"Quagmire?" The voice was like a whisper, amplified a thousand times. *"Kitten?"*

"Meow," he answered. His eyes caught the light as Matilda's presence seeped back into the earthly world. Her spirit looked around. She wasn't certain what she hoped to find, until something caught her eye. In the corner, near Quagmire's empty food dish, was a bit of shiny foil.

"Did you do this?" she asked the cat.

He licked his paw and then his face.

"Oh, you clever thing!" The relief was just beginning to set in. Matilda had been dead before, but always with the confidence that she'd be back for supper. *"I should have known. You watch everything I do as if your life depended on it."* She was coming back into herself in bits and pieces, and it felt like . . . well, it didn't feel quite like anything else.

Her spirit slipped inside the aquarium and settled with a moist sigh into a pickled female body. She came up gasping, flexing unfamiliar hands, shattering the illusion of shimmering koi and nearly cracking the heavy plexiglass. Matilda squooshed onto the floor. Human. Human again.

"Meow?" said the kitten. There was some slightly sour haddock in the icebox, and Matilda used up one small spell to set out the fish for Quagmire, even though her readjustment would require lots of energy.

"I owe you, kitten," Matilda said.

With a series of small shudders, she became whole again. She shook herself, spritzing preservatives at the ceiling. She put the finishing touches on her appearance: an appendix scar, a mole, a larger pair of . . . Then it hit her.

"Quagmire, where did you get the gypsum salts?" He made a figure eight around her damp ankles, let a purr slip out, and went back to his meal. "I guess it doesn't matter, but I know for a fact there were none at the druggist's."

The cat flicked at his piece of aluminum foil, pounced on it as if it were alive, and abruptly lost interest.

"Kitten?" No answer. "Tell me, what became of Madame?"

She bent to look into his topaz eyes, but Quagmire had become deeply interested in the haddock.

THE PLAGUE

Written by
A. C. Bray

Illustrated by
Lee White

About the Author

*Amanda Bray lives in Sydney, Australia.
About her becoming an SF writer, she says,
"I experimented with The Lord of the Rings as a child, and
never quite recovered. I said to myself, 'Oh, it's just a little epic
fantasy. I'd never get involved in the hard stuff. I can stop
anytime I want.' Then my friends gave me some Ursula K. Le
Guin and I was hooked. There's only one way to support a
habit like that: deal! I began writing science fiction last year; it
was either that or ripping off VCRs."*

About the Illustrator

Lee White's illustrating career began six years ago while working as a graphic designer in San Francisco. One day a client needed a small illustration and was in a rush. Lee took on the job and has been illustrating ever since. Some of his clients include Apple, Sunset and Hitachi.

After a few years doing advertising, he realized that the work he was really interested in was narrative illustration. "I love to take a scene from a story and turn it into reality," he says. Lee has just finished writing and illustrating his first fantasy book, entitled "Book of Wings."

In 1999, he enrolled at Art Center College of Design in Pasadena to master his drawing and painting skills and to get his degree. He plans to become a teacher at university level and continue illustrating books and showing in galleries.

moved out to Wolgola to survive. You try setting up a GP practice in the city and see how far you get—a bloody good way to starve to death, if you ask me. There must be a doctor for every three people in Sydney. Forget it. So when the plague came, there I was—Dr. Jane P. Fairchild, country GP. And surgeon, psychiatrist and tooth-extractor extraordinaire; in fact, the only doctor for a fair-sized chunk of the state. Not exactly what I'd had planned, but there you are.

The plague started harmlessly enough; rat numbers went up just a bit. The farmers complained, but then farmers are always complaining, so nobody paid much attention. They bought up warfarin—you know, Warfarin, Ratsak, whatever you call it—and spread it around. Rat numbers went down again and everyone was happy. Except the rats, presumably.

Then one or two showed up again. Out came the warfarin—nothing. No internal bleeding. No dead rats. The resistant ones bred, so they brought out another poison. Same thing, resistant rats. Over and over again—each poison a bit more toxic than the last. By the time I started my practice, there wasn't a lot of native fauna left around Wolgola, but by God there were a whole lot of rats.

The day Evans turned up I was in my surgery treating more infected rat bites. My surgery wasn't much to look at, but then neither was the town. Wolgola's a quiet place—forty-six houses, a general store and post office, a hairdresser who also takes in laundry, and of course a pub, the only building higher than one story. Forty-six families—mostly wheat farmers and the shop owners who kept them clothed and fed. And drunk, usually. There isn't a lot to do in Wolgola except drink. I don't mind a drink myself, although I'm always on duty, so I try to stay sober enough to drive and operate. It's taken a lot of experimentation to find out exactly how drunk that is, and the night before Evans came I'd been gathering data.

The light seemed more than usually brilliant that day. I had the blinds down in the surgery and I was trying not to make any sudden moves. I figured if I made it through the morning, I had a better than average chance of surviving till sunset.

My last patient before lunch was Nina, a five-year-old with plump legs, stringy black hair and a scream that was hacking its way through my skull right into my brain. Her mother had one of Nina's chubby legs pinned to my operating table while the rest of Nina gyrated in time with the screaming and gnashing of teeth. I'd never seen anyone actually gnash their teeth before and, despite my precarious health, I was impressed.

This was the third time Nina had been in to have her infected rat bite debrided. She'd practiced a crescendo of protest for three days and her performance was now extremely solid. I patted her foot weakly.

"There now, that wasn't so bad, was it?" The wailing grew louder, if that were possible. I motioned to her mother to take her out, and stripped off my gloves.

"See you tomorrow, Doctor," her mother said, grinning as she went past me with Nina clamped, squealing,
under one arm. I winced.

I locked up the surgery and squinted my way out
onto the street and down a few doors to the pub. I was
completely sick of rats and all rat-related phenomena.

I'd seen too many infected rat bites. Too many ulcers
that wouldn't heal and too much septicemia. I'd already
lost a couple of old people and one baby. The kids were
catching all sorts of infections from spoiled food, too.

The farmers were on the verge of bankruptcy
because rats ate half the grain and contaminated the rest.
Nothing kept them out for long and if just one pregnant
female got into a silo, you could forget whatever was
inside. Wolgola looked like turning into a ghost town,
and what would become of the good Dr. Fairchild then?

Okay, perhaps I wasn't completely honest about my
motives for moving out here. The Medical Board will
put up with a lot from a GP who agrees to work in the
country, even drinking on the job. They know the alternative. You guessed it—no doctor at all. And I swear I
stayed mostly sober during business hours. If people
didn't care to consult me after four in the afternoon, they
could always see Dr. Hadfield—a hundred and twenty
kilometers away.

After lunch, I stepped out onto the pub veranda and
squinted up and down the main street—well, the only
street. Nothing moving in either direction. The red
air shivered and shed its load of dust over every available surface, which led to a certain predictability in the
color scheme. Houses were whitish red, the tarmac
blackish red; my station wagon outside the surgery
struck a daring note of greenish red. And there were
those little buggers right out in the main street, sniffing
around an empty chip packet.

Illustrated by Lee White

The bloody things were everywhere! The only way to keep food safe was in tins. They even got into the fridge—chewed through the door seal. Rat shit everywhere, of course—impossible to keep the filth out of your food preparation unless you washed and dried everything right before you used it. Even then, they could have shat on the tea towels in the linen closet.

Everyone slept in hammocks now, after too many nights feeling them running around on the sheets and pissing on the pillow or biting the kids' faces.

Disgusting to have to pick your way through rats to reach the outside dunny and sit with your legs pulled up so they didn't bite your ankles, and then listen to them scuttling around underneath you while you went. I felt like I'd never be clean again.

It was while I was walking back to the surgery for the afternoon's rat bite parade that I saw the cloud of dust. Then a dirty white van came into view and pulled up outside the pub. The van had EVANS' RODENT ERADICATION on the side. That was interesting enough to make me drift on back to the pub veranda. A few other people had materialized out of their houses, so we all stood in the shade watching Evans climb out of his van and saunter into the front bar where Bill, the publican, was cleaning rat shit off the glasses.

Evans gave a general impression of tidiness and littleness, from his thinning red hair to his small neat shoes. He was dressed in what passed for formal wear in Wolgola—jeans and a brown checked shirt tucked in. He gave us a smug little smile as he walked past, as if to say, wait till you see this.

"Mind if I bring my cats in?" he said. "They need some water—been on the road all day."

"Yeah, mate, no worries," Bill said. "I reckon we can handle a couple of cats. See if they can catch a rat while they're here, ay?"

Two brown rodents scuttled under a bench out of Evans's way as he walked back out to the van.

With a flourish, Evans swept open the van's back doors. Two cats jumped down and picked their way to the veranda. They sat with their eyes fixed on Evans, ignoring us completely. Then another two jumped out, and another two—they just kept coming out of that truck, a stream, a river, of short-furred, well-muscled felines. All colors, all sizes, they hit the ground running and ran to sit in line on the veranda.

This was the bit I couldn't believe—I swear those bloody cats lined up in double file and then just sat down and waited for Evans. Not a miaow, not a little bit of a lick to get the dust off. In the end there must have been fifty cats lined up there.

We all looked at each other and said clever things like, "Well, would you look at that," and "Shit, ay." Nobody patted them though—for a start, Wolgola isn't a patting kind of place. Pets tend to be useful things like dogs that can guard the house, or lambs that can be killed and eaten when the kids get sick of them. But, also, these cats radiated a businesslike atmosphere, as though patting wasn't really their thing.

Evans closed up the van then went to stand in front of the column. He made a kissy-kissy noise and walked off into the pub with the cats following in a neat double file. It was more than a little spooky, I can tell you.

I went in too, of course, if only to see Bill's reaction. He looked up from cleaning the glasses and saw them all filing into the pub. His mouth fell open and the cigarette dropped off his bottom lip. In complete silence, the cats lined up against the back wall.

"Er, the water?"

"Sorry, yeah. Umm . . ." Poor Bill rubbed the back of his neck, clearly stumped.

I decided to help. Before long we had bowls, baking trays and saucers of water lined up on the floor, and the cats, after another kissy noise from Evans, were lapping away.

Evans accepted a light beer and smilingly deflected questions. The pub was filling up; people had phoned other people to tell them there was something going on. Like I said, not much happens in Wolgola. Even Bruce from the shop had closed up and come to see what was what.

When Evans had finished his beer and the cats had finished drinking, he gave a complicated whistle and the furry feline backs formed up into their column again. Evans stood up and waited till he had everyone's attention.

"Publican, with your permission I'd like to offer you a free demonstration of my product. My product is Rodent Eradication and I've heard that you people here might have a rodent problem."

Enthusiastic murmurs of assent from the crowd.

Bill scratched himself and shrugged. "Yeah, mate, righto. Free, you said?"

Evans nodded. "Would it be possible to open up a space for them to get inside the walls?"

Bill was rubbing the back of his neck again, so I stepped in.

"How about where Bruce knocked the plaster in with his pool cue? We could open that up some more."

We all trooped off to examine the hole—Bruce looking rather proud of himself. Bill broke off a couple more pieces of the old plasterboard until the hole was wide enough to fit a biggish cat. Evans decided it would do, and we all went back to the front bar.

For the first time, he used a spoken command. "Hunt."

Suddenly, the cats erupted out of their rows and scattered all over the pub. Ten shot up the stairs; about fifteen went through the hole in the wall; a few vanished under the bar. The rest split up and covered the ground-floor rooms.

"Jeeeesus," Bill said.

To our amazement, the cats seemed to have some sort of system. The little ones would get into spaces too small for the rest of them, and a minute later the rats would come streaming out, falling over each other trying to get away.

Fifteen of the bigger cats had come back to the common room, and they were rounding up the rats. Yes, that's what I said, rounding them up. They had them herded into a corner and they were keeping them there. Every so often they'd open up a gap and add a few more rats to the pen. The rats were trying to climb up the walls, scrabbling with their claws, squealing and biting each other—absolutely petrified.

One huge rat got through the line of guards and made a break for it, but the second line of cat defense got it—four stringy looking felines obviously built for speed. One of them killed the escapee with a bite to the back of its neck. Not one of the cats tried to eat a rat. This was not predation; this was a carefully planned and executed slaughter.

Rats came pouring out of the walls, from under the bar, down the stairs, running into the mass of rats in the corner pen. There was a rustling and squeaking from the cellar hatch and a stream of rats ran up from the basement with about five muscly hunting cats behind them. The cellar rats were rounded up and herded in with the others.

By now there must have been more than three hundred of the buggers squealing in the corner. The cats formed up around them in three concentric arcs, tails switching and every muscle tensed. You could see every muscle in their bodies tensing up.

Evans had been sitting at the bar sipping another light beer through this whole performance. He gave us another one of those tight little smiles.

"This is about to get messy. Anyone who doesn't have a strong stomach might want to leave." Nobody moved. The room was silent except for the squealing and rustling from the rats.

He gave the command in his soft voice. "Kill."

The cats in the first row launched themselves at the mass of rats. They pounced on each rat in turn and bit it on the back of the neck. The smaller rats had their heads bitten right off. That corner of the room just turned red. It was pretty gruesome.

The other two rows hung back. I figured out their job when a few rats slipped between the front-row killers and bolted for the door. They didn't get far. Only two rats made it through to the third row and they had no more luck than the others. It was over in three minutes.

We were all open mouthed at the carnage. There were dismembered rat parts everywhere, pools of blood all over the floor, and the wall in the corner was smeared

red. The whole place stank of blood and rat piss. I felt sick and I could hear Bill clearing his throat, trying not to throw up.

The cats sat back and panted for a moment and then they started to lick the blood off themselves. They picked the solid bits of guts off with their teeth, and when they'd reached all they could on their own, they licked each other's faces clean.

When they'd finished, they stood to attention. Yes, I know, but the whole thing had a certain military feel to it. Evans whistled at them, and they each picked up a rat and carried it out to the truck. Then they came back and did it again until all that was left was blood.

"You might want to hose the place out now, before the blood sets," said Evans. "They'll be back in a minute to clean out the babies from their nests."

As you can imagine, every farmer in the place was queuing up to book Evans to do his or her property. His prices were pretty steep, but everyone knew that this was their only chance to pull in any kind of harvest this year. Evans had timed his appearance for maximum desperation. He got his price.

Well, you couldn't turn around after that without hearing about Evans and his bloody cats. Everyone thought he was just the duck's nuts, except yours truly. I don't know what it was about him I didn't like. Maybe it was that creepy little smile; maybe it was the way he acted the mysterious hero, pretending to ignore the adulation when you could tell he was really lapping it up. Bill told me I was just jealous, which was bloody ridiculous.

I think Evans knew I wasn't overwhelmed with enthusiasm, because he kept trying to impress me. He obviously couldn't bear the fact that somebody wasn't a fan.

He'd moved into the farm that had been left empty when the rats ate Jane Stokeson's wheat last year, and all her savings in the process. He had dinner at Bill's pub every night; I mean, there wasn't anywhere else to eat.

Since I have a moral objection to cooking my own meals, I was there most evenings too. I couldn't shake him off; the silent treatment only made him more talkative— usually about himself. This went on for a week, and I think he was getting desperate for a response, because then he started talking about the cats.

He never had before—all he'd tell anyone was some bullshit about them being selectively bred for the herding instinct. Maybe the atmosphere of the town had got to him though, because he was drinking more than when he first came. I think that might have loosened him up a bit.

Anyway, one night I was ignoring him as usual when he got my attention by mentioning my own university. He thought he was impressing me—probably thought country doctors were trained at Dingo Flats Technical College, not the Most Prestigious University in the Land.

"My so-called colleagues look pretty stupid now, don't they? Where are they—cleaning test tubes for some egomaniacal half-wit so they can be fifteenth author on his papers? Geneticists! Yeah, right! They wouldn't know an intron if they bloody fell over one. My cats . . ." He suddenly registered that I was paying attention. "Wouldn't you like to know, sweetie? Wouldn't you like to know?"

Now if there's anything I hate more than being patronized, it's being patronized by someone who gets staggering drunk on light beer. I thought about telling him where he could stick his intron, but I decided it wasn't worth it, so I just went home.

What he'd said about genetics and cats stuck in my mind, though. I was pretty sure that letting genetically modified animals roam the countryside was illegal. It was possible that he'd been talking about his selective breeding program when he mentioned genetics, but I didn't think so. Why would some big-city genetics techie leave it all behind and tour the country killing rats? Got to be running away from something.

I don't usually stick my nose into other people's business. In fact, I don't usually do anything that involves extra effort of any kind. But I was the closest thing Wolgola had to a scientist, so I couldn't help feeling that this *was* my business.

The next day, Evans was due to de-rat Fred Finley's farm. I decided to go along to Jane Stokeson's place and have a look at Evans's setup while he wasn't there. No harm in having a look around, was there?

At nine the next morning, I watched him trundle through town in his white van. I told my secretary I'd be away for a few hours and headed out to my old station wagon. She didn't ask any questions—I think she unfairly assumed I was going for a drink. Actually, I'd already had just a small one. I drove as fast as the old rustbucket would go and pulled into Jane's just after ten. The place was deserted.

I got out and circled the house, looking in the windows. Nothing to report, except that Mr. Evans was an exceptionally tidy person. Not an unwashed cup in the place, and I thought I caught a glimpse of nested spoons in the cutlery tray. Figures, I thought. I've never trusted people who nest their spoons.

I nearly gave it up and went back to town, but then thought I might as well have a quick look in the barn first.

Jane's barn was an old corrugated-iron thing. She'd had some impressive farm machinery before she went bust, so the barn was pretty big. The doors were padlocked, but when I went around the back I saw that one of the corrugated-iron sheets had rusted around the nails that held it on. I yanked on it, but all I managed to do was open up a bloody great big cut on my palm with the rusty edge. Terrific, I thought, another bloody tetanus shot. I tried to tear a strip off my shirt to bind it up with, but shirts don't rip up neatly into bandages in real life the way they do in Hollywood. One of the seams ripped open so my bra showed, the scungy gray one with holes in it. I decided to ignore both the laceration and the indecent exposure and just get on with it.

Another yank and a couple of vengeful kicks and the iron sheet came off, leaving a hole big enough to climb through. It took a moment for my eyes to adjust after the glare outside. The first thing I saw was a rat.

I was so used to rats that it was a few seconds before I realized how weird that was. I mean, surely Jane's farm would have got the best rat destruction treatment in the country. Then my eyes adjusted properly to the light.

There were lots of rats, and they weren't running across the barn squeaking or anything. They were standing around in neat little groups, eating grain. There were rat pens all over the floor. Some had been cobbled together out of chicken wire; some were real cages built of steel mesh. I remembered that Jane had made an abortive attempt to make her fortune from chinchillas when things were going bad with the wheat. Those might have been her chinchilla cages.

I picked my way between the enclosures near my impromptu door towards the middle of the floor where an empty corridor ran from one end of the barn to the other. I wandered up and down a couple of times and peered into some of the enclosures. Not only were the rats in cages, but—get this—they were graded in order of size. Little ones at the back of the barn and big ones near the door. Then I noticed that the rats on one side of the walkway were pretty frisky. They were jumping around and trying to eat through the steel mesh when I walked past. The ones on the other side just sat there eating and wriggling their whiskers at one another. Were they being graded for temperament as well as size, or had one lot maybe been doped? What the hell was Evans up to?

I poked around a bit more but couldn't find anything else, so I headed back to the car.

Evans was in the pub as usual that evening, sinking those watery light beers one after the other. I wondered when he'd drop the pretense that he wasn't really drinking that much and get onto full-strength. Or whisky. I gave whisky a go myself for a while, but beer is really my drink. Ah, just thinking about it now makes me want one, cold and clear, hitting the back of my throat. . . . Just a minute.

Sorry, yes, like I was saying, Evans was still kidding himself with that watery crap. I plonked my beer on the counter next to his and sat down. He must have thought I was finally a convert to the Evans is Fabulous camp. I quickly disabused him of that notion.

"What the hell are you doing up at Jane's place, Evans? You breeding a rat army to take over the world or something?"

You should have seen Evans jump. It was heart-warming.

"You've been trespassing, Dr. Fairchild! I should call the police!" He was spluttering slightly, but I thought he didn't seem as angry as he should have been. Actually he looked more frightened. And distracted. I put some sneer into it.

"I know you're doing illegal genetics research, Evans—if that is your real name." I glared at him significantly, feeling very much the steely-eyed investigator. "If you can't satisfy me that your dealings are above board, I'm afraid I'll have to notify the appropriate authorities." I'd had a few beers myself, so this last bit took me a couple of goes, but I got my message across.

Evans smiled his nasty little smile at me.

"Very well," he said. "I'll meet you out the front."

And before I could say anything, he'd gone. I levered myself to my feet and followed.

Outside, the night was cool and starry. Evans was waiting for me in the van. I opened the passenger door and climbed in. I know what you're thinking. Why on earth did she get in the van with Evans the Creep? Answer: Seven or eight schooners of Victoria Bitter, and a level of curiosity that qualified as a notifiable disease. Which, unlike my judgment, I have not yet been able to dissolve in alcohol.

We pulled up at the farm at about nine, by which time the booze had started to wear off. There were cats everywhere, of course. Evans unlocked the front door of the house and we all went in. I mean me, Evans and fifty cats. It was quite a squeeze in the kitchen, and I wasn't one of the lucky ones that got a chair. Evans didn't shoo the cats off so I could sit down either—in fact, he seemed a bit afraid of them. To be fair, there is something intimidating about fifty simultaneous unblinking stares.

"So enlighten me," I said, ignoring the cats and making myself as comfortable as possible against the kitchen bench.

He dropped the cute little smile and rubbed his hands through his hair. Funny to see a hair out of place on him.

"Okay, they are genetically modified," he said. "Look, how much do you know about NMDA receptors?"

I made a cautious, noncommittal sort of noise and he looked at me as though I was some sort of mental cripple.

"NMDA receptors are critical in processes like memory and thinking," he said. "They're especially concentrated in the temporal lobes." He gave me another mental-cripple look. "In the brain."

"Hey, Evans, I know where the temporal lobes are, okay?" Dickhead.

He ignored me and went on. "Mice whose NMDA receptors have been genetically modified to stay open longer show a significantly greater ability to learn and recall information. The modification is achieved by the insertion—at the zygote stage, of course—of the gene coding for a certain NMDA receptor subunit protein, which—"

"Yeah, yeah—smart mice," I said. "What about cats?"

"I was getting to that." He sounded a bit testy. Evans preferred expounding to conversing.

"It was my idea to try cats," he went on. "Nobody else could be bothered. 'What's the point?' they said. 'Mice, cats, aardvarks, who cares? The ethics committee will never let us try it on humans or chimps. We've shown we can do it with lower mammals, let's move on.' Small-minded fools!"

Actually, I thought they sounded pretty sensible.

Evans was just warming up. "They were wrong, of course, and I've proved that now. Cats have tremendous potential. Their speed of information processing is already fantastic. Their range of instinctive behavior is impressive. Of course, their intelligence is limited by the need for a predator's skull shape, and the oversized cerebellum. Until now. With this NMDA receptor gene, they can cram everything they need into a brain the size of a hazelnut.

"As I said, nobody supported me, and the ethics committee refused my application. I did the research anyway, of course."

Of course.

"When they found out, my so-called superiors sacked me. I stole my cats from the lab and left town. Now the cats make a living for all of us. When I have enough money, I'll be able to continue my research."

"So how intelligent are they?" I glanced down at Evans's chair where a tortoiseshell tabby was licking its anus.

"At the moment, only as bright as, say, the average eight-year-old. But they cooperate closely—pool their knowledge. The next generation will be much brighter, because they'll be taught from birth by intelligent parents."

"Pardon me, the next generation? This thing is heritable?"

"Yes, that's the really clever bit! Only a proportion of the embryo cells take up the gene, so the cat's sperm or ova don't always carry it on to the next generation. But so far only the intelligent kittens have survived. They selectively eat the others after a few weeks. So, the kittens that will be born to this younger generation will almost all be supercats."

Supercats. Hmmm. He obviously put a lot of thought into that one.

Forgetting himself, Evans tweaked the tortoiseshell tabby on the ear. This time he was the one on the receiving end of the mental-cripple stare.

"So what are the rat cages for? Are you selectively breeding a tastier rat for them? Why can't you just open a tin of cat food like everyone else?"

I was getting sick of that look.

"You don't get it, do you? *I'm* not breeding the rats. *They* are."

Come again?

"They started straight after we got here. They must have found those old cages in the barn, because when I got up the next morning, they had it all set up. Not as many rats, just what they could catch here, but you could see they had a system. It was fascinating! I decided to help out by making a few more enclosures out of chicken wire, to see what they'd do. How far they'd go. The effects of the NMDA receptor gene surprised even me!"

He'd stood up during this explanation and paced around waving his hands. I stayed out of his way. When he tried to sit down again, a cat had taken his seat. He tsk-tsked a bit, but left the cat alone.

"Then they started keeping prime stock from the farms we've been working on and bringing them back here. They seem to be building up a selective breeding program for size and docility. The perfect characteristics for domesticated meat animals. Their methods are really quite sophisticated." He sounded genuinely enthusiastic.

The idiot hadn't even wondered why the cats wanted to be self-sufficient.

What had he done to this lot when he'd had them in the lab? He didn't seem like the type to bother with time-consuming nonessentials like anesthesia. If their memory was as good as he'd said, they could probably hold a pretty impressive grudge.

They would have scattered already if they'd wanted to. Every cat for itself. Perhaps they'd been putting up with him so far for the chance to develop an organized society. What they'd do when they no longer needed him, I didn't know. They were already showing him less respect, and he was a little bit scared of them. He was about to get a lot more scared. Me, too.

"Anyway, the question is now purely academic," he said. "Finley's fee will make up what I need to resume my research. You can help me—be second author on the papers. I could use an assistant and you'll certainly never get another chance like this one. We'll find somewhere quiet, buy the surgical equipment we need. Some of the females are pregnant. The kittens will make wonderful research material for us, especially in utero—no danger of environmental contamination of the results. . . ."

He went on and on, oblivious to the increasing agitation amongst the cats, which were prowling back and forth and switching their tails. I started backing away from Evans at this point. I found his use of the first person plural pronoun highly disturbing. Something bad was coming and I didn't want it to involve me.

When my back hit the kitchen door they'd begun to yowl in unison. Evans had finally shut up and was looking around with frightened eyes.

I fumbled the door open and made for the van. I expected to be pursued by the feline horde, but they must have been busy with Evans because by the time I opened the driver's side door he'd started screaming.

I slammed the door and locked it. The keys were still in the ignition, thank God. I started up and sat there for a minute, waiting for Evans. He didn't come, but a couple of the cats wandered out, licking their faces. I got the hell out of there.

The first thing I did when I got back to town was have a quick one to soothe my nerves. Actually, it took ten or twelve quick ones to soothe my nerves to my complete satisfaction. Then I called the police. Maybe if I'd done those things in a different order . . . In retrospect, I can see that I probably didn't make a lot of sense over the phone. I couldn't get the words to come out right, and we're talking about little words like "cat" and "dead."

When the police finally did understand me, they just sniggered—the first in a proud tradition of laughing at Crazy Doctor Fairchild's cat story. I called everyone. The Most Prestigious University's genetics department hung up on me; the Army wouldn't let me past the switchboard; the minister for health sent a polite note asking me not to call again. You get the idea. The police had me on their prank caller list, for God's sake. You're the first people who haven't actually laughed out loud, and that's only because you're trained professionals.

In the end, I bought a gun. I took shots at a couple of them, but my aim's a bit off—it just put them on their guard. There's always one or two of them around now, keeping an eye on me. God, I listen to myself and I can't believe how insane I sound.

Look—I know it's time to go, and I don't mind. Really. At least I'll have clean sheets while I'm waiting.

What? For them, of course. The pregnant females will have had their kittens by now. The next generations will be smarter, faster, bigger. I wonder if there is a practical limit to how big they can get. Unlike us, they have no scruples about their selective breeding program. In fact, cats aren't big on scruples in general.

I was thinking about those rats, trying to scrabble up the sheer wall to get away from them. What will it be like to live in a world full of highly intelligent predators, do you think?

Can I bring my beer? Yeah, fair enough.

BOOS AND TABOOS

Written by
L. Ron Hubbard

About the Author

L. Ron Hubbard's remarkably versatile career as an internationally best-selling writer spanned more than half a century of literary achievement and wide-ranging influence. In scope and productivity, it ultimately encompassed more than 530 works—over sixty-three million words—of published fiction and nonfiction. Esteemed as a writer's writer, with an unstinting personal dedication to helping other writers, especially beginners, become more proficient and successful at their craft, he also carved out significant careers in other professional fields—as an explorer, mariner and aviator, filmmaker and photographer, philosopher and educator, and musician and composer.

He grew up in the ruggedly open terrain of a still-frontier Montana, was riding horses by the time he was three, and by the age of six had been initiated as a blood brother of a Blackfoot Indian medicine man. While still a teenager, before the advent of modern commercial air transportation, he journeyed more than a quarter of a million miles by sea and land into areas of the Far East then rarely visited by Westerners, broadening his knowledge of other peoples and cultures.

Later, as a master mariner licensed to operate ships in any ocean, he led three separate voyages of discovery and exploration under the flag of the prestigious Explorers Club. He also served with distinction as a U.S. naval officer during the Second World War.

Returning to the United States from his early travels in the Far East in 1929, Mr. Hubbard studied at George Washington University where he became president of the Flying Club and secretary of the Engineering Society, and wrote articles, stories and a prize-winning play for the school's newspaper and literary magazine.

A daredevil pilot, he barnstormed across the United States in gliders and early powered aircraft, becoming a correspondent and photographer for the Sportsman Pilot, *one of the most important national aviation magazines of its day. Then, at the age of twenty-five, with his reputation as a writer of popular fiction already prominently established, he was elected president of the New York Chapter of the American Fiction Guild, whose membership at the time included Dashiell Hammett, Raymond Chandler and Edgar Rice Burroughs. He subsequently also worked in Hollywood, writing the story and script for Columbia's 1937 box-office-hit serial* The Secret of Treasure Island, *and as a screenwriter and script consultant on numerous films for Columbia, Universal and other studios.*

Over the broad spectrum of his professional career, all of this—and more—found its way unforgettably into his writing, giving his stories a compelling authenticity and an exciting sense of the textures of life, or of the way things credibly might be in some possible future or alternate dimension or in the deep vaults of space, that continue to captivate and engross readers everywhere.

Beginning with the publication in 1934 of The Green God, *his first adventure yarn, in one of the hugely popular all-story "pulp" magazines of the day, L. Ron Hubbard's outpouring of fiction was prodigious—often exceeding a million words a year. Ultimately, he produced more than 250 published novels, short stories and screenplays in virtually every major genre, from action and adventure, western and romance, to mystery and suspense, and, of course, science fiction and fantasy.*

Mr. Hubbard had, indeed, already attained broad popularity and acclaim in other genres when he burst onto the landscape of speculative literature with his first published science fiction story, The Dangerous Dimension. *It was his groundbreaking work in this field from 1938 to 1950, particularly, that not only helped to indelibly enlarge the imaginative boundaries of science fiction and fantasy, but established him as one of the founders and signature architects of what continues to be regarded as the genre's golden age.*

Such trendsetting L. Ron Hubbard classics of speculative fiction as Final Blackout, Fear, Typewriter in the Sky, *the Hugo Award nominated* To The Stars, *as well as his capstone novels, the epic saga of the year 3000,* Battlefield Earth, *and the ten-volume* Mission Earth® *series, continue to appear on bestseller lists and to garner acclaim in countries around the world.*

*The single biggest science fiction novel in the history of the genre—and a perennial international bestseller for nearly two decades—*Battlefield Earth *was given hallmark recognition, among its many other accolades, when it was voted the best science fiction novel of the twentieth century by the American Book Readers Association.*

At the same time, an original L. Ron Hubbard screenplay about look-alike spies, Ai! Pedrito!—When Intelligence Goes Wrong, *novelized by Kevin J. Anderson, became an immediate* New York Times *bestseller on its publication in 1998. The following year,* A Very Strange Trip, *an uproarious L. Ron Hubbard screenplay of time-traveling adventure, turned into novel form by Dave Wolverton, also became a* New York Times *bestseller—and the fifteenth Hubbard fiction title to appear on that list—directly after its release.*

The culmination of L. Ron Hubbard's enthusiastic commitment to actively fostering the work of new and aspiring writers of demonstrated ability came, meanwhile, with his establishment in 1983 of both the Writers of the Future *Contest, now the largest and most successful merit competition of its kind in the world, and the* Writers of the Future *annual anthology of the winning best new original stories of science fiction, fantasy and horror. The anthology also provides an influential showcase for winners of the companion Illustrators of the Future Contest, inaugurated in 1988 as part of Mr. Hubbard's continuing legacy to the field.*

L. Ron Hubbard's earliest work with fledgling writers, however—undertaken while still in his twenties—was marked by lectures he gave at such schools as Harvard and George Washington University on how to get started as a professional.

He also began, as early as 1935, to publish incisively practical "how to" articles and essays about writing as a craft and profession, which appeared regularly in major writers' magazines and continue to be used today in writing courses and seminars, and as the basis for the coveted Writers' Workshops held each year for the winners and published finalists of the Writers of the Future *Contest.*

In the article that follows, titled "Boos and Taboos," L. Ron Hubbard challenges the restrictive "taboos" of writing for publications that bind stories in formula straitjackets and siphon off what he cogently calls the "delightful plasticity of ideas." Urging writers to flout by-prescription storytelling, he describes his own conspicuous success in doing that, with a final, telling reflection on creative energy, sales—and writing stories that will be remembered.

When Ye Editor recently popped up at an American Fiction Guild luncheon, she found me lime punch drunk against the bar.

Said Ye Editor, "Write me an article on something, will you?"

Said I, "Certainly, on what?"

Said Ye Editor, "'Why You Sold Your Last Story.'"

I pondered it for a bit, couldn't remember what I had sold last, and then put the question to two very learned gentlemen of our exalted fraternity.

Said one, "Why did I sell my last story? Well, editors do go blind, you know."

Said t'other, "Why? Because I needed the money."

Said half a dozen more, "Because I needed the money."

Said Ye Editor, "Certainly, but you can't put that in an article. It doesn't make sense."

Well, here it is in an article, but neither does it make sense.

There was reason behind that last sale. Not facetious reason, but actual cold, hard writing reason. Now that we get right down to the meat of it, the reason I made my last sale a few days ago was the farthest thing from your mind.

I broke all the taboos. Which brings us to the scene.

All writers agree on one thing. Strange but they do—on that one matter. Writing is the screwiest profession man ever invented—as witness our double existence. Writers were originally minstrels, of course, and the minstrels used to wander about sleeping in haystacks and begging their wine, getting paid only in gifts.

We have become elevated to respectability as far as the world is concerned but we still live that cup-to-lip existence of our long-dead brethren, and our lives, whether we strummed a lyre or a typewriter, are pretty identical.

And every once in a while we like to upset our own traditions just to see what will happen.

So I broke some half-dozen strict taboos and sold the story.

Now, of course, there's a hitch to all this which I must mention, later, even though it smacks of conceit.

But to the taboos. This particular house, in common with the other pulp dynasties, enumerates their taboos in no uncertain terms. But I don't think, after this experience, that they believe them any too strongly.

Their heroes must be strong, virile, upright.

Of heroines they will have none whatever. No love interest!

No first person whatever. All third.

And there were others which I can't name because they would identify the yarn too clearly.

This yarn, not yet published at writing, was told in first person by a gentleman whose deeds smacked of crime. He went to great lengths because of a girl, and was, in fact, entirely motivated by that girl.

Which makes a very unwholesome lesson. Pulp taboos have been handed down, down, down until they bind a story into a narrow, viselike groove, and like water which runs too long in one place, the limited plots are wearing down like stone. In ninety percent of the present pulp stories, tell me the beginning and I'll tell you the end.

All too true. One day an editor told me that, grinding the editorial teeth, little suspecting the answer to it. And so I set out to write a yarn which wouldn't foretell its ending. To do that thing I found out I had to break a couple taboos. I shivered over it as a Polynesian shivers over his own particular *tabus*.

But the story sold. It was just enough out of line to be interesting, just enough inside to stay in keeping with its brethren. Like a golf shot which slices over out-of-bounds and then sails in for a landing on the fairway.

It is even possible to apply to detective stories—and that, coming from an adventure writer, says a great deal.

These taboos! They're like fetters to a convict—and a writer chained to his mill is enough of a convict already. The story must not be over such and such a length. Well, you get to be an automaton after a while, so that you can write without numbering your pages—as I do—and still arrive at the required length. A sort of automatic alarm clock which shouts "Ending!"

That's a taboo, to overlength something, but not very serious.

Another taboo consists of virile heroes. Anything but clean-limbed gentlemen with a gat in each hand wait outside. And some of the mightiest stories ever written have been about nervous, anemic, shivering shrimps afraid of their own cigarette smoke. But no, sayeth the pulps, the hero must be lithe, tall, dark and handsome.

The heroine must always be pure as snowdrifts, unsullied, unsoiled, and the greatest worry is about the intentions of the big, bad, sneering, leering, rasping, grating, snarling villain. Dear girls. Most women are married in the mid-twenties. And with all due respect to everybody, the most interesting, witty, quick-thinking ladies are past that age. Dear me, can't we have some really interesting females in pulp?

One outfit puts a ban on anything where adventure fails to go after a reward of some kind. No mental rewards. The clinking clatter of gold and the brittle sparkle of jewels must be in the fore forever. I searched for gold once, twice, but any adventures I might have had, bad or good, dull or interesting, dealt with quantities far more intangible than gold. Esteem, self-respect, loyalty . . .

Ah, but I'm being too unkind. I could list taboos by the hour and boo at them, showing, of course, my great superiority over mind and matter, demonstrating that I dwell in a void high over all else. But I don't— honest, lady.

My cry is this. Writers are foolish enough, from what they've told me, to believe in a lot of those taboos to their own detriment.

As a consequence, what do we find? The rut, the pit, the caldron of lost hopes and the rain of sweat. That's a pitiful picture.

A man can clatter out just so much in one pattern before the pattern becomes as solid as a prisoner's bars. Don't argue. I've been through it. It gets so that you can't write anything but what you have written before. You lose all that delightful plasticity of ideas. You are hampered by vague demons who jump up and down and scream in your ears when you fail to place so many words of straight action in a story. You groan at the thought of writing something new, because you know the conflict which will take place in your own head.

You'll drown in a sea of already written words, and the tide of youngsters will come up and sweep over you, and Davy Jones, in the form of the reject basket, will swallow your bones forever.

And mainly because of Old Man Taboo.

What courage it takes to break free! You stare at a vision of an empty cupboard. You seem to feel your toes peeping through your shoes; you already listen to the angry words of the landlord as he helps the sheriff toss your writing desk out into the street.

And you remember the taboos, and you know that if you fail to mind those taboos, if you fail to stay walled in and blinded by those ruts, you'll go broke.

And yet, if you don't jar yourself some way, then how will you climb, advance, put markets behind you and see others looming to the fore?

It's a bad spot. About a year into the game, every writer faces it, doesn't quite know what it is, groans and writhes about, and then, when the gentle news is broken—if he has friends friendly enough to break it, to tell him that his stuff is still in one place, that he must advance, for nothing can stand still—he is apt to lose months of work.

The taboos do it. You must mind the taboos, but if you do, you stand quite still for a space and then begin to slide—backwards. I wonder how many writers have wrecked themselves that way?

The solution wasn't rammed at me in the cold dazzle of day. It sneaked up on me through black nights of worry. "Damn the taboos!" And I thought about damning them. They were fetters. I couldn't actually face the fact that my stuff was juvenile. How could that be? Didn't I give it my all? And I tried to write for better markets. Markets I knew I couldn't touch. I had to make a break. I felt need of that plasticity of mind which would allow me to do something with a hero besides letting him bump off natives and kiss the girl, and I had to do something with the girl besides letting her kiss the hero and dread the villain.

But the taboos stuck and stuck until I deliberately set out one fine day and sorted out all the taboos of a certain market. Maliciously, I broke them, one by one, stringing out an off-length story.

But the thing retained its stamp. It was, after all, action for action's sake. It didn't live. It wasn't the best I'd done. And so I set out to break more taboos, bigger and better taboos.

For many, many words I wrote for the wastebasket, and then suddenly I saw a change. Plasticity was coming back. Satisfied and smug, I sat myself down and wrote a yarn and sold it higher than I had ever sold anything before.

The formula to end all formulas had worked.

The whole summation is this. Any magazine, big or small, will take something different, just off their beaten path, if that something is better to their own way of thinking than anything they have purchased before.

"What?" you say. "You mean you have to write twice as good for the same market? You mean you have to spend more time on a yarn? You mean you have to deliberately coax them out of their ideas with quality? Well, to the devil with that!"

Ah, but the glory of it! The feeling that you have done something real! And then those yarns can go higher and still sell lower the second time out. Not that I ever sell a reject, you understand. Oh, cross my heart, never. But you can sell a good piece of cloth to a native who dresses in gunnysacks and palm bark. You can sell a good fast cruiser to a fisherman used to a one-lung sloop. You can peddle can openers to people who open their cans with an axe.

And you can sell a high-class, fast-action, counter-plotted, characterized, pulsating yarn to a mag which has heretofore purchased only the action.

It can be done, is being done, and to clinch the deal, unless you're one of those who likes to lie in a rut, keeps you from slopping about in the muddy plain of medi-ocrity. You'll get rejects, but when you sell, you'll be remembered. Never fear, you'll be remembered.

Give them all their own demands plus everything you want to put into a story. Do it so well that they don't even know their taboos are being broken, and through this, escape from the pit. We'll all be saying, "Well, well, made the awards, did he? Yes, I knew him when."

EL PRESIDENTE MUNSIE

Written by
Tony Daley

Illustrated by
Lee White

About the Author

Tony Daley is a graduate of Northwestern University, where he completed their writing program. Currently, he's finishing studies in Latin and Spanish at the University of Illinois. His professional background includes directing and writing award-winning theatrical productions, writing for television and film, and contributing to numerous magazines and newspapers as an editor, illustrator and writer.

On *Calle de Huron* in Chicago, behind the recent crater where the Abassids, in their fierce awe of Allah, had left fifty town homes little more than a vitreous waste, the auxiliary group of *Los Gatos* called their members to order. To the south, the city hunched under a night sky that looked like a pile of yellow-and-brown guts, a reminder to each gang member of the true controller of their lives. Here, in the wasteland, the air stank of cabbage, gas, and ammonia. There were no cops around except for the odd security checker patrolling the worst sections of the area like a gigantic jittery cockroach. *Calle de Huron* was in the so-called "punk zone"—extrajurisdictional and, from an alderman's viewpoint, politically and socially negligible. Here were the remnants of the old neighborhood, separate but part of Chicago, *la ciudad del infierno*. Only here could *el Presidente Munsie* call the initiation to order.

But, to be safe, Jesus, *agente secundario de Los Gatos y primer pistolero*, made a sweep for surveillance, just in case a squad *de policia negra* were nearby. The black police, rogues and reprobates mostly, could recreationally hunt for gangsters.

"*Esta claro,*" Jesus said. "*No miro policia para nada.*"

Jesus was talking about how he hadn't seen the black police.

"The palmer runs a statistical regression program to figure out probable patrol events within the safety margin of a few thousand percent. We should be okay in the punk zone for approximately one hour, fifty minutes, according to the nonlinear curve estimates under a normative confidence parameter."

Munsie nodded, satisfied that the scene was clear, that there was a low probability for arrest, and eyed his initiates, *tres guerreros nuevos*. In his head, a few dozen times, Munsie had considered, in terms of calculus proofs, all the ways in which events subsequent to this meeting could turn out. He wasn't a great mathematician, he was a little raw on theory, but he intuitively understood enough underlying concepts in order to work probabilistically within the gang framework. The events to follow had a high confidence level for success.

The three new potential soldiers were doves, greens—shitbirds. They stood in a nervous group against one of the retaining walls of a bomb-scarred building. They fidgeted and brushed at their rheumy eyes, and each of them probably wondered if they'd live out the night, let alone get into *Los Gatos*.

Munsie was pretty sure they'd measure up. They'd been handpicked, like athletes, from the rotating talent pool, selected according to individual abilities and, of course, physical dexterity and endurance. Each gang-banger had good immunity, called gomune status, which was important in *la ciudad del infierno*. And each dude had a sharp brain, partly as a result of gomune, partly because of fortuitous circumstances in the hood.

But each of the soldiers was *muy nervioso*. Even Frankie, *un hombre duro*, big and bad, was shooting his cuffs and adjusting the sweat-gray collar of his shirt. Even a guy like Frankie was just a dove, a green, a shitbird.

Fear or no, these guys were going to see if they measured up. They wanted the money and safety and

Illustrated by Lee White

prestige of the gang. They wanted *mujeres* too—women in the infernal city, a place where women were obtained chiefly through financial transactions.

And *Los Gatos* wanted members to maximize the club's overall earning potential. Money was what it was all about, was what it had always been all about.

There was something else as well—something to be aspired to. Brotherhood in a small world of focused honor and filial respect, where family still meant something, where family wasn't an archaic term for a certain outmoded system of principled conjecture. *En Los Gatos* was a band ideology culled from the Roman historian Tacitus, who had, in his *Germanica*, described the concept of the *comitatus*. This concept of loyalty was *muy importante para las guerras de Los Gatos.*

Munsie grinned, remembering his own *dias de inocencia,* days of innocence, of youthful glory and rebellious spirit when, as a dove, he, too, had desperately wanted to join, to belong, to be part of something.

Tapping himself on the chest for emphasis, Munsie said, "Listen to me. Our saying is *pugnatas et pugnatas.* This is Latin for 'you fight and you fight!' No matter what, you uphold the code *de Los Gatos,* the warrior code that is as good in enterprise as it is in the field *del barrio de la ciudad del infierno."*

"Remember our own president," said Jesus. "When Munsie killed Fabs, he didn't hesitate, he didn't flinch or shirk, *porque el presidente es grande!"*

Munsie nodded solemnly, eyeing Jesus and feeling a touch of some unaccountable sensation. But he had no time to dwell on it.

He directed Jesus to tell the doves about their destination. The organoplex was a layered, tiered, splintered section of refraction within the city, a locale more than a place, that teased the corner of the eye and forced a kind of rushed seeing. Most visitors drank *cerveza* or Mexican beer before going to the organoplex, and it was good to be gomune. Once laced with narcotics, the experience was better, if you were a mere visitor out on a revel in *la ciudad de Chicago*. The amusement park bore the weight of thousands of hourly visitors, who poured in every day to play orchestras and suspend themselves in id pools. The organoplex, serving rich and poor alike, was like the old extra-London pleasure center of Shakespeare's time, taken to an exponentially increased degree of excess.

A select number of card-bearing folks went to the gaming levels and wired into worlds. Here, at the far end of the Midway, the old carny flat store chiselers and bunko artists now ran stuff like *la vida para ti* and *lex et rex*. The city allowed the flimflam as part of a complex payola scam. Things still happened in Chicago because of money, *dinero solamente*, like unlimited creds and non-indentured genetic lines.

At the top level of the plex, in the rotunda, which was in a polymorph-constructed section, an array of infini-ported time machines rested in a bay of black-and-gold rococo. Chesterfield chairs and chaise longues of Victorian cerulean and carmine velvet ran through the aisles of shafts, finials, and rods composing the skeletal fretting the cyberplasm. Each machine resembled a device of coercion and torture, furniture out of the paintings of Bacon, a sewing machine needle-stitching neurons. No smoking was permitted in the cyberplasm.

"They've cracked simcode problems on the timers," Munsie told the doves. "Now the sims are real, without any virtual flux or distortion. Whatever I want is there."

Timers playing history role-playing games were squares and yip-yops and yahoos. Timers were being used for evolutionary practice sessions for new genus development routines being done at all the multiversities on Earth and across the Synod.

But role-playing games were still way cool.

Gilly, a big-time game boy, was excited.

"Are the sims really *that* good?"

Munsie shrugged. "Computers have traditionally had a hard time duping complex systems. Variable data issues, *verdad?* Like weather systems that can't account for all gas exchanges, diverse pressures, and molecular movement on global bases in climate modeling. But the timers should be perfect sims because they're using new proofs."

"The Meninger Twister equation," Jesus said.

"Right, that equation and some others," said Munsie. He outlined a few equations in dust particles that phosphoresced then vanished.

Now came the part of explanation about the *pugnatas et pugnatas.* The initiation was compounded of old customs and rituals, most of them lost in the recesses of other tribal associations that had one time underlain the matrix of heroism and chivalric code.

Physical exertion was still part of the pattern, especially the exertion of gomune individuals, either man or woman, who had proven themselves as streeters. Each of the green dudes had worked in Logan Square, had killed and avoided being killed, and had therefore aced certain tribulations *mano a mano.*

Physical exertion and trial were connected to the idea of energy being used in a holy, sacred way for only *Los Gatos.* Energy was built up over time in a status of holding, waiting to be vented, like steam expanding to make power available as a rotating torque to a flywheel or crankshaft in an engine.

The gang was the engine, the members its potential sources of energy. And physical exertion, in the initiation, was a clean use of tested will and nerves against a very real, very dangerous challenge. Custom and rule and precept were governed by considerations of the stable natural. And it was all deemed good for the club.

Using the organoplex and its timers for ritual in a gamer context initially excited the doves.

At the moment, Gilly wasn't thinking about the ritual.

"Oh, yeah! Meninger redefined the axioms based on a new quantum state paradigm. The games should be incredible, now."

Frankie nudged him in the ribs. "*¿Te gusta la simulación? Chocha?*"

"*¡Sí, me gusta!*"

"I knew it. You just been waiting for total sim, pussy," Frankie laughed.

"And you weren't?"

"I don't need any sims when I got real *chocha todos los dias, mi compañero del barrio.*"

Jesus took out a small gelatin cap suspended in a solution phial. The cap was about two inches long and its insides swirled with milky fluid.

"Damn, it looks just like a horse tranquilizer," Gilly said. "Where'd you get that timer processor?"

Jesus, ignoring the question, said, "We're currently maintaining a good confidence level on probability of success on the timer switch scenario."

"How randomized was the sampling on invasive procedures?" Frankie asked.

"Pretty much so," replied Munsie, looking at Jesus. *"¿Eso es correcto, señor?"*

"Sí, sí, señor presidente," Jesus said with a slight smile.

"But how're we gonna do a switch in a place like the organoplex, with that hard cover?" Gilly asked doubtfully.

Munsie smiled. *"Estas muy curioso, Gilly.* You always want to know things. *¿Te gusta soltar la lengua?"*

"Shut your *agujero!*" Frankie told Gilly.

"And you shut it, too," Munsie snapped. "You're a greenie and a dove and a *puta,* just like the others. All you maggots—shut it."

As terrible as Frankie's expression was, it was nothing to Munsie's look of casual annihilation. Everyone knew that *el presidente* was at ease with many things beyond the comprehension of the average *caballero.*

"We're going to enter a pseudo-Eocene sim," Munsie explained. "You all know about the period from the dials I gave you. The new cap will give the current hybridized paleo-sim that researchers are using.

"The period will have one nasty-ass order of fauna, *Creodonta.* Creodonts resembled, morphologically, *Carnivora vera,* the regular carnivores. Creodonts were different in terms of skull and teeth, and were apex members of comparative predatory niches for a substantial amount of time."

Munsie changed the air. A roughly bear-sized animal with a golden pelt was soon rotating in a shimmering field.

"This is a *patriofelis.* It is one bad motor scooter. Look at this *bomba.* Admire it. Get to know it. Because tonight, it's going to get to know *you.*"

The doves nearly shit a collective brick.

Munsie laughed with pleasure. Doves always freaked when he showed them an animal.

"I'm putting all you three bone smokers in a simulation of Patty's hunting ground."

"What do we got to do?" asked Frankie.

"Survive."

"Do we get some firepower, at least? Even in a sim, you get firepower."

"You get a hand laser good for cutting wood," Munsie grinned. "Figure out what to do with it, and be glad you're lucky enough to get the laser. When I went heads up a few years back, I didn't even have clothes on my back. And I went up against that new gigantic species of *Deinocheirus* that made even T-rex look like a Chihuahua, in the best Mongolian sim then available for time travelers.

Jesus's mouth twisted to the side at Munsie's last remark.

"How long we got to stay in the sim?" Gilly asked nervously.

Jesus did some palmer calculations.

"A few minutes, true time. But maybe a day *en tiempo, señor*. We'll have to work fast, before security tumbles and shuts down the unit."

Gilly couldn't stop shaking. "I don't know about this," he muttered.

Munsie put his arm around Gilly's shoulder and led him to the side.

"You don't want your brains beaten in, Gilly. And you don't want to be eating through a straw for six months. And I know having a bag on your hip would cramp your style."

Gilly looked almost cross-eyed with grief.

"Don't back out now," said Munsie. "You'll only look bad to the troops."

"But that *thing*—!"

"Why throw away membership in the club? You know what we do?"

Gilly shook his head.

"We have fun, man. And fun ain't easy to come by in the sun—not if you don't have the right connections."

"I just don't know."

"You shirking duty to the club?" Munsie asked sharply.

Gilly looked up in horror. "I'd never do that!"

"You're doing it right now! Maybe you think this is all some kind of joke."

"No!"

"I thought you had loyalty."

"But going heads up against that monster . . ."

"It's a *simulation*, right?"

Gilly floundered. "Munz—maybe this was easier for you. I—I mean, that wasn't even a current sim you went through—"

A dark look passed over Munsie's face. When he resumed, his voice was tight.

"I put my personal feelings aside for the sake of responsibility. Without us all contributing to the club, we have nothing. The Romans created the keystone civilization in the West, and you know how they did that? They put their personal feelings aside and supported the club. And Rome became great and stayed great because the men were brave and loyal and were willing to do anything to support the club.

"Now what're you telling me? Are you saying you don't have what it takes to measure up? Are you saying you're not going to support the club?"

Gilly looked painfully uncertain, even though Frankie was daring him with a fierce look.

Finally, Gilly shook his head and almost wildly said, "I can do this thing, Munsie. I can go heads up against—" he gaped at the creodont. "But I was just saying that you can do stuff like this, Munsie. You're *el presidente*. It's easier for you."

"So if it's harder for you, Gilly, then aren't you making that much more of a sacrifice, and isn't your membership in the club going to be that much more valuable? Think about it."

Munsie cuffed Gilly's head—like a mother lion might do to a mischievous cub.

"Now get back in line. What do you got on the stove at home that's so important to cook up? Forget it. Just remember our slogan: *pugnatas et pugnatas.*"

Gilly nodded, smiling weakly. He repeated the slogan to himself.

"You keep saying it."

A moment later, Jesus asked Munsie if Gilly was really squared away.

Munsie licked his teeth. "Well, either Gilly's really that scared . . . or he's a ringer."

"A spy from the Simon City Royals?"

"Maybe. The Royals have wanted to crack us down for all that turf we grabbed last year. They've tried infiltrating us before."

"You think Gilly is doubling?"

"*Posiblemente, señor,*" Munsie said. "Gill asks too many questions. But more than that, he puts me on edge for some reason I can't say. I have instincts about these things."

Jesus's eyes widened. "So what do we do?"

"We let him go through the initiation. If Gilly tries bailing, we nail *sus cojones en la mesa.*"

"Fabs was in the Royals," Jesus said.

He glanced sharply at Munsie, though the president didn't see the look.

"Maybe it wasn't such a good idea killing her. All that retribution shit. *Para acciones malas,* they have the same slogan we do—*pugnatas et pugnatas.* Maybe you shouldn't have killed Fabs."

"Mention that diesel dyke again," said Munsie quietly, "and I'll do something to you. *¿Entiendes?*"

"*Sí, señor presidente,*" said Jesus, after a moment.

•••

When the gang got to the ziggurat of Fun City, Munsie worked out the program exchange with Jesus.

The evening guard change on security was coming up. During an interval, the time machines shut down for the next round of gaming. A complex procedure of military-style calls and passes was observed, from the Deck Manager on down to the comp personnel who actually ran the consoles, with a security sequence calibrated to hijack illegal gamers skimming the sims.

During this change-up, Jesus would use a phony card to override the biosensors long enough for him to replace the standard programmer with the new cap.

Surrounded by gamer's rainbows, Munsie huddled Jesus and the recruits on the second-level play grid.

"Use these," Munsie said, handing out dream cards. "Jesus's overwritten them in quantum code so that your projected time period, geographical location, and climate level will trigger our customized travel routine. Present your cards to the watch robot. The cards will start the timers once Jesus has reconfigured the system. Any questions?"

No one had questions, but Gilly stared vacantly at his dream card.

"Are you cool?" Munsie asked him sharply. "*¿Estas tranquilo, señor?*"

Gilly nodded, gazing emptily at his card. "Sure, *señor presidente.*"

Munsie jerked his thumb toward the lift. "*¡Luego vamos con las mujeres!*"

Suddenly, Munsie stopped and biffed himself on the forehead with his palm.

"*¡O Madre!* I forgot to explain something! In these sims, you can die."

Even Frankie did a double take.

"Jesus H. Christ!" blurted Mickey, the quiet one. "You should have said something before!"

Munsie frowned. "Would it have made a difference, Mickey? Would you have pussied out of coming up here? Realism is a *good* thing," Munsie added angrily. "This is going to *test* you. You can always bail, but if you do, you're going to get shitcanned. Now I already gave my little inspirational speech to the Gill Man. *¿Tienen más preguntas?*"

Gilly quickly shook his head. "No questions, *señor presidente.*"

Frankie laughed halfheartedly and flexed his powerful muscles. "Ah, Munsie, you know this ain't no thang."

Mickey looked around for a moment, blowing air up his face, ruffling his bangs. Finally, he shrugged and gave a lopsided grin, scratched his ear and kind of chuckled and said, "Hell, *es verdad.* This ain't no thang."

"*¡Bueno, chicos!*" Munsie smiled.

After the doves had gone on ahead, Jesus grabbed Munsie's arm.

"You're not going up there too?"

Munsie smacked away Jesus's hand.

"But with the new cap, *you* could die," said Jesus. "Besides, if we get caught, we'll all be doing time in Pontiac on a short chain. *Escuela dura con putas.* You should stay out of the loop. You're the goddamn *presidente,* Munsie. *Tienes responsabilidad con Los Gatos.*"

"*Mi compañero, mi hermano,*" Munsie said, soothing and sharp-eyed, patting the kid's cheeks.

His hand slid down to Jesus's throat and suddenly squeezed.

"I'd hate to lose you. But you can wind up in veggie bags, just like anybody else, if you don't follow my orders without question."

Ten minutes later, real time, the boys were in the pseudo-Cenozoic.

•••

Mickey smelled the strong ammonia scent of spoor still glistening wetly on an oak at the edge of the creodont's territorial range. The sky was deep blue and clear and fleeced with clouds, so different from the miasmic hue of shit and piss hanging over the megalopolis. There were flowers everywhere, real flowers that had been carefully reproduced down to the curl of petals and bend of stamens, with a moist fan of sweet odor. Mickey didn't doubt that he was in a beautiful place.

Beautiful, except for the *patriofelis*.

Clutching the pin laser, Mickey walked diagonally, without any real direction or plan, moving along a path that cut and wended through dense underbrush. Here, a heavy row of flowers flattened under his boots as Mickey approached a clearing ringed by gigantic old-growth trees that reduced the sunlight to a misty emerald twilight.

Suddenly there was a loud droning buzz to his right, and Mickey tripped and fell back into a thicket without noticing right away the shooting pain in his left hand. He sprawled, clutching for the pin laser that had spun away out of his pain-weakened grasp.

He noticed his palm, reddened and shiny under a balloonlike swelling.

He yelled with the throbbing pain, scrambled out of the weeds and fell face first into a wide clearing. A swarm of bees droned in fury and dogged the air.

Something passed like a vibrating shadow over Mickey's face.

His throat had closed up, preventing his scream, and his whole body felt on fire with a series of clenching tendons of heat that seemed to clamp around each of his bones, tightening and closing, as his stomach gave the first spasms of agonized nausea.

Mickey crawled as the swarm coated him, the thousands of bees lighting again and again, relentlessly stinging. He realized that he had no voice left to give the exit code out of the simulation, and that Munsie had probably planned it that way.

•••

Frankie emerged on the edge of grassland, where the land sloped into the wide tufted plain running across to the other side of the valley. Large rat-faced carnivores were hunched in a clearing, finishing off the carcass of a proto-elephant, whose tattered rib cage curved up from a red welter of meat. The air stank of blood and feces from the ripped intestines littering the grass.

Growling and snarling, lashing out at one another in a greedy melee of desperate hunger, the carnivores ignored Frankie in their zeal to gather as much nourishment as possible before the inevitable onslaught of other predators or scavengers.

Frankie—who called himself *el mejor hombre* because of his prowess *con las chicas*—backed away into the underbrush as his jockey shorts filled with urine. No simulation had ever been *this* real.

A rippling crash of shrubbery snapped his head around.

In the dim shadows a hulking shape, roughly the size of a bear but with a cat's blunt, telescoped muzzle, lurked among the layered foliage.

Frankie ran. Branches cracked, and vines and creepers tore in the undergrowth behind him as he plunged through dense brush that pulled and yanked at his clothing. He turned toward another clearing, hearing behind him the chuffing roar of the beast. He fell, clawed himself upward, and ran again.

He saw a tree rising like a leaning totem pole out of the low weeds and ran for it, thinking that if he could get up into the higher, thinner branches, he might be safe from the creodont, not realizing that even some large bears climbed trees very well.

He was just seven feet up the trunk, shimmying frantically, clawing at the bark, when the animal's paw fell on him with almost loving gentleness.

Frankie slammed to the ground. The impact punched the air out of his body. A ragged pain, like a jigsaw pattern lined with jolts of electricity, shot down his spine, though instead of loosening, his sphincter muscles clenched.

Then, feeling behind himself to assess the damage, he detected a nub of bone sticky to the touch and flecked with wet shreds of skin. But now he didn't really feel much pain, just a vague tickling pressure that seemed to feather delicately along to the end of his tailbone.

He sprawled on the ground. The animal had cuffed the side of his head with enough force to bang the brain inside its case. Frankie, who had boxed throughout high school, recognized the blurring sensation, the abrupt wave of disorientation, which soon flooded over his eyes in a gray tide.

Still half-conscious and going into shock, he saw a golden flash of movement as the gigantic predator lunged.

Frankie squeezed the laser's trigger, but only managed to singe his own leg, though he didn't feel the heat beam cut through, only an airy absence of sensation that crawled up his body.

He couldn't scream because his throat had been torn out, but there was still enough cerebral blood in his cranium to nourish cortical activity, so that he could, for around fifty seconds, watch the predator chewing his left thigh.

• • •

As Frankie and Mickey were dying, Gilly fell forward, the grass-tufted ground rushing up to meet his jaw. He moaned from the impact and rolled over through moist, clinging weeds, and vomited in a delayed convulsion of panic and fear.

Around him was a fringe of forest. It was thick with ancestral species of linden and thorn-studded fir, and ringed by the hills of a small valley, which sloped down into the denser patches of dark green thicket and deadfalls.

A storm must have just passed through because, bark torn off by wind or slashed by lightning, and moldering leaves and offal sent their dark odors upward from the valley floor. A white mist curled through stands of trees that shadowed the deeper gullies. Through a break in what looked to be mixed oak and elm trees, Gilly saw part of the steppe stretching beyond the valley in a flat, gray-green table almost bereft of trees. Here the sky was a blue bright enough to hurt one's eyes, and was striped by clouds racing after the tail of a storm still visible as a gray murkiness on the western horizon.

Gilly smelled what he thought to be territorial scent—a kind of harsh pheromone odor—but couldn't be sure whether it was the creodont's. He hoped that it wasn't. But maybe it didn't matter one way or the other in an ecosystem teeming with myriad predators. A smaller animal, even fox-sized, could do considerable damage. Looking upward, Gilly saw small rodents leaping through the branches. They called in sharp, rasping sounds, scattering flocks of birds and smaller mammals, which fanned in a chattering rush over the rain-darkened boughs. Patters of rain, shaken from the upper branches, fell in Gilly's face.

He tried figuring out what to do: If he could only hold on, prove himself to Munsie, to the rest of them. If he could only hold on, he might put himself in a better position in the club than even *el presidente* could have imagined, having gone heads up in the best simulation available, having toughed it out under circumstances that most people could never endure.

What might be Gilly's reputation then, with the *real* leaders in Chicago, the cats controlling downtown and all the radiating neighborhoods?

If he could hold on, if he could prove himself in this situation, there might be no limit to his advancement.

One thing Gilly knew was that on the steppe or here in the valley, he didn't have a chance, because he would be too exposed on all sides, given scant hope of defense or cover.

But the woods looked formidable, shadowed enough in the brake so that even a large animal such as *patriofelis* could use deep cover in order to make a strangling kill.

There was one hope, the only hope, really, and that was to climb a tree. If the *patriofelis*, or any other beast, tried following, Gilly could turn and whip out the pin laser and fire at short range into the animal's face, at least to put it off and make it realize that *this* prey wasn't worth the trouble in energy expenditure.

Gilly brushed away sweat. He stood immobile for a moment. There was another smell, ripe with carrion, lying heavily around him. Again he looked up, letting his gaze drift along the heavier, lower branches, and finally saw the dangling limb of an animal.

The limb had been raggedly shorn off and was now a flyblown crimson bundle, glistening with muscles and yellowish-white ribbons of fat on the glints of carti-lage and bone. The meat was just like the food larder a leopard hoards in treetops, above scavengers and competitors; and the size of the limb suggested the kill of a rhino or elephant—just the sort of animal a large creodont was adapted to hunt.

Gilly said the exit code, but nothing happened.

He repeated the code, in a high, frantic voice—and nothing happened.

Then, in a fluttering spray, a covey of birds took wing, and the rodents groped wildly along the vines and boughs, squealing in terror as a striped form slid out of a nearby thicket.

The animal's golden eyes watched Gilly. Its black gums silvered with spittle.

Then the animal, in a rasping, barely human grunt, said, "Surprise, Gilly."

•••

Medics pulled Mickey out of the formfitting chair and gave him cardiac shocks and revived him. Coughing phlegm, eyes tearing, Mickey nodded in understanding to the medics' questions, and willingly lay on the ambulance stretcher, knowing he was eventually going to jail for a long time.

Nearby, Frankie was already recovering. He was dizzy and weak and didn't understand what was going to happen to him.

Meanwhile, police walked onto the timer deck, eyeing the contraption of the main simulation console, where Jesus sat behind a panel, expressionless as he looked into the timer pit.

Munsie sat in front of the timer, grinning, eyes glazed over.

•••

"The others lasted, Gilly. But you aren't strong enough, even after I acted like a father toward you. You don't have the mustard, *amigo. No lo tienes.*"

Munsie settled on his haunches and pawed the ground.

• • •

On the simulation deck, two officers had to hold Gilly up as he wobbled between them. His eyes gaped and he kept repeating the exit code cycle in a terrified voice.

• • •

Gilly hadn't yet vanished.

"You're caught like a rat," Munsie growled. "You're going to squeal on the others. You're going to tell me who's trying to sell us out to the Royals. *¿Eres agente de la policia?* The police, Gilly?"

The creodont's golden eyes did not waver.

"It will seem like forever, subjectively," Munsie promised. "Being in here, living in the sim. You've probably heard about a recycle patch, programmed to run this scenario for as many times as I want. That's what I've done, Gilly, used a recycle patch to keep us here for as long as I want, for as long as it takes to slowly rip you apart, over and over again."

• • •

When the cops took Jesus off the timer console, he was through with his business anyway. He limply submitted to them, but simple surrender was not enough for this infraction.

A nightstick whistled through the air and cracked Jesus across the face. He reeled back, holding his broken nose.

"What have you got to say?" the cop asked.

Jesus shook his head, flailing blood.

Technicians were trying to undo the damage Jesus had wrought on the equipment.

The cop finally gripped Jesus's shirt front.

"How do we get the cap out?"

"*Pugnatas et pugnatas,*" Jesus muttered.

•••

"*Con el tiempo,* Frankie and Mick died quickly," Munsie told Gilly. "But I won't be quick with you. Because you sold out the club."

•••

The cops tried *thumbing* Jesus, the worst thing you could do to a suspect, even to a gangster.

Grinning through his pain, Jesus nodded toward the timer area, where the medics were struggling with the grips holding Munsie into the timer lattice. Then a doctor rushed over and belayed the disconnect order.

"The sim's still going in cycles," the doctor barked. "A disconnection will kill this man!"

Jesus's head rolled. He was thinking of a young woman he had known, with whom he had lived on the streets of *la ciudad del infierno,* with whom he had shared the broils and brawls *del barrio.*

•••

In the Eocene, Munsie tried yelling at the glittering shadow of Gilly as it faded, but suddenly no human sound emerged from his throat, only a roar of cheated anger.

•••

"Turn it off!"

The cop kept yelling at Jesus, whose split nose dribbled blood.

"Let him stay in there awhile," Jesus murmured, eyes half shut with pain.

He gave a weak laugh and drunkenly waved his good hand in a gesture of dismissal.

"Just a few minutes more. It's not a long time. What's in a few minutes. Oh, yes, for him . . . for him, it's different, of course. For him subjective time's a bit different, indeed."

Jesus's face suddenly twisted as he struggled up against the restraining hands of the policemen.

"He *wanted* to be an animal! That's why he went up on the simulation deck and locked in, connected up to the cerebral lattice in the timer. He wanted to go *back* there and *torment* Gilly, because he thought that poor little bastard was the shill for the Royals. But with Munsie it wasn't just about retribution or payback or punishment. He likes doing this stuff. He's done it before. I've seen him do it."

Jesus laughed wildly.

"He did it to me, when I was a *caballero de verdad!* He spent three subjective days with me. But I didn't let on or let up. He never found out that I'm the shill."

Then Jesus looked almost pityingly at the cops.

"But I didn't do it for the *dinero*. ¡No, señores—no solo por dinero!"

Jesus banged on the glass overlooking the arcade.

Munsie now slowly thrashed and strained, pushing in a quiet, slow, silent struggle against the villi that flared in widening, vegetal arrays out of the translucent canopy.

"Stay in there, Munsie," he cried. "For what you did to Fabs . . . you just stay in there!"

As the cops herded Jesus into the paddy wagon, the precinct commander nudged the detective managing the crime scene.

"Who the hell was Fabs? Name doesn't check on the palmer."

"Junky code for alpha fem, rival gang. His mother," the detective said.

He spat in his palm, looked around, then wiped it on his coattail.

"She was a killer too, like the rest. We shoulda thumbed her too, right out of the womb, like they do some of them who the probability stats show as likely criminals. We shoulda thumbed Fabs and then she wouldn't have bred."

• • •

The creodont stalked prey. As an apex carnivore, this particular female—more robust than most others in the dynasty, which had lasted for twenty-five years in this valley's territory—could live a very long time on the substantial kills, because of its superior speed and power.

Perhaps she could even last longer, through specially controlled environmental conditions, or stochastic variables programmed for lesser competition than the usual ecosystem pattern, all because of algorithms in the deck system.

The memory of Gilly faded like those of other cheated prey.

All variables in species behavior had been mapped and gauged within the local environment. The animal's existence repeated its nuances of activity within a pattern, and Munsie's thoughts were submerged into the programming of the creodont life cycle, and he was unable to resist the predatory impulses of the host animal. A phrase in Latin he had known since he was a boy slipped from his ever more tenuous recall. And then it was gone. She saw a group of herbivores drinking at a pool. She padded slowly through the grass, carefully staying downwind from the snorting, shuffling animals. She succumbed to the hunt.

And when the moment came, she ran the prey down, killing with a crushing grip of fangs around its neck.

Then, occasionally pausing to rend the air with roars of threat and warning, the creodont tore the pig-thing's flesh, digging greedily through blood and entrails and cracking bones until marrow oozed through their jagged splinters.

When the time of mating came, the creodont hunkered on a bluff or ridge overlooking her territory. Her mate beckoned in a long cry that descended from crescendos of almost painful, desperate need, and the drive to maintain the dynasty took over her instincts, and she succumbed.

Eventually, a male loped near, tentatively, and the female showed that she was not aggressive so that the male wouldn't kill her. By sliding on her back and presenting her limbs at a certain attitude, chuffing with quiet, snarling invitation, she demonstrated her readiness. Then, in a sliding, quick motion, the male mounted her, his haunches bunched and trembling as he repeatedly stabbed urgently to impregnate. She roared in a paradoxical fury of violation and complacency.

And Munsie had, in all probability, fifteen years left on the plain.

TIME OUT OF MIND

Written by
Everett S. Jacobs

Illustrated by
Andy B. Clarkson

About the Author

Everett S. Jacobs has lived in the Kansas City area all fifty-one years of his life. "Jake" has a bachelor's degree in business administration, a master's degree in public administration, and is currently working on a dual Ph.D. in public policy and social science. He has been a fantasy and science fiction fan since the age of twelve, but only a serious writer for the past five years. He has been married for thirty years to his loving wife, Tina. He has three daughters, two granddaughters, one grandson, two dogs, three cats and about a dozen goldfish the last time he counted.

About the Illustrator

Andy Clarkson lives and works in Columbus, Ohio. He graduated from the Columbus College of Art and Design in May of 1999. He has been freelancing as an illustrator and mural artist in Columbus since then. He likes to work in a range of moods from serious and direct to the bizarre and unexpected. He doesn't try to limit subject matter for his artwork, as he is always expanding on what interests him. His career goal is to do cover art for SF books and graphic novels.

The rotting carcass of an apatosaurus blocked the intersection of Highway 9 and Needham Road. Its head lay across the collapsed roof of Petree's Amoco station, its tail extended some sixty feet down Highway 9. Thomas Randall coasted his dust-covered ATV to a stop before it, letting the engine idle down to a bubbling purr.

Ignoring the overpowering stench, Thomas surveyed the scene with studied concentration. A pair of vultures returned his gaze from their perch on the roof of the tractor-trailer rig that had crashed into the dinosaur's body. At least another dozen of the scraggly birds paused and eyed him suspiciously before returning to their prehistoric buffet. There were no signs of more dangerous scavengers, so he cautiously maneuvered around the rotting hulk.

As he cut through the Amoco parking lot, he glanced at the mound of earth and the lopsided wooden cross in one of the landscape beds. The poor trucker. The guy had had no warning, no time to avoid colliding with the apatosaurus when it suddenly appeared in its displaced bubble of time. At least Thomas had given the trucker a decent burial.

Before pulling across Needham Road, Thomas stopped the ATV again and studied a good three or four miles of the road in either direction. It looked placid in the afternoon stillness—sun-washed asphalt stretching into an infinity of forsaken cornfields. Round time-bubble traces randomly cratered the fields like the surface of the moon. His artist's eye caught the subtle shadings and strong autumn colors that dominated the scenery. For a second, he longed to capture this surreal landscape on canvas; but there were more urgent matters at hand.

He looked at his watch, 2:15—almost four hours since the last time-wave. There should be another one any moment. Another time-wave meant another chance for time-bubbles to form.

He waited, fingers tight upon the handgrips of the ATV. He still got the creeps when the time for each wave occurred—wondering if the whole world would change around him. He believed he was one of the lucky ones—someone who had not just up and disappeared like so many others. God, how awful—in one time one moment, and then gone the next, to who knew where or when.

Impatiently, he inched the ATV forward to cross the pavement of Needham, then gunned it suddenly as a faint movement to his left caused familiar panic to grip him. The sturdy little vehicle roared across the road and onto the trail he had worn into the former farmland, with his trips between Smithton and Weberly. He glanced fearfully back, but the movement had only been dust devils whirling down the empty road. He clenched convulsively on the brakes and the ATV slid sideways to a stop in the rutted trail. His heart pounded heavily as the surge of adrenaline ran its course.

Suddenly, a thunderclap of displaced air reverberated across the fields, announcing the formation of a time-bubble nearby. Thomas spotted an iridescent shimmer about a mile down Highway 9. It looked like a giant soap bubble winking into existence. The strong smell of ozone washed across him. Another deafening thunderclap came and the bubble melted into nothingness. Inside its hundred-yard circle of time-shifted earth, a half-dozen Conestoga wagons materialized. Men shouted, horses reared, and women screamed in shock. A team of horses ran off, dragging half a wagon with them; the other half left behind in whatever time lay beyond the bubble's perimeter. Thomas lowered his head and let loose a deep sigh. *Why not?* he asked himself. Highway 9 ran along part of the old Santa Fe Trail.

He watched the dazed pioneers mill around for a few minutes, then he quickly made a head count. At least twenty of them, not counting children or others who might still be in the wagons. Damn! More mouths to feed. He'd let Gloria know as soon as he reached Weberly. She would send somebody out to explain their predicament and help as much as they could. He needed to worry about other things at the moment.

He checked the closures of the flaps on his ever-present backpack, and inspected the clip in the semiautomatic rifle in the scabbard duct-taped across the ATV's handle-bars. He took one last look at the pioneers—they were pulling the wagons into a circle. Squinting into the sun, it was difficult to see them clearly. For a moment, he thought he saw black stripes across the beige flanks of a number of the horses, but he could not be sure.

Revving the ATV's engine to a dull roar, he lurched forward. The trail got rougher ahead, and he needed to concentrate on maneuvering through the narrow ravines along Little Blue Creek. He prayed he would not run across another saber-toothed tiger.

• • •

Illustrated by Andy B. Clarkson

The stoop in front of Weberly's City Hall, a former bingo parlor in headier days, shone clean from a fresh sweeping. A pot of wilted red geraniums beside the door looked more alive than Elmer Jenkins sitting next to it did. A shotgun rested in the crook of the old man's arm.

"Looks like you made it all right, Tommy," Elmer said, squinting at Thomas's bulging backpack.

"Well, I didn't get all the medicine we need, but enough to tide us over until we can make a run into Springfield."

"Good, good," Elmer muttered. "Gloria's inside worrying over the food stocks again."

"Well, I've more news for her to worry about," Thomas said, jogging up the wooden steps.

"Gloria!" he yelled through the tattered screen door, then swung it wide to enter, allowing the ever curious Elmer to step inside behind him.

Thomas slipped the backpack off in one smooth motion and lifted it to the faded, linoleum-covered counter that separated the mayor from the rest of Weberly.

"Back here, Tom," Gloria responded from the shadowed office beyond. He squinted into the darkness. The grating of wooden chair legs against wooden floor made Thomas flinch. Any sudden noise had that effect on him nowadays.

"Did you get the meds all right?" she asked, reaching for the backpack. Thomas held on to one of the backpack's straps, never wanting the pack and its precious contents out of his reach.

Gloria smiled as she opened the flap of the pack and pulled the needed drugs out, one by one, arranging them in a careful row across the countertop.

Gloria had been a beautiful woman once, Thomas thought, until age and extra weight changed her outward appearance. But she shone with a special radiance when she smiled. Thomas figured her to be in her mid-fifties, twenty-five years his senior. She had been a high-school classmate of his dead mother.

"Ampicillin, great!" Her smile grew wider as she checked off the items from a tattered list. "Can you run the insulin out to Ronnie tomorrow?" she asked, looking at Thomas across the top half of her eyeglasses. Her eyes shone cerulean blue.

"Sure. I can take it first thing in the morning if you want."

"That'd be so helpful." Her smile formed again. "Well, you done good, Tom. I don't know where we'd be without you doing all this running for us." She paused, but he could tell she wanted to say more, to ask the question that always waited on everyone's lips: "See anything new?"

"A wagon train just appeared near Needham and Highway 9. I counted about twenty people—but there's probably more than that."

"Dammit," Gloria said, closing her eyes and rubbing her brow. "How are we gonna help that many?"

"Maybe we should just let 'em fend for themselves," Elmer said, scratching one age-spotted ear. "They'll have their own supplies and they're accustomed to hunting and such. There's nothing that says we have to offer 'em help."

"I can't ignore them, Elmer. You know that. At least we're sophisticated enough to try to understand what's going on—but those folks? It's gonna be hard enough explaining *when* they are. They won't even begin to understand how they got here. To them, it might as well be the work of the Devil." She frowned, processing the new information and planning what would be needed.

"I'll send Bob Lucas and his oldest boy out to talk with them."

Thomas smiled to himself. He admired her spirit so. She managed to keep the town going and helped everywhere she could, despite the setbacks. She was the reason he stayed on in Weberly. She took everything that life threw at her with calm acceptance and a rigid backbone. He appreciated that more than he wanted to admit.

"Anything happen here while I was gone?" Thomas asked.

"Nothing serious that I know of yet," Gloria said. "Tolliver's bean field's full of two-hundred-year-old oaks now—that happened just after you left. No one reported anything else."

"Good," Thomas said. "Well, I'm gonna head home. I've got some work around there I need to tend to." He turned for the door.

"You do that, Tom," Gloria said wearily. "Thanks again. Say, what are you doing for dinner tonight? I'm baking one of those old hens from Ronnie's place, and there'll be apple pie for dessert."

Thomas stopped and smiled. He was unable to resist Gloria's apple pie. "7:30?"

"7:00, if you want to help set the table."

"7:00 it is. See you then."

He rolled the ATV to its parking spot behind the hardware store across the street, and then shouldered his rifle and backpack, walking the two blocks to his house.

Weberly had not been much of a town before the time disruptions began. It felt even smaller and more deserted now, six months after the first time-waves. Most of the townsfolk had moved to the government camps that dotted the rural landscape from Ohio to Colorado. Only a few people had stayed on in Weberly and, like him, they accepted the hand fate dealt them—they'd rather be in their own homes than in a makeshift tent-city patrolled by the National Guard.

As Thomas walked up his front steps, he glanced across at Lydia Smith's house next door. She and a perfect sphere of her garden plot disappeared during the first week of the time-waves; a weathered crater marked the spot where she had last stood. *The poor old soul,* Thomas thought. The scientists said that there was no predicting where—or more rightly, *when*—someone had disappeared to. He just hoped she was someplace pleasant.

Thomas pushed his front door open and checked for any changes with a cursory glance around the living room. Everything looked the way he had left it that morning. He pulled off his sweat-stained T-shirt and tossed it over the back of a chair.

Walking into his cramped kitchen, he approached the one convenience left to him, an old refrigerator hunkering in the corner. Miraculously, power still came across the lines into town. Before the state troopers quit driving in once or twice a week, they had warned everyone to use electricity sparingly. Well, the power still flowed, but no one had seen a trooper in weeks.

He counted ten bottles of beer left and decided that his successful return from Smithton called for a celebration. He pulled one of the long necks out and twisted off its cap. The beer splashed delightfully cold against the back of his throat.

He wandered into his studio, a long high-ceilinged room with large windows to catch the light. The afternoon sun slanted in, softly gilding everything with a golden hue that only occurred this late in September. He sat down and contemplated the large, unfinished landscape mounted on its easel. It reflected the photographic detail that had made him the darling of the art world: the meticulous rendering of individual leaves on the towering oak trees; the subtle shades and texturing of a wildflower field; an unfinished cabin reflected in a winding trout stream.

He studied the painting thoughtfully, then turned away from it. The New York banker who had commissioned it was probably dead by now, or at least no longer interested in a Thomas Randall original. Still, Thomas could not abide a painting to go unfinished, and who knew, maybe the banker would show up one day for it? He laughed softly to himself as he imagined the banker's black limo negotiating the narrow, potholed streets of Weberly.

Monty, Thomas's agent, had thought him insane for moving back to this little Kansas town. But New York had proved too hectic a lifestyle for Thomas. Besides, he could paint anywhere, and he felt most comfortable in Weberly, surrounded by the more pleasant memories of his life.

"Living here saved you, bud," he said to himself.

He had last spoken with his agent over six months ago. Briefly, he wondered if Monty survived. New York had been hit hard.

In just a few months, the sudden alterations in time had ended much of the modern world. The big cities like New York were in chaos. Places where people, buildings, and vehicles concentrated were impacted the worst by the time-bubbles.

Thomas imagined driving along one of the freeways with cars, buildings, and trees from the past materializing right in front of you, or even in the same place as you—like the apatosaurus at Needham and 9. The radio reports said that millions died or disappeared those first few weeks. The end of the world, at least as humanity knew it, came from an unexpected direction—the past.

Lying on his worktable was one of the flyers that the National Guard helicopters had dropped all over the area. It tried to explain how you could expect the bubbles on a regular basis; they coincided with the rotation of the anomaly. Somehow this huge anomaly, this *singularity*, out in space, had wandered near the solar system, rotating and sending out powerful particle waves. As the waves crossed the earth's path, they generated time-bubbles that altered time—broke it into pieces and then scattered them. They could predict when the waves would occur, but their outcome—that was another problem altogether. People and things disappeared, other people and things from the past appeared, often displacing whatever had been in the present. The only predictable pattern was that things only moved forward in time, not back. Nothing from the future had ever appeared anywhere. The TV evangelists said that was because there was no future—at least not for humanity.

Paradoxes and such should have cropped up, or maybe they had, but reality kept changing to accommodate them. God, how the scientists argued about it. He supposed they were still arguing about it, somewhere. Time-arrows; time-bubbles; multiple timelines—it was all very confusing. The scientists believed that because the anomaly arrived in 2002, that made the year a time *nexus*—everything changing in relation to it.

Thomas shook his head and took another long swig of beer. Just thinking about it gave him a headache. He glanced back at his painting and sighed. Picking up a brush, he dabbed it into a glob of yellow ocher and began to concentrate on the wildflowers.

•••

Candlelight shone through the front windows of City Hall as Thomas went up the steps. Gloria lived in the back now. She had a little kitchenette, a cot, a dining area and a bathroom—all the comforts of home. She only returned to her house on the west end of town to get clothing or books and such. She'd been a widow for years and claimed the house was just too big for her, but Thomas knew better. She was closer to the action here, closer to the only friends she had left in this world.

Thomas heard the rattle of pots and pans from the kitchen as he entered. He slipped his backpack and rifle off and set them next to his chair. The last time-wave had passed around 6:15, so he could relax a little, for a while.

"Gloria?" he called. "Need some help?"

"Of course I do," she gasped, bustling into the dining area with a stack of dishes. She pushed a stray lock of gray hair away from her face. "Do your male thing in there and carve the bird," she said, nodding her head toward the kitchen.

The meal was delicious. Elmer joined them briefly, taking just enough time to down ample portions of chicken and mashed potatoes before he headed home. Thomas stood at the front windows watching the old man's scrawny form disappear up the street. The night outside was quiet and dark, as only a small town's evening can be. *A nearly empty small town*, Thomas thought.

After clearing the dishes, they resumed their seats at the table. The light from the two candles warmed the room like a slow sip of wine. Gloria's face glowed from the darkness reminiscent of a Rembrandt portrait.

He liked these private moments with Gloria the best. With a good meal under his belt and the comfortable feel of friendship permeating the room, he could almost forget about the state of the world. He and Gloria had been close since his return to Weberly. There was an unspoken bond between them. Despite their age difference, an attraction existed that neither of them acknowledged verbally. Remnants of social taboos or the societal displeasure with May-December romances still restricted their contact, still inhibited their thoughts.

They could spend hours chatting about their favorite books or the humidity in August; the topic didn't matter. Being together certainly did, though. *We cling to each other like shipwreck survivors,* he thought.

Gloria reached into the Hoosier cabinet behind her chair and brought out a half-full bottle of brandy.

"We might as well make this disappear before a time-wave does," she said, smiling as she tilted the bottle over two snifters.

As he swirled the glass in the palm of his hand, the aroma of the liquor filtered into his senses, musky and sharp.

"Bob Lucas stopped by after he spoke with the wagon train folks," Gloria said. "He doesn't think they believe him. They said they were going to take a vote whether to stay here or move on to Mexico." She shook her head. "Bob said there was something different about them, but he couldn't quite put his finger on it. Poor people. They don't have a clue as to what is happening, and I guess I don't either. Look here at what Bob brought over—found it at the Johnson's place after half of it time-shifted."

She handed him an old high-school history book, the cover worn smooth and pale along the edges. *A History of the Modern World,* it proclaimed. The copyright date was 1960.

"Turn to page 134," she said.

The slick pages slipped through his fingers as he searched. A multicolored map of the Western Hemisphere covered page 134. The legend called it *The United States of North America.* The blue, yellow, green, and pink states flowed uninterrupted from the upper reaches of Canada to the southern border of Mexico.

"What the hell?" he muttered.

"It's from another timeline. In the place it came from there was no United States of America. Look where the capital is," she pointed toward the middle of the map. "St. Louis."

"My God," he whispered, and abruptly dropped the book as if a spider scuttled on the pages. The pastel colors of the map mocked his senses. Here was physical proof of not just time-shifting, but world-shifting.

"There was something interesting on the afternoon news, too," Gloria said. She glanced at the grandfather clock across the room: 8:25. "Get the radio. They'll probably repeat it this evening."

Thomas went to the counter and hefted the old Crosley radio, sitting it down between them on the checkered tablecloth. It crackled and sputtered as he searched for a clear station. Soon the room filled with a deep hum and the static-laced voice of a broadcaster in Kansas City.

". . . at the White House continue to state that the president's recovery is progressing well. He will regain full use of his right arm. The assailant has been identified as a Secret Service officer from the Kennedy administration who had been time-shifted to the West Wing of the mansion. No charges will be filed.

"To recap our top story, scientists at the Johnson Space Center in Houston have determined that the singularity is moving away from our solar system. Based on data from the Pegasus probe in orbit around Jupiter, they believe the particle waves generated by the massive object have dropped in intensity over the last four days. The time span between the waves has also widened. To quote Dr. Victor Stinson: 'This is a positive indicator that the singularity has made its closest approach and is receding once again into the depths of interstellar space.' Dr. Stinson will be providing a complete news briefing at 1:00 P.M. Central Standard Time tomorrow.

"In local news, residents of the exclusive Mission Hills area south of the Country Club Plaza reported a herd of woolly mammoths stampeding along Ward Parkway . . ."

Thomas turned off the radio with a quick flick of his wrist and looked at Gloria.

"Do you believe it's going away?" he asked her.

"Why not? They've said all along that it was just passin' by. Maybe soon we won't have any more time-waves to worry about," she said.

"Time-waves, true. But time-bubbles—we'll probably be experiencing them forever."

Gloria raised her eyebrows.

"Think about it," Thomas continued. "If things are being displaced into the future, then when that future becomes our present there will still be things materializing from the past."

"You're right, I hadn't thought that far ahead. Thanks a lot, boy." She feigned cuffing the side of his head. "I was getting hopeful that this craziness would end soon." She took a sip of her drink. "God, it's not gonna be very pleasant having to continuously worry about that."

"I suppose we'll get used to it—death, taxes, and time-bubbles," he said with a grin.

"Not much in the way of taxes at the moment," Gloria answered. "But I suppose the boys in D.C. will be back in control in no time."

"Who knows," Thomas shrugged. "Maybe, maybe not. The world's not gonna recover overnight. It's not just the time-bubbles themselves we have to worry about. It's what they bring with them too—strange people and creatures, long-extinct diseases. And who knows what else from very different timelines. Life is gonna be difficult at best from now on." He slowly shook his head. "I just wish things could be a *little* easier."

"Life's never been easy, no matter what situation you're in," Gloria said. "This just makes the future all that more interesting."

"If you believe some people, there is no future."

"Humph!" Gloria scoffed. "They don't have any more of a clue than we do. Our time in this world is what we make of it. We each shape the world in our own way—the past was shaped by us, and so will be our future." She raised her glass for a toast.

"To the future," she said softly.

"To the future," he echoed, draining his glass.

The toast sent a shiver down Thomas's spine. The warm splash of brandy down his throat did not dispel it.

Slowly, he pushed away from the table and stood. "I'd best be heading home. Can I help you wash the dishes before I leave?"

"Naw," Gloria said. "They can wait 'til morning. Get outta here. You look tireder than Elmer after church." She smiled brightly at him as he bent to kiss her on the forehead.

"See you tomorrow," she said, squeezing his hand.

His rifle and pack felt somehow heavier on his shoulder as he walked home.

• • •

The alarm clock woke him at 7:30. He still kept to his regular schedule—hating to waste daylight hours. He'd slept right through the 6:15 A.M. time-wave. He shook his head; it was amazing what the human mind could grow accustomed to. He cautiously peered out the bedroom window. Everything looked normal. A light fog coated the old sycamores along the street like a watercolor wash.

After brushing his teeth and shaving, he returned his toothbrush and razor to his backpack and made a cursory check of its other contents: a change of clothes, toiletries, allergy medication, ammunition, and a flashlight nestled in one compartment. Another zippered space contained several packets of freeze-dried food, camping essentials, maps, and a compass. A large pocket on the side contained a sketchpad, pencils, and some pastels. All were essential items he felt he would need if he ever disappeared into Time.

Two pieces of toast and a cup of coffee later, he left to pick up the insulin and deliver it to Ronnie Sowers, on the opposite side of town. He grabbed his rifle and pack and slung them across his shoulders as he stepped out the front door.

Walking to City Hall, the golden peacefulness of the early morning oozed around him, capturing him like a fly in amber. No place else could feel like this, like home. No wonder he had stayed here.

As he passed the Tolliver place, he stopped to admire the massive oaks that had displaced the careful rows of soybeans. The trees were huge, majestic in a way that had not been seen in this area for centuries. A trick of the early morning light made him pause to stare at them more closely. They looked uncannily like the oak trees in his landscape painting. He shook his head and laughed at the coincidence.

As he turned the corner onto Main Street, he stopped abruptly. The buildings on the east side of the street were gone—the old feed store, Olga's Beauty Shop, and City Hall had been time-shifted. An overgrown meadow, crowded with wildflowers and lichen-covered boulders, spread in a perfect circle encompassing the place where they had been.

My God! he thought, *where's Gloria?*

He stumbled into the middle of the street, oblivious to everything but the meadow before him.

Where is Gloria?

"What's happened?" a startled voice behind him spoke, and he turned to see Elmer trudging down the sidewalk toward him, hastily adjusting the suspenders on his baggy overalls.

"Gloria's gone, and the medicine, and everything . . ." Thomas's voice wavered. He turned back to study the sun-dappled grasses, the nodding coneflowers.

"Oh, no!" cried Elmer, as he stopped beside Thomas and stared. "What'll we do?"

"I don't know," Thomas answered.

What will I do? he asked himself.

He looked back over his shoulder twice as he headed home, hoping.

•••

Thomas stood at the kitchen window, staring out into his carefully manicured backyard. The bushes in his rose garden were beginning to drop their leaves as fall encroached. An orange and purple butterfly bigger than his hand fluttered among the fading blossoms. He ignored it.

He was dazed, punch-drunk. So many extraordinary and unusual things had happened over the past six months; he felt numb and disconnected from reality. But Gloria's disappearance struck a chord within him that resonated with his emptiness. He'd been a loner all his life; but now he actually *was* lonely. It seemed Gloria filled some void he never realized he had, until she was gone.

He glanced at the kitchen clock. It was 1:45. The time-wave due at 10:15 had not arrived until 10:27, so perhaps the scientist on the radio had been right—maybe the waves would gradually slow down and end as the singularity moved away. Why couldn't it have moved a little faster, so that Gloria would not have been taken? For the hundredth time he wondered futilely where she had ended up.

He looked through the open doorway leading to his studio. It pulled at him. He knew the feeling. He always took comfort in his painting, and perhaps that was what he needed now. Gloria's disappearance hung about him like a heavy weight. Maybe if he lost himself in his painting it would help assuage the emptiness he felt at her absence.

He busied himself in preparation—gathering clean brushes from a drawer, laying tubes of paint across the top of his worktable. He kept glancing at the painting and the banker's photographs he was working from, making sure he was choosing the right colors. He paused. The oak trees did look remarkably like the ones not two blocks from here. That one had the same twisted dead branch reaching into the sky, and that other one bore the same gaping scar from a lightning strike. He stopped in disbelief and stared at his painting again. The wildflower meadow stretched away from the stand of oaks. Purple coneflowers and black-eyed susans bent in a gentle breeze among strewn glacial boulders. A meadow much the same as the one that appeared in town this morning, the one that had displaced Gloria. *How could that be possible?*

He was losing his mind. Time was not only shifting and changing, but reality was changing somehow in relation to what he painted. He shook his head in disbelief. This was crazy. Why would his painting have an effect on time-bubbles? Could he be somehow creating a *new* reality?

He *knew* he was losing his mind now. It had to be the shock of Gloria's loss. He'd be cutting his ear off next.

He sat for a long time with his head cradled in his hands, tears filling the empty space between his fingers, but his thoughts kept coming back to the similarities of his painting and the recent time-shifts.

He wiped his eyes, grabbed a sketchpad and headed for downtown. He had to see how closely they matched.

•••

Later, sitting in his studio, he continued to marvel at the similarities. They were the same trees, the same meadow. They had to be!

The absence of Gloria gnawed at him. It was ludicrous, but he kept wondering that if he painted Gloria, brought her to life on canvas, then somehow that would bring her back to him in reality. He pulled a gessoed canvas panel from the shelf and placed it on the easel, exchanging it for the half-completed landscape. He stared at it blankly for a few minutes then shrugged his shoulders. *If I am crazy, I might as well be happy in my insanity.*

With a few broad brushstrokes, he began to fill in background colors and realized how right it felt. The smell of the oil paints, the sound of his brush caressing the canvas, the clear afternoon light falling across his palette—all drew him into this singular act of creation. It did make him feel better.

Two hours later, he put down his brushes in dissatisfaction. He just could not get her smile right. Gloria's face, her expression, was so much more than what he had captured on the canvas. He closed his eyes in frustration. He just did not paint well from memory. He usually needed a model or at least photographs to work from. That was it. He would get a photograph of her.

•••

He found her photos in the hall closet—an old cardboard box brimming with albums and photo envelopes. It took him over an hour to sort through the pictures. He chose three that represented her best—one appeared to be a college graduation photo, a beautiful young woman filled with promise. The second was a candid shot of her marveling at the beauty of a yellow rose. And the third, a more recent photo—perhaps within the last couple of years. Thomas tucked them carefully into his backpack.

• • •

He painted until the day faded into dusk and the colors bled into grayness. The painting was almost complete. He would make any final changes to it tomorrow with fresh daylight and a steadier hand. The photographs helped him catch that elusive quality she always seemed to radiate. He wished she were here to see it.

He heated a can of pork and beans for supper and watched his reflection in the darkened kitchen window as he slowly ate. A beer washed it down. He heard muffled thunder in the distance and thought it funny he saw no lightning.

The time-wave took him completely by surprise.

There was a loud groan, a feeling of vertigo and a jolt like an electric shock. The house shuddered. The room glowed around him, pulsating light and dark like some spastic strobe light in his head. He fought against throwing up his supper—the urge to vomit was so strong he could barely overcome it. He fell out of his chair and pressed his nose against the cool tile floor while the world spun about him. He pulled his backpack closer to him, clutching it like a life preserver.

In a few seconds it all stopped. Weakly, he lifted his head to peer cautiously around the room. Everything looked the same. He pulled himself to his knees, and then stood shakily. Harsh sunlight fell warmly across his face. Sunlight? It was almost 10:30 P.M. There should be no sunlight at this time of day. Then it hit him. He was no longer in his time.

He staggered to the front door and flung it open. A hot humid breeze brushed against his face, carrying the sharp smell of ozone. He studied the surrounding area carefully. His house sat off-center of a forty-foot circle of displaced ground. His short-clipped lawn within the time-bubble perimeter ended in a ragged border of over-grown weeds and low bushes. The other houses on his block looked as if they had been abandoned for years. Lydia's front porch roof was collapsed. The Tyler house directly across the street was a pile of charred rubble.

He shook his head in despair. It was not supposed to happen like this. Was anyone else in this time and place?

• • •

Main Street looked like a ghost town from an old B-movie. Dirt had blown in and across it for years; weeds choked the gutters; gangly trees sprouted through the upturned sidewalks.

Thomas froze in place as he noticed the door to City Hall standing open. City Hall should not be here. The buildings on the entire block had been shifted in his time; somehow they were back in place in this time, this future. Or had they ever shifted?

He slowly walked across the street and went up the sagging stairs. It was not the same City Hall. There was no counter dividing the office space. A faded poster advertised bingo on Tuesday nights. Rotting tables and folding chairs cluttered the entire first floor. There was no backroom, no kitchenette, and no sign of Gloria ever having lived in this place. He closed his eyes and fought against sudden nausea. He wasn't just in a different time, he was in a different timeline.

He went outside and walked behind the hardware store. His ATV wasn't there. It probably had never been parked here in this world.

He walked over to Elmer's house. It was empty; long-deserted. He trotted on over to the Lucases's place, but it was long-vacant too. This was not good. He could be five or twenty-five years into the future. The country should have recovered by now. People should be back in their homes, getting on with the life that the singularity had disrupted. But only wind whispered in the deserted streets. He really was on his own now. And he had no idea as to what he should do.

•••

Later that night, a sudden burst of noise jarred Thomas awake. He raised his head from where he rested it at the kitchen table, cradled on his folded arms. He braced himself for another time-wave, but nothing happened, though the noise grew louder. He stumbled through the dark house—there was no electricity in this time. As he opened the front door, an old VW Beetle roared down the street, headlights washing the houses like a searchlight as it passed.

"Stop!" Thomas yelled, but the driver could not possibly hear him above the engine's din.

He ran to the kitchen, snagged his rifle and pulled his flashlight from the backpack. He heard the rattle from the VW's engine fade into the evening air as he followed its path through the deserted streets.

He found the VW cooling and popping in front of a large brick house. He stopped and watched a dark figure lighting a candle in the first-floor parlor. Thomas, excited by the thought that he was not alone, did not want to do anything to startle or surprise the person inside. He stood at the foot of the front porch stairs, wondering what to do. At last he decided, and shouted.

"Hello! I've just been shifted here and I thought I was alone! I'd like to meet you."

The candle inside went out abruptly. A few seconds later, he heard the unmistakable sound of a gun being cocked.

A voice near the front door spoke. "Who are you?" It was a woman's voice, hesitant but strong.

"My name is Thomas Randall," he replied. "I thought I was all alone here." He paused.

"I've been alone here almost two weeks," came the reply. "Was there a nuclear attack?"

"I don't think so. At least I hope not." He glanced around, frustrated. "Do you remember the singularity out in space in 2002 that disrupted time? I lived here then, er, still do live here, but now it's all different . . ." His voice died away in frustration.

"2002?" she said, her voice quavering with doubt. "I don't know a thing about something out in space. All I know is that one day I was headed over to the junior college in Smithton, and the next thing I knew, there was no Smithton. The road just ended at this huge crater! I came back to Weberly to find it like it is now—dead and deserted." There was the sound of the screen door creaking open and then her voice closer. "Let me see what you look like," she demanded.

Thomas angled his flashlight upward to shine on his face. "I don't want to frighten you," he said. "I just thought I was all alone here, and now, well, now I feel better that at least one other person has survived. Can you tell me what year it is?"

"I thought it was 1964, but I'm not sure of anything anymore." She paused, a dark silhouette against the darker wall behind her. He could feel her scrutinizing him from the darkness.

"Well, you look harmless enough," she said finally. "Come on up and I'll let you tell me all about this space thing and shifting stuff. I don't know anything about it. All I know is that one day everything was normal, and the next I thought I had died and went to Hell or something."

So she had been shifted, too. He waited until she went back into the house and re-lit the candle. Then he slowly opened the screen door and entered. The young woman turned to face him in the wavering light.

She still held the pistol loosely in her hand. She appeared to be about twenty years old, slender, with deep blue eyes and dark hair. She was studying his face closely as he walked near, then she smiled hesitantly. And then he knew. He had no need to study her.

"You may not know *me*, but I know you," he said, a smile warming his voice as he held out his hand.

"It's a pleasure to meet you, again, Gloria."

BROTHER JUBAL IN THE WOMB OF SILENCE

Written by
Tim Myers

Illustrated by
Carlo Arellano

About the Author

Tim Myers is a writer, songwriter and professional storyteller who currently lives in Plattsburgh, New York, where he also teaches writing at Plattsburgh State University. He has won a national poetry contest judged by John Updike. Part of his story, "Brother Jubal in the Womb of Silence," was inspired by his sense of the inevitability of country music someday being played on the moon.

About the Illustrator

Carlo Arellano was born in the Philippines and raised mostly in California. After not quite finishing art school, he toiled in obscurity for five years before meeting the woman who is now his wife. In 1999, with her encouragement and that of a friend in the FX industry, he managed to get a freelance job designing monsters. Having subsequently quit his day job, he got his first professional gig from a national publisher, Dragon Magazine, *and also won his place in the L. Ron Hubbard contest.*

He continues to make monsters for movies and create SF art, but now it's his turn to encourage his wife, who wants to be a writer and a photographer. He bought her a camera with the prize money.

As he eased the little hoverbug over the humped white bank of a rill, Brother Jubal was still thinking about the base he'd left an hour before. Behind him, the bare luminous heights of the Carpathians were receding, along with the rounded metal-dark outlines of the com-towers and domes of the base; ahead, the open rock-strewn expanse of Oceanus Procellarum stretched away in aching silence to the slightly curving lunar horizon: the Ocean of Storms—his home—which had not known any fundamental disturbance in three billion years.

But Brother Jubal was disturbed; visiting the base was always a trial. Still, he had no choice. Every six months he'd mount the little vehicle and make the weary eleven-hour journey to Drake Lunar, perched like a tick at the foot of the mountains on the jagged boundary between Mare Imbrium and the vast western reaches of Procellarum. "Back for oxy, Father?!" the loading hands in the big entry bay would raucously greet him, and he'd nod, blinking under the bright lights and trying to smile, his ears pounding with their sudden loud voices. Even in their oldest cruisers, the base police could do his eleven hours in fifty minutes—but Brother Jubal wasn't interested in speed.

Now he was crawling, it seemed, across an uneven dazzling whiteness, an utterly empty landscape, while the sounds and smells of the base still boomed through his mind, ricocheting off his mole-like thoughts: rock music thundering from overhead speakers; mechanics shouting to each other across the echoing motor-pool dome, clanking their tools, banging sections of sheet metal; the clatter and sizzle and hissing and incessant voices from the big kitchen and cafeteria; odors of hamburger, cheese, juice, soup, tacos, the bland soy scent of "lunar lettuce"; the body smells of men and women, strong or subtle, some off-putting, some intense and volatile—all of it making a wild cacophony in Brother Jubal's overburdened brain.

But he was used to this. A base visit, he'd tell himself, was like a meteor shower. In time, his thoughts would grow quiet, arrange themselves, flow again in their accustomed channels. In time, the Moon's limitless silence, deeper than anything on Earth, would envelop him again, and he would go burrowing into it like an egg into the rich warm lining of a womb. And the first minutes alone, cruising at a snail's pace above the floor of the Oceanus, always soothed him. *Maybe it's like this when it comes,* he thought, scanning the open basin from north to south in the overpowering lunar daylight; *an emptying just like this.* As he watched a tiny meteor streak somewhere off to the south, the words of Shankara's prayer came back to him, as they often did:

Oh Thou, before whom all words recoil . . .

But the base wasn't letting go of him so quickly this time. With the moly-hover shaft vibrating inside the seat beneath him, he tried to pace his thoughts to the sound of his own breathing. But, instead, he found himself thinking about Ronnie again.

Ronnie worked in the food service at Drake, bright eyed and almost always smiling, pale skinned but solidly built, his face usually reddened with a blemish or two. He was in his early twenties, it seemed, but still boyish. After picking up oxygen and helping load it on his hoverbug, Brother Jubal was required to report to Diggins, the base supervisor; his superiors in the order made it clear that such safety precautions were mandatory. News of any kind traveled fast in a community as isolated as Drake Base, and Ronnie would usually catch up to him at some point between the entry bay and Diggins's offices.

The young man just wanted someone to talk to, Brother Jubal realized. And he had plenty to say, went at it cheerfully and energetically. It wasn't that he babbled—and he was a good listener, seemed genuinely interested in Brother Jubal's life—but the monk knew loneliness when he saw it. And he was the *last* one who could help someone in that predicament.

Above the luminous plain, he rode on, feeling the hours slowly pass, his leg muscles beginning to ache from lack of movement. Slowly, he felt his swirling thoughts unravel as he eased himself back into the silence and immensity of his real life. But even this soundless ride across the littered white basin wasn't yet the peace he craved, the peace that was his greatest tool; navigating the lunar surface required at least part of his mind to be constantly alert. Just beyond the three inches of his suit was a crushing, burning airlessness, so hot in the sun's unobstructed glare that his blood would instantly boil were he exposed to it. The hoverbug—officially a "D-7 liftsled"—kept a good ten feet above the ground, but its safe operation required careful steering over the contours of faults, small domes, rill banks, hummocks, slopes, intermittent boulders and the endless crater walls. *Lunar geology*, he thought, *is more like some kind of pathological dermatology.* It would be very

Illustrated by Carlo Arellano

good to return at last to the great upland tranquility of his cell.

As he rode on, he happened to look up—to loosen his stiffening neck—and suddenly it was there in the black sky, huge, blue white, phased and ominous. He looked away. At such moments Benedict's *lectio divina*—an emphasis on reading sacred texts as part of monastic life—comforted him greatly, and as the moly-shaft vibrated endlessly beneath him he set to repeating some of the words that had given his life its shape: *The nature of God is a circle . . .* , someone had written (he didn't know who, but such anonymity was unremarkable to a hermit). *The nature of God is a circle of which the center is everywhere and the circumference is nowhere.* Here on the Moon these words rang twice, he felt—in the metaphorical sense that had thrilled him as a young man on his parents' farm in upstate New York, and then in the physical sense here, where the foreshortened lunar horizon always made you feel at the center of something, even though travel could never bring you to any edge.

And then, as the heights of the Aristarchus Plateau appeared in the west, his journey near its end, he remembered St. Thomas's words and felt them again pierce his heart, revealing the very spiritual pinnacle where he always stood: *Man: a horizon between time and eternity.*

His arrival at the plateau always made him feel strange, though he was used to that too. Skirting the walls of the great Aristarchus Crater as the hoverbug climbed, the scree of the crater's ejecta blanket rushing beneath him, he felt the usual mix of familiarity and dread. His cell near the rim of the deep, winding Schroter Valley was "home," as much home as a seeker could ever have, and he felt all the anticipation of the suburban vacationer for easy chair, couch and bed—though

Brother Jubal owned none of these. The great plateau with its canyon, craters, cliffs and broken uplifts was where he belonged; he knew that.

But Aristarchus was a vast, empty, crater-pocked, cliff-broken, crust-heaved, forbidding place. Its loneliness didn't frighten him; once he was home again, he would pour that over his head, annoint himself as with a salve. And he didn't fear the emptiness either, though at times it had crushed his spirit. The work was what weighed him down, the return to his quest and its exhausting concentration, its watchfulness, its endless inner journeying—all the heaviness of devotion brought to utter action. *I will go out into the desert,* he thought, remembering how one of his books described the desert wastes: "a region of . . . malevolent spirits . . . the place of trials . . . a terrain of struggle . . ."

Now he could see the little outcrop before him, the intricacies of its rocky shape as intimate to him as the face of a spouse. The great littered jumble of Cobra Head and then Herodotus Crater lay beyond. As always, he felt his reluctance and weariness begin to lift as he drew closer. Throttling down, he parked the hoverbug in its little alcove in the basaltic ridge, then climbed off and tottered toward the air lock, his legs achingly stiff and raging with pins and needles. Before he stepped in, he looked around.

From the east, the terminator was approaching, its line razor-sharp in this airless world. *Terminator,* Brother Jubal thought, recalling one of Pope Yushio's poetic names for God. The long lunar day—two weeks in Earth terms—was drawing to a close. Ink-black shadows crept slowly eastward from every rock, ridge, crater wall, cliff and humped mountain shoulder. Down in the immense canyon just thirty feet from his door, utter blackness was creeping across the ancient floor, reaching blindly for the eastern walls. In the strange lunar twilight—a heightening of day and night rather than a mixing of them, stars shining fiercely as ever—he felt his strength returning. Blaze of light, black nothingness of shadow: These were the truths of the universe, its fundamental duality—and with one foot in each, he was ready to work, to battle, to seek. "I am like an owl in the desert," he whispered, recalling the Psalms.

He went through the air lock, stepped slowly out of his suit—fighting off a violent charley horse in his left thigh—and then hurried downstairs to the little underground rooms. But he didn't even pause in the kitchen with its hydroponic chambers, potted flowers and climbing vines; the soy-alfalfa patties, the dry wheat crackers, even the water his throat so desperately wanted, would have to wait. Nor did he turn on the lights; only the generator and systems warning bulbs, flashing red and green, gave any illumination.

Exhausted, his joints and muscles aching, Brother Jubal groaned as he knelt before the crucifix, laughing for a moment at "Brother Donkey"—St. Francis's name for his own body. Then he fixed his gaze on the divine body and spoke in the words of the Psalmist, words he'd repeated each day for the last ten years and yet still whispered with a lover's passion:

> Hear my cry, O Lord . . . Hide not thy face from me . . .
> My heart is smitten and withered like grass . . .
> When shall I come and behold the face of God?

•••

Within a decade of the first flush of lunar activity, the Vatican had paved the way for a new monastic order dedicated to off-planet eremitism. For almost a century the international influence of the Church had grown steadily; the scope and tolerance of its doctrines had expanded too, though some disapproved. A presence on the Moon—particularly the kind of dramatic presence the Anchorites would make—was of great importance to the hierarchy, and both money and political leverage were applied to procure the requisite agreements. Many in the Vatican were keenly aware of the political value of such high-profile spirituality; others were humbly and genuinely desirous that the Church be a greater light to humanity. So international protocols were signed, construction ordered, equipment moved, all at great cost. More importantly to the Anchorites themselves, a papal council approved special sacramental dispensations for lunar Anchorites; the highlight of Brother Jubal's year was taking the Eucharist with his fellow monastics at Tycho Base during Earth's April.

There were others on the Moon besides him, and others had gone before. His own cell had been home to, in succession, Brother Ambrose, Sister Ananda, Sister Kiwa, Brother John, Brother Bruno and Brother Mbulo. Seven Anchorites were currently living out their lives at widely scattered spots on the near side. Jubal knew some of them: Sister Cecelia in Mare Nectaris, Sister Macrina far to the south in Mare Humorum, Brother Kwa at the Bay of Rainbows. There was no one on the far side; though the order had no rules forbidding habitation there, the Anchorites avoided it. Even such solitaries as they were, it seemed, couldn't stomach such a location, despite its obvious advantages for isolated living—there were, for example, no permanent human settlements except for the mining operations at Mare Moscoviense, and even that was staffed on a frequent-rotation basis. And, of course, on the far side you never saw Earth.

But Brother Jubal rarely thought about his fellow monastics, or about the great concerns of the Church, or the doings of people or nations. At Aristarchus, his solitude was perfect, broken only now and then by some curious base employee out joy riding in a cruiser (illegally) or a geology team taking samples and seismological readings along the barren length of the canyon—and, from time to time, by the winking lights of a great orbiter high overhead. As always, his return to Aristarchus brought a slow and welcome descent into the silence he loved, and a honing of his thoughts toward (in words he remembered from Deuteronomy) "the precious things put forth by the moon." As the sensations of the base visit faded from his memory, his life resumed its natural shape: Beneath the brilliant stars he would rise early—"clock-early"—pray for an hour, take a spare breakfast, look to his garden and check his plants and life-support and power systems, read until "noon," pray again, exercise for at least two hours, pray again, take a modest and unappetizing dinner, rest for a time, and then go to meditate—the climax of his day, the height of the spiritual athleticism he sought. After these exhausting sessions—invariably two or three hours, often more—he would wash himself, do some more reading, pray, and then retire to his mat, seeking the Divine even in what dreams came during his six hours of sleep. Fortnight by fortnight, in deep lunar darkness or blazing solar dazzlement, he lived as the loving spouse of silence.

One day five months after his return from Drake, he went to meditate at the talus slope beneath the cliffs a few miles northeast of the canyon. The long lunar night

had descended, temperatures plummeting as the terminator again swept across the unprotected surface. As he
bounded easily along in the kangaroo style he'd
mastered—keeping a keen eye on the rubble-strewn
landscape over which he was leaping, under the pale
illumination of bright Earth and stars—he listened to
his breathing and began murmuring Simone Weil's
words, his starting point for that day's meditation:

> *There is a silence in the beauty of the universe which*
> *is like a noise when compared with the silence of God.*

When he reached the foot of the great brownish-
white cliffs, he stopped, then walked a few bouncy steps
to the dim shadow-edge of a boulder the size of a small
house. Seating himself carefully in the pale dust, his
back firm and straight, he gathered his thoughts,
emotions and sensations, trying to reach down even to
the chemical and electric firing of consciousness itself, to
press together all the scattered forces of his being,
silently igniting them with a single desire. For a time,
staring into the deeper shadow of the boulder as if
down a well, he worked to calm the babble of his
thoughts; only then would he be ready to begin shaping
all he was into a single strand, a weapon of ecstatic
pursuit. When his mind strayed or tried to tempt him
with its silly needs or rational feints, he simply looked
more deeply into the blackness of the shadow, the *via
negativa* that led, as surely as righteousness and love, to
the foot of the Throne. Slowly, slowly, as he sat there
beneath the bleached and monstrous cliff, his mind
began collapsing inward toward its singularity.

That was, of course, when the assault of images
came, like the flurry of demons Athanasius reported as

incessantly attacking St. Anthony in the Egyptian desert.
Brother Jubal had never seen horns, claws or hooves, but
he recognized temptations all the same. He'd known
they would come; they always did. Suddenly he saw
himself as a boy, sitting thirty feet up in the crook of his
grandparents' willow, watching the swift, narrow river
rush past their Adirondack cabin. He glimpsed again the
bright reddish-brown gleam of maplewood, his parents'
coffins, felt again the burning pang that had humbled
him, even at college age, to the snarling, stinging grief
of a child, the pain of a wounded animal. He relived
that lunar "dawn" when, eight months after his arrival
at Aristarchus, he'd fallen to the floor of his cell and
wept uncontrollably at the memory of green shoots in
spring mud. But all of these had come before, had now
been defused by time and the steadiness of his spirit, still
wandered through him but only as impotent ghosts.
One by one he dismissed them. Looking down into the
void of the boulder's shadow, he watched them float
away, swallowed up. When the last was gone, he exerted
himself simply and quietly, his mind—as the Upani-
shads counseled—motionless as a candle flame in a
windless place.

But then another image came, very quietly. He
almost didn't notice. Again he was a boy in his parents'
house, not fond of school, not playing much with the
other kids in that neighborhood of old houses and
towering oaks and maples. He'd climbed to the attic, sat
there in a forgotten corner watching dust motes dance
silently in columns of warm sunlight. And then he saw
that pencil drawing in the museum hall at the Anchorite
monastery near Reno, the one that had so attracted him:
an ancient Greek Orthodox monastery atop a huge
rocky outcrop in Thessaly, tile-roofed buildings perched
on its summit like Simon Stylites on his pillar, so isolated

that bundles of food and firewood had to be pulled up by ropes. For an instant, he even saw a zany and colorful picture from some old children's book: a little boy in a feathered hat painting the pinnacle knob of a flagpole above an outlandish striped dome, in a city crowded with such whimsical domes and flagpoles.

The intrusion of these images disturbed him—not so much because they were unexpected, but because he must exert himself further to expel them. But as he did, he felt reason—stubborn old opportunist—leaping back in. He found himself thinking how, for as long as he could remember, he'd been trying to get away, to climb out of, to travel past—always seeking the desert, the wilderness, the infinite ocean of silence, as if he'd known from childhood he had some great appointment there.

Again, he peered down into the boulder's shadow—and suddenly, for one searing instant, everything but the blackness of the shadow disappeared—all things swallowed up in it—an infinite void opening onto Nothingness itself—and an overwhelming sense of the vanity of all existence moved through him like a physical force. Brother Jubal was shocked, stifled a cry. The hair rose on his neck; he thought he might vomit. Swinging his head up wildly, he searched desperately to be sure the universe was still there: cliff edge above him, boulder before him, shattered scree to either side, beyond it all the stars, in that moment more beautiful to him than flowers.

But the sense of their beauty drained away as suddenly and violently as the horror had come. He quickly stood up and then set off for home, bounding too fast, his own breathing wild in his ears, preposterous amid the silence. He felt himself growing lightheaded, but he didn't slow down. When he reached the air lock he rushed through, tore off his suit and clothes, turned up his thermostat, and then lay shivering on his mat beneath two blankets, repeating uncontrollably the words of the koan: . . . *drink from the empty cup . . . empty cup . . .*

Sleep brought no respite. He dreamed that something had gone terribly wrong with the orbits of the planets—watched in unspeakable terror as the great blue-white disk overhead grew monstrous, huger and huger as it rolled ever closer, certain to crush the Moon and everything on it—and as the dream suddenly turned quiet, he saw whirling fragments of white rocks amid a veil-like dust in empty space. . . .

> *Because thou lovest the Burning Ground,*
> *I have made a Burning Ground of my heart . . .*

He decided the next evening that he wanted to be buried on the Moon.

• • •

A week later he was still reeling, but he'd taken hold of himself. *This is an opportunity,* he argued with the silent man inside him. *I'm not alone! Pachomius, Elia, Osee, Paphnutius, Pambo, John the Baptist . . . they all went through it. . . .* So, as he sometimes did when his spiritual life grew convoluted, he sat down at his little desk to write—to "prune," as he put it, the tree of his spirit:

> *Lord, I am your creature, so I live between the two*
> *great forces: change and changelessness. Thy will*
> *be done. But I'm pulled in two directions,*

sometimes torn into pieces, into Nothingness.
Before Galileo, they thought the Moon was changeless,
a perfect sphere! This pocked and rubbled globe,
where volcanoes flowed for seven hundred
million years, where meteors fell like rain—still
fall, the tiny ones, at 70,000 mph, they say, but
so tiny you need a microscope to make out
the endless pitting of the surface. And residual
outgassing—the reddish "fog" I sometimes see
drifting from Cobra Head. And the slump of things,
what that survey geologist called "mass wasting,"
even here on this frozen-corpse world: slumping
and settling, gravity eerily constant, everything
slowly drawn into dust.
And yet there's a kind of perfection here, too,
a changelessness—almost nothing profoundly
altered for three billion years. A bootprint will last eons.
This is a place without sound, where the human soul
can step past all the terrible noise of the world. Here.
"Nothing in all creation is so like God as stillness,"
Pascal said.
That's your gift. Forgive me. I have confused silence
with emptiness.

He set down the pen and hunched on his stool, profoundly tired. Suddenly he remembered the rover—he'd meant to tell them about it at the base. It was an old model, from the days before wheels were outlawed on the lunar surface. He'd found it in a cooling-crack gully near Herodotus, the relic of some early mission. For days he'd used it as a focus for meditation, a memento mori like the skull St. Jerome gazed at in all those woodblock prints. The environmental people at the base would want to pick it up; maybe it had historical value. He wondered momentarily why it had been abandoned—and who had abandoned it.

But suddenly he heard a banging sound from his air lock, leapt up in terror thinking it a meteor impact, rushed to the foot of the stairs, peering up toward his small observation dome, and saw the unthinkable: in the background, a smaller and somewhat battered company cruiser from the base; in the foreground, Ronnie—his face clearly discernible through a tri-bex bubble-helmet—grinning from ear to ear, having knocked on the "door" like a neighbor coming over for coffee.

Brother Jubal was stunned. Then anger surged through him. *How dare he!* . . . But he caught himself; this was hardly Christian charity. Perhaps there was some emergency. Yes, that must be it. As he mounted the stairs in panic, Ronnie came through the air lock.

"Hi, Father!" he chirped. "Hope I'm not disturbing you!"

"Is something wrong?!"

"Oh, hell, no!—whoa. Sorry. No, nothing's wrong. I was just passing by—gotta pick up some information canisters from a sampling station . . . well . . . north of here."

Brother Jubal knew just how far north the sampling station was. This was more than "stopping by."

"But—how did you find my cell?" he asked, knowing his voice was too loud.

Ronnie smiled sheepishly. "Diggins's records. You know what they say—no security system's perfect! So I, you know . . . looked up your coordinates. Figured you wouldn't mind."

Brother Jubal crossed his arms, looking as stone-faced as he could. But if Ronnie noticed, it didn't stop him.

"Quite a place!" he blurted, looking around. "Geez, Father—what do you *do* out here all day? I mean, I know you got important spiritual stuff to do. I just wonder about you sometimes."

Brother Jubal remained silent, dropping the broadest possible hint. *I don't have the oxygen for this!* he fumed to himself. But Ronnie ended the awkward silence with a laugh.

"And all you've got is that little moly-hover rig out there?" He jerked a hand back over his shoulder, pointing. "Don't you worry about it conking on you? Leaving you stranded in the middle of nowhere?"

"We're trained to repair them," Brother Jubal answered directly. "I can take care of most problems."

"And you don't even have a communicator!" Ronnie went on excitedly, looking around with the familiarity of someone in his own house. When he crossed to the battered desk and picked Brother Jubal's journal up, his reluctant host's annoyance rose precipitously. Ronnie read the shocked expression.

"Oh, Father—I'm sorry!" He set the journal down hastily and reverently, backing up. "It's living at Drake, I guess—you get used to sticking your nose where it doesn't belong. I didn't mean to come barging in here. It's just . . . well, it's pretty dangerous all the way out here alone. I know you can take care of yourself—but what if you got sick or hurt or something? You know?"

Ronnie's eyes were bright. There was genuine concern in them. Brother Jubal felt a kind of tremor run through him. "Life," he said, trying to sound dry and judicious, "is always dangerous."

Ronnie's usually cheery features clouded even more. "Yeah," he murmured, hanging his head. "I know."

Neither spoke. In the silence—this one an altogether different kind—Brother Jubal recognized the beginnings of a sick feeling down in the pit of his stomach, which he might have ignored if Ronnie hadn't been standing right in front of him.

"You've . . . had some trouble?" he asked gently.

"Oh, it was a long time ago," Ronnie answered, rousing himself. "My dad died when I was a kid. We were kinda poor, lived up in U.P.—you know, Michigan, Upper Peninsula. Everybody calls it the U.P. So when my dad died, my uncle—they never got along, see, my dad and my uncle—so right after the funeral, my uncle sold our house, told us we had two weeks to pack up and get out." Ronnie stopped, almost wincing. Brother Jubal sensed that he couldn't bring himself to tell the worst. But then Ronnie looked up and smiled quietly. "That's it," he said.

The older man had no idea what to say. "How old were you then?" he ventured.

"Nine," Ronnie answered, and here his voice began to break. "I was a little kid and I was . . . it was so . . . my dad . . . then my uncle, the asshole, throws us out! And things got bad . . . moneywise."

Brother Jubal looked down, overwhelmed and ashamed. *What did you expect, old man?* he asked himself fiercely. *A life of crime? Addiction? Wasn't losing a father enough? Don't you remember?*

"But like I said, Father—I didn't mean to barge in," Ronnie went on, his usual smiling self again. "Actually, I was kind of hoping you might . . . uh . . . recommend some books for me . . . like about what you do. We can get pretty much anything downloaded from the Sat System."

Again, Brother Jubal was taken by surprise.

"Yes! Of course!" he nodded quickly. "I could. I will! Yes! I'll make a little list. But are you sure your supervisor will let you use mainframe time for something like that? I mean, just between you and me, he's rather"—he searched for the term—"hard-nosed. Isn't he?" This was a generous description, he thought; the Drake supervisor had struck him from the first as grasping and venal.

"Who, Diggins? Oh no, Father, he's not so bad!" Ronnie sat down on the floor, leaning against the wall, and Brother Jubal realized he hadn't even offered him the chair. "Diggins is definitely a company guy—and, of course, they're always breathing down his neck. But he sticks up for us. Last year, one of the guys in Plant started flipping out—thought his girlfriend back home was two-timing him. Then he gets the idea that all his messages to her were getting lost in space—you know, eaten up in the void, that kind of weird stuff. Kinda typical, really. The bigwigs down in Yokohama wanted to red-sheet him, and that, of course, meant they'd drum him out once he got back to Earth. But Diggins went to bat for him, and then he worked with the guy and the counselor, and they smoothed it out. He's okay now. You'd like Diggins if you got to know him, Father. He won't let them show the pornophobes at Drake. They do at the other bases, you know—not supposed to, of course, but it's a backroom thing—smuggle 'em in. Diggins won't put up with it."

For a moment Brother Jubal couldn't speak. *Too much longing for the goal,* he finally told himself, *and not enough effort on the way. Forgive me.*

Suddenly Ronnie stood up. "Well, Father—I gotta go. Still got samples and shit to pick up—whoops. Sorry. And I'm burnin' your oxy!"

Once the young man was gone, Brother Jubal stood in the center of the little room, feeling silence flow back into its many places.

•••

The next day, still ashamed but practical by necessity, he checked the oxygen. It was down some, but only a hairline or two; Ronnie's visit only meant he'd have to go in a day early.

He shut down all but the essentials, climbed into his suit, went through the air lock and then climbed to a high ledge in the jumbled rocky hills above the Schroter Valley. Standing there, he looked out over the canyon's immense meandering course—all dust-dry, the flow channel of ancient vulcanism out of Herodotus running its barren length from the plateau to the darker mare below. But again he found himself thinking about Ronnie. In the brilliance of lunar day, he stood lost in unformed thoughts, letting the easy flow of emotion fill him, like water filling a low place. Just then, with the image of Ronnie's face in his mind, he glanced up and saw Earthrise.

It was as if he'd never seen it. Beyond the empty reaches of the dry Oceanus, it lifted with such perfect colors and vital shapes of cloud, sea and landmass that Brother Jubal gasped.

Ronnie was born there, he found himself thinking. *I was born there.*

One dead world, one teeming with life, coupled endlessly in space as if spouses in a dance of love—and then it came, flashing into his head with a dizzying rush, amid images of reeds, insects, frogs, noisy streets, boat-crowded harbors. Words unbidden came with it:

The worlds bend down for such as these . . .

But even before the words had fully formed in his consciousness, before their sounds had achieved balance in his silent brain, they blazed past themselves into something else, as if the individual letters had burst into flame, then the flame burst into air—and then it all exploded mutely past anything he'd ever dreamed of.

Presence. Melted and formlessly reformed, he felt himself become a silent implosion of paradox—pandimensional eruption so violent it could pierce the walls of the universe itself, but without so much as nudging a single pebble at his feet.

It passed. He sobbed like a child at its departure. Then a completely irrational thought formed momentarily in his head: He wondered if he should check his seismograph when he got back.

And that set him to laughing as he hadn't laughed since grade school.

•••

Plodding uneasily beneath the great lights of the main dome, people streaming past him in both directions, Brother Jubal moved reluctantly toward the office wing to complete his mandatory check-in with Diggins. Another six months had passed; another eleven aching hours of travel, and then his descent into the babble and confusion of the tacky little company city. *Babel*, he thought. *Babylon. Close enough.*

Today there was country music blaring over the speakers, twanging juiced-up guitar chords pressing into every inch of stale-smelling space. Looking around for Ronnie, he noticed three young women with dyed-blonde hair sitting over drinks at the neon-spangled café, swaying and singing with the music:

> *You think we're rowdy—*
> *Well, boy—howdy!*
> *We'll show you how it's done . . .*

But the moment he entered Diggins's plastiwood-paneled office, he knew something was different.

Diggins was on the communicator, a balding middle-aged man with fierce eyes and an expanding middle. He always wore a suit; the suit was always rumpled. When he saw Brother Jubal at the door, he impatiently motioned him to sit down.

"Greer—she *has* to go out today," Diggins was saying. "It's angina. You'll have to re-route. Dammit, you know my people here don't have the juice for this level of treatment! Okay. Okay. Okay. No!" Diggins had suddenly shouted; Brother Jubal jumped up from his plastic chair, startled.

"Just think for a second, Greer, what it's going to cost if you stick with the policy and something goes wrong! They could haul *your* ass in court—it won't be just the company! So tomorrow, by 1500. All right. Okay. Good-bye." Before he'd even hung up he was looking straight into Brother Jubal's eyes.

"Brother—I need your help."

The monk looked back at him in confusion, said nothing.

"I'm losing my counselor," Diggins went on, talking too fast. "You heard all that. Heart trouble. She's history." Diggins fiddled with a paper clip for a moment, then looked up.

"Listen—I took the liberty. Checked your records. I know you took some psych courses at university, sociology, that kind of thing. You even taught school for a while. That's enough background, for legal purposes."

Brother Jubal shifted uneasily in his seat. "None of that," he replied quietly, "worked out." Then he looked up, confused again. "But I don't understand—why would you check *my* records? What could that possibly . . ." Then it hit him.

Diggins saw his eyes go wide and jumped right in. "Now, look, Brother—I *need* somebody to help me keep the lid on here! The only thing I'm more afraid of than a pressure blowout is my people freaking on me. It's not easy for anybody up here! We've got three hundred employees, everybody knows everybody, there's no place to go—hell, we're 240,000 miles from frigging Earth and it's a frigging small town! Worse than a soap opera! And I get a few doozies here too, despite the screening. Your friend Ronnie's got his troubles, but *he's* one of the healthy ones."

Brother Jubal felt as if he'd had the wind knocked out of him. He stared at the supervisor without blinking. "Mr. Diggins, I understand your predicament. I sympathize, of course. It's unthinkable, however, that I should give up my work, nor am I suited . . ."

Diggins held up his hand. "Brother Jubal—just think about this. Look at it from where I sit. I'm *responsible* for these people. Now the company picks management pretty much on the basis of technical knowledge. Oh, they shove you into some Work Psych courses and leadership seminars—but that's not their main thrust. I know about titanium, scandium, hafnium, yttrium. I know low-g manufacturing, exploration support, R & D. Hell, I know how to run a food service, an infirmary and a goddamn rec program! Excuse me. But it's not about that! It's all personnel! That's the whole ball-game! And I need your help!"

Diggins looked down, momentarily at a loss for words. When he looked back at Brother Jubal, there was something like pleading in his eyes. "Look—it'll be a year at the most."

Brother Jubal's head dropped. He gazed at his hands.

"Brother, " Diggins said quietly. "These people need you. You took an oath or something, didn't you? Not to turn the other cheek when people're in trouble, right? I've got quotas and deadlines to meet, Brother Jubal—I won't bullshit you about that. But we've gotta have a halfway healthy community up here, or people are going to get hurt."

"I don't know the first thing about it," the monk murmured.

"You could learn."

How could he talk to this man? What could he say? How could he express the struggles he'd been through, his anxieties at the assaults on his solitude, his dread of such a life?

"My superiors would never allow it," he added definitively.

Without a word, Diggins reached into his desk drawer, pulled out a tele-fax, and set it in front of Brother Jubal. "I already talked to them," he said quietly. "They say it's up to you."

It was too much. Mumbling some refusal, Brother Jubal rose and rushed from the office, hoping the hoverbug was already loaded.

As he plunged into the great din of the main dome, he noticed he was sweating. He'd wanted to tell Ronnie about that moment above the canyon—the reeling stars, the terrible loveliness of the rising Earth—especially about the lightning that had burned his blindness away, the knife that had split him like a fish, the revelation that all worlds moved to strange, beautiful, mysterious purposes. But that would have to wait—if it could ever be said at all.

But now he was here, standing beneath the center of the dome, music blaring, crowds pressing all around him, people brushing past, the beating of rhythm in the blood, lives all tangled and hot and blowing into and through each other like vapors—all the hurt and pride and longing, all the hating and loving and screwing and forgetting and creating and destroying—and just for a moment he realized how *familiar* it all felt.

But how could you trust people? Even to do the simple things that were good for them? And how even *begin* to trust them to seek God?

He turned and retraced his steps. Almost before he knew it, his hand was on the knob to Diggins's office door. And just then he heard St. Basil's words echoing in his head, words he didn't realize he knew: "If you always live alone, whose feet will you wash?"

He trembled a little, knew he was now entering a much greater wilderness.

THE SHARP END

Written by
Kelly David McCullough

Illustrated by
Dwayne Harris

About the Author

Kelly David McCullough lives in Menomonie, Wisconsin, with his physics professor wife and two cats. He's been working primarily in science education as an editor and writer. He's currently working as the staff science fiction writer for the Constructing Ideas in Physical Science project. CIPS, a project funded by the National Science Foundation, is developing a middle-school science curriculum with a science fiction content. He's had one story published in Weird Tales and another in Tales of the Unanticipated. He's completed one novel and is working on another. He'd like to dedicate this, his first publication in an actual book, to his wife, Laura.

About the Illustrator

*The illustration for the story that follows was
done by Dwayne Harris.*

Eric Waters was the last astronaut. There would be no more after him. He sat at the desk in his tiny dorm room and looked at the meager pile of belongings he'd managed to amass in two years at Mare Imbrium Base, Luna. He had an eBook reader, a few articles of personal clothing, a laptop, and a photo of himself and his advisor in front of the prototype magnetic field generator that had landed Eric his NASA appointment. He also had the standard kit including uniforms, toiletries, and the small black case that contained his "passport." The syringe full of poison had been part of the package since the Mars expedition disaster.

Mars had been the first step toward dissolution for NASA, and now Eric was about to take the last. It was 1:45 P.M. Greenwich mean, almost time to close up shop. Sighing, he swept the clothes and other gear into his vac-capsule. The high-tech foot locker wasn't big, but it easily held the lot, and in the low gravity of Earth's moon it weighed next to nothing. Eric balanced it on his shoulder as he headed for the building's main air lock.

He mounted the capsule to his suit's carrying rack, and carefully checked the suit over. He'd done the same thing earlier when he'd hiked to the main building for lunch. It was unlikely that anything had changed significantly since then, but taking things for granted got people killed. When he was sure everything was as it should be, he wriggled into the suit and attached the helmet. Then he stepped into the rack that held his air and belongings. Sighing, he turned away from the air lock.

It was less than fifty feet from the entry to the dorm's control room, but it felt like miles. One by one, he shut down the building's systems until only air and power remained. The latter wasn't his problem. Power would be cut off remotely after Eric had cleared the air lock, but the former . . .

He held his trembling hand over the cover of the evacuation switch for a good minute before finally flipping it aside. The exposed switch would pump the air into tanks for storage and redistribution. With a small simple motion, Eric laid the last NASA training facility to rest.

He felt there should have been some ceremony to honor all the effort and blood that had gone into the astronaut program, but there wasn't. Every single human being who cared was at the launch site trying to get NASA's last mission ready before Congress could kill it too.

It was less than a mile to the launch pad and Eric covered it in a series of long bounds. The *Phoenix* was tanked up and ready to fly. She was an ungainly flattened cylinder, designed and built in microgravity with no intention that she ever enter atmosphere. Misshapen lumps and bumps marred her hull where various bits of equipment had been added as afterthoughts. These gave her the impression of having some kind of nasty skin condition. Eric smiled. She was the prettiest thing he'd ever seen. He lovingly touched his glove to the weld holding one of his shield projectors in place. There was a slight irregularity where the wirefeeder had hiccuped. To anyone else it would have been invisible. To Eric it was like a signature that said, "I did this, no one else." He smiled to himself and turned away. It was time to board.

•••

They were at T minus one hour and counting. In the ship's tiny fusion room Eric went over the final checklist with Nadia Gladysheva. He was glad to be working with the Russian. If anyone understood how he felt, it was Nadia. Seven years earlier she'd been the last trainee through the *cosmonaut* program. The Federal Republic of Russia had ceded its place in space to commercial interests, just as the United States was about to do.

"Look at this pile of junk," said Nadia, affectionately patting a bulkhead. "We must have ten thousand kilos of experimental equipment."

"And all of it jury-rigged," responded Eric. "Every scientist with a pet research project and some clout tried to get in on this mission. It's like vultures circling a dying horse."

"I don't know. There will be many space scientists looking for work after this. If anyone wants us to succeed more than we do, it's them."

"I suppose, but it won't do us any good. The new space corporations make some mighty big political contributions and they think NASA's a dinosaur."

"They're right," said a voice from the doorway.

Eric whirled in anger. The space-black face of Scott McGregor was split by a wry grin.

"What the hell is that supposed to mean?" demanded Eric.

"NASA is a dinosaur. We've become a bureaucracy in the worst sense of the word."

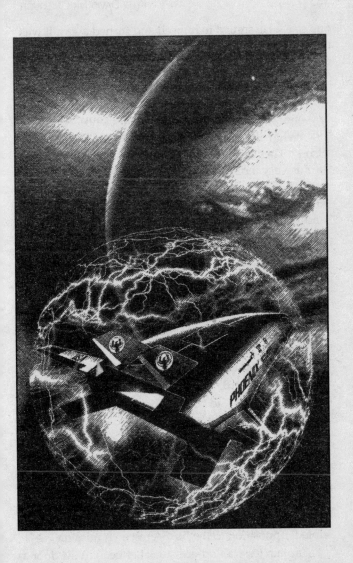

Illustrated by Dwayne Harris

"Ha," said Nadia, "so speaks the American. NASA is a gleaming and efficient machine compared to Russian bureaucracy."

"She's still a dinosaur," said Scott.

"That's not true," said Eric. "NASA's the last organization interested in doing real space science."

"What about Consolidated Mining?" countered Scott. "They're working on the first asteroid mining ship at this very moment."

"That's not science," snapped Eric, "it's glorified engineering. They're taking principles we developed and refining them for commercial use. If it weren't for NASA, they'd still be a half-bankrupt strip-mining firm. When the commercial interests control space, the real *I didn't know that before I started* research is going to be deader than the surface of the moon."

"That's not what Congressman Thacker said in his latest address," replied Scott. He mimicked the finance chairman's motor oil Kentucky drawl, "It's time for big government to stop stickin' its nose where it don't belong and let the *free* market set the agenda in space."

"He's a bastard," snarled Eric.

"Wait for it," said Scott. "There's more. He also said the *Phoenix* was the biggest waste of federal dollars since the Advanced Stealth Submarine."

"Isn't Consolidated Mining and Refining headquartered in Kentucky?" asked Nadia.

"Yes," spat Eric. "The only military spending Thacker's against is the kind that happens in someone else's district. But that's got nothing to do with his 'principled' opposition to the NASA research mission."

Captain Jessica Radford stuck her head in the door as Eric was finishing this sentence. "What's got you so riled, Eric? Is Scott picking fights again?"

"I was just trying to take the tension off," said Scott.

"Scott says NASA's a dinosaur," replied Eric.

"Really?" replied Jessica, turning her gaze on Scott. "So, why are you still here? Consolidated's offering some mighty hefty bonuses to experienced pilots."

"Hey, she may be a dinosaur, but she's my dinosaur," said Scott defensively.

"Ah," said Jessica, laughing. "My dinosaur right or wrong?"

"Yeah," replied Scott, sullenly.

"He quoted Thacker at us," said Nadia.

Jessica's dark eyes flashed dangerously. "On my ship that's a hanging offense. Do you know what Thacker said this afternoon?"

"Apparently not the worst of it," answered Eric.

"He called us a fat government bird made for roasting, and said this was one *Phoenix* that wouldn't be rising from the ashes." The bitterness in her tone was like over-brewed coffee.

Eric felt the same way. *Phoenix was* named in hope of a resurrection, but it wasn't something anyone at NASA wanted to talk about. There was a superstitious dread that actually voicing it would kill their luck. To have NASA's primary congressional foe spouting off on the subject on the day of their departure filled his belly with cold lead. No one had much to say after that, and the four went quietly back to work.

Forty-five minutes later the *Phoenix* rode its flaming tail into the heavens. NASA's last mission was on its way to Neptune.

• • •

"Eric," said Jessica over the cabin speaker, "we have multiple radar traces on the scope. It looks like we've found you a dust storm. Do you want to try out your new toy?"

Eric let out a whoop as he reached for the intercom button. They'd been searching for a good concentration of space dust ever since they'd hit the asteroid belt three weeks earlier. It had begun to look like they wouldn't find any.

"That's a roger, Captain," he said. "I'm on my way." He grabbed the small bundle of his skinsuit and headed out the door.

"Hello, Eric," greeted Nadia, as he entered the reactor room. "I hear you will finally test your micro-meteor screen. Congratulations." The fusion plant was her baby in the same way that the experimental meteor shield was his.

"Thanks, Nadia, but it's not really mine. Professor Garten came up with the idea and did most of the design work. I was just his grad student."

Nadia bowed her head briefly. "My condolences, Eric. I was very sorry to hear about his lymphoma."

Eric smiled sadly. "Thanks. If he hadn't pulled every string he could get his hands on, I'd never have landed that last cadet slot. Putting me here with this," he patted the shield control unit, "was Garten's final project." He straightened his shoulders. "At least he lived long enough to see this mission approved."

He leaned over and turned the computer on. As soon as it finished booting, he began typing the commands that would activate the magnetic field generators. He felt Nadia watching interestedly over his shoulder. The meteor shield was a close relative of the magnetic bottle at the heart of her experimental fusion reactor. Her advisor and Eric's had studied under the same professor at Harvard thirty years before, which made Eric and Nadia into the academic equivalent of cousins.

The next ten minutes were spent going through a carefully prepared checklist. Turning the shield on was almost anticlimactic. Eric slid the cursor over the "activate shield" button and double-clicked. There was the faintest of hums as the reactor compensated for the added load, but that was the only indicator that the device was running.

"Shield active," he said into his headset.

"Roger that," replied Jessica's voice, "shield active. We should be entering the dust cloud in about two minutes. Scott's running the meteor tracking program now."

Eric was too tense to sit still. "Damn, but I wish I could be up with the monitoring system."

Nadia touched his shoulder sympathetically. "In any rational world, that's where you'd be. But with all of this," her hand swept in a gesture which took in the various experiment pods that were attached to every surface in seemingly random order, "and more up front..." She trailed off.

Eric sighed his agreement. He was lucky to have a dedicated command console. Over the past several years, all of NASA's nonresearch functions had slowly been privatized. And now, thanks to the unremitting efforts of Thacker and his ilk, even that function was being closed down.

Eric went to the port and looked out. There was nothing else he could do from where he was. If he squinted his eyes, it seemed he could almost see a faint shimmering distortion like heat over a highway. It was wishful thinking, of course. The little reactor could never sustain the kind of power the shield would need to ramp up to visibility. But it would be so nice if he could just see that it was working.

"Entering micro-meteor shower," said Scott.

Suddenly, tiny rainbow sparkles began to bloom along a plane parallel to the window.

"Wow!" said Scott, "Can you see this from back there? The shield isn't just deflecting them, it's vaporizing the little bastards."

"Yeah, Scott, I see it," said Eric, forgetting for the moment all of his NASA-speak. "It's beautiful, but I haven't the foggiest notion why it should be—"

The blare of a klaxon cut him off and an electronic voice said, "Reactor overheat likely."

Without thinking, Eric dived for his skinsuit. Nadia passed him going the other way. It took less than fifteen seconds for the pair to go from First Alarm to Full Suits.

Eric was hooking up to the *Phoenix*'s air supply when Jessica's voice came over the com. It was unnaturally calm. "Reactor, we are showing a red light on the fusion board. Do you have that there?"

"Yes, I do, control," came Nadia's voice, equally calm. "I have an overheat warning at stage two. I'm trying to lock it down."

"Understood, reactor. If it goes to level three you will have fifteen minutes before I order a scram."

"Acknowledged. At level three, fifteen minutes and then emergency shutdown. I'm working on i— *Chorte!* Sorry, control. Level three on reactor. Shutting down in fifteen minutes."

"Shield, this is control. Shut anti-meteor system down now."

"Shutdown in process, control."

Eric wanted to scream. Instead he forced himself into the ritualized dance of proper command and response. The precise military language NASA used had been invented for situations like this one. It provided the emotional distance necessary to override the body's natural fight or flight instinct. Even as his adrenal glands went into overdrive, Eric's hands were sliding calmly across the computer's keyboard. He didn't know what was wrong, but the fusion reactor had been fine until the shield started vaporizing meteors.

"Control, this is reactor," said Nadia. "I've located part of the problem. The meteor shield is overdrawing. Repeat, shield is pulling too much power."

"Shield, this is control. Did you copy that?"

"Roger, control. I copy. I'm experiencing software failure. My board is locked up. Initiating manual shut-down." He reached down and physically removed the power plug from its socket. There was no apparent effect. He slammed a hand down on the board. "Control, this is shield. Manual shutdown has failed. Repeat, manual shutdown has failed."

"Excuse me, shield, did you say manual shutdown has failed?"

"Yeah, that's what I said, Jessica. I pulled the plug and the computer clicked off, but I can still see those pretty little rainbow bursts out my window."

"Well, shit," replied the captain. "Scram reactor now, Nadia. I say scram reactor now."

"Scramming," came the reply, followed by a burst of the foulest sounding Russian Eric had ever heard.

"There's no time for that, Nadia," came Jessica's voice over the com.

"Control, this is reactor. The computer has refused the scram order. The whole damn control system is locked up. I'm going to have to cut the feeds manually. This could take some time." She'd already pulled her suit's umbilical loose from the panel and was squirming into the space between the reactor and the hull.

"Reactor, what's the status on the overheat?" asked the captain.

"Control, this is shield. I'm at the reactor board. Overheat is at level three and holding." Eric checked a quick readout. "The containment field should be good for another thirty-five minutes at this level. Nadia is working on the feeds, but that could take more time than we have. I'm going EVA to see if I can shut down the shield by disconnecting the projectors."

"Negative on that, Eric," said Jessica. "I need you to help Nadia. If we only have thirty-five minutes you won't have time to go EVA anyway."

"I will if I don't put on my hardsuit. If I just strap on some mag-boots and a tank I should be able to get out there in five."

"Are you crazy!?" Jessica's voice rose fifteen decibels. "Without a hardsuit you're going to be a popsicle inside of ten minutes."

"Better than a radioactive cinder," said Eric as he headed for the lock.

There was only silence at the other end.

•••

Eric clomped slowly across the outer skin of the *Phoenix*. The closest shield projector was mounted outside the reactor room window. It wasn't a long walk from the air lock, but if he didn't want to lose contact with the ship and float away he had to move slowly. The cold went through the skinsuit like it wasn't there, and he felt as if he were going to freeze solid. In the middle distance he could clearly see the tiny circle of the sun, but this far out its heat was negligible. He was still twenty feet from the projector when an electronic voice came over the com.

"Reactor overheat level four. Containment field failure imminent."

"Control, this is reactor. The feeds are all shut, but I don't think I got to them in—"

Nadia never finished the sentence. Instead, the small star at the core of the fusion reactor went nova. The containment field was designed for low-grade fusion. It was never meant to handle the stress of a nova-type reaction. The magnetic bottle shivered under the strain. For just a moment more it held, but the miniature star would not be denied its freedom. A weak point on the hull side of the field failed. It was less than a centimeter across, but that was enough. A spear of superheated plasma shot out of the tiny nova, punching through the wall of the reactor, the reactor room's bulkhead, and Nadia Gladysheva. The last cosmonaut died instantly as the middle two feet of her flashed into steam.

Eric was looking sunward, away from the ship, when the plasma erupted through the skin of the *Phoenix*. Across his entire field of vision, the stars went away. They were replaced by a mad rainbow of color as the blast from the reactor struck the meteor shield and amped it up to a power level beyond all design specs.

Like a vampire sucking a corpse dry, the shield fed on the runaway energy of the nova reaction. The drain prevented a complete failure of the fusion bottle, a circumstance that would have vaporized the ship. Instead, all of the enormous power of the fusion over-load went into the shield. Eric stared at the wildly coruscating field, transfixed. It was the most beautiful thing he'd ever seen, and the most terrifying. In less than ten seconds it was over.

Before she'd died, Nadia had managed to close the reactor feed lines. Without fuel, the miniature nova was unable to sustain itself. The rainbow of the shield faded and the stars returned, only there was something wrong.

"The sun's gone," Eric whispered into his mike.

"Could you repeat that," said Jessica's voice in his ear.

Mechanically, he responded, "I said the sun's gone, Jess."

"What do you mean, the sun's gone?" snarled Scott. "It's a bloody great big ball of burning gases. It can't go away."

But Eric wasn't listening anymore. Despite the reactor failure, despite the sun vanishing, despite everything, his feet had carried him steadily on toward the nearest shield projector. Now he squatted near the bent and blackened remnants of that piece of equipment, but he wasn't paying it any attention. He was looking at the ragged hole where the plasma jet had exited the ship.

By some twist of fate, the explosion that killed Nadia had left her floating with her face just below the hole. When he first reached the damaged area it was still glowing redly, framing her features in a pulsing halo of fire and lending them an illusion of animation.

For a brief instant it had been possible to believe that she was alive. A closer inspection revealed the truth and the ravages of decompression. Eric didn't want to believe it, but there was no question that his vivacious Russian friend would be going home a martyr rather than the hero they had all dreamed of. He reached a hand through the hole and brushed his fingertips across her helmet. The voice in his microphone called again.

"Eric. Eric, do you read?" asked Jessica. "Eric, please answer me."

Eric didn't know how long the voice had been speaking. He didn't really care.

"Eric, are you there? Goddamn it, answer me."

Finally, he roused himself to answer. No matter how much he hurt, he had responsibilities. It was time to return to them.

"Control, this is shield. I read you. I am on the surface inspecting damage from the reactor failure. There's a hole in the ship's hull. It appears to be about forty centimeters across. The shield projectors are toast. I think the overload cooked the whole system."

"That can wait, Eric. You're near a port, aren't you? Can you see Nadia? The reactor room's in vacuum and we can't open the hatch. She hasn't been responding."

"She won't, Jessica, not ever again." If there was any reply, Eric didn't hear it. Gently, he touched Nadia's helmet one last time, and then he stood. "I'm coming in. There's nothing more I can do out here."

He was shivering uncontrollably before he'd gone three feet. He might have no conscious memory of the time he'd spent staring into Nadia's face, but his body knew that he'd been out in deadly cold for far too long. Scott met him outside the lock. If he hadn't, Eric would have died too. His hands were too stiff to work the controls.

• • •

Eric winced as Scott rubbed salve into his frostbitten fingers.

"You're an idiot," said Scott. "You know that, don't you? Did you think you were immune to cold?"

"No. I thought I could manually disengage the shield. I wish I'd thought of it sooner. If I had, Nadia might still be alive."

"That's bullshit," said Scott. "Even if you'd gone out the minute the alarm went off you'd never have made it to the generators in time. It happened too fast. You know that as well as I do."

"What I know," said Eric, his tone deadly quiet, "is that the system that I brought aboard this ship failed. It failed and my friend died because of that."

"That's true," said Jessica, "but it's not currently relevant. We have a more immediate problem."

"Hey," said Scott. "Cut the kid some slack. He's hurting pretty bad."

"No," she said. "Self-pity isn't something that we have time for. While you were bringing Eric in and getting him out of his suit, I was looking at the navigation systems."

"What's that got to do with anything?" asked Scott.

"Eric was right about the sun going away."

"I don't understand."

"I'm sorry," said Jessica, "I misspoke. The sun isn't exactly gone, it's just . . ." She trailed off. "Let me try again. I used the spectroscopic telescope to find a couple of reference stars. The only problem was that when I used that data to point the 'scope at the sun, it wasn't where it was supposed to be."

"What are you trying to say?" asked Scott.

"I'm getting there, but I have to edge up on it, because it scares the liver out of me. I took a sighting on where the sun should have been and I did eventually find it. It was right where it was supposed to be, but it was a lot dimmer."

"What?" said Eric, as realization hit him, cutting through his despair. "Did you double-check the figures?"

She nodded grimly. "We're a long way from home, boys. I did some rough calculations. If I'm right about the apparent size of the sun, we're somewhere way the hell out past Pluto."

"But how did we get there?" Scott asked. "Assuming, that is, that you haven't just flipped your lid."

"Look," said Jessica, "there's no reason to take my word for it. Why don't we go look at the instruments and see what we can find out. You have no idea how happy I'd be to discover that I was hallucinating."

It took about an hour to establish that they were indeed a very long way from home. In the eight seconds that the shield had been hyperactivated by the reactor failure they'd traveled eight billion kilometers, over seven light hours.

"What happened?" Eric asked for about the thirtieth time.

"I'll tell you what happened," said Scott. "Your advisor didn't invent a meteor shield. He invented a hyper-drive."

"I think you're right," said Jessica. "He did one more thing as well."

"What's that?" asked Eric.

"Well, as grateful as I am for the way the shield took the bang out of the reactor, it was only a delaying action."

"I don't think I see where you're going," replied Scott.

"If we can't get the reactor running again we're going to keep drifting until we hit Alpha C."

"Oh."

"That's not all the good news," she continued. "In addition to setting us well on our way to deep space, the shove that the shield generator gave us pushed us off to one side. We're on the wrong side of the sun for contacting Earth. For the next three and a half months we're completely on our own."

• • •

Eric relaxed his grip on the arc welder. The blue pinpoint sputtered and went out. He flipped up the smoked-glass visor and eyed the patch warily. It was as pretty a piece of welding as he'd ever done, but . . .

"Are you sure this is going to work?" asked Scott from the doorway. He was wearing his full hardsuit, as was Eric.

"No, of course I'm not. In theory, all that the reactor vessel does is supply a magnetically active conducting surface for the fusion bottle to conform to. The patch *should* work almost as well as the original reactor wall. And if you believe that, I've got some land at the Luna retirement center I'd like to sell you. It's got a lovely crater view, and when we get around to installing an atmosphere it'll be on some of the finest shorefront in near-Earth space."

"You know," responded Scott, "as tempting as that sounds, I think that I'll have to find some other way to invest the enormous salary that NASA pays me."

"Your loss. Now, why don't you close that door and I'll try jump-starting this thing."

"All right, but if it goes boom, is the door going to make any difference at all?"

"Well, no," said Eric, "but it provides the illusion."

"Right." Scott ducked into the hallway.

The pressure door closed with a sharp clunk and Eric was alone in the reactor room. He said a quiet prayer, asking Nadia to intervene with whichever Russian Orthodox saint watched over nuclear plants. He flipped the switch. At first nothing happened. Then the reactor indicators began a slow climb. When they hit 80 percent he locked the feeds down. That was as high as he dared push it.

•••

Eric was hunched over the shield computer, trying to figure out what had happened when the field took the power spike from the reactor. It wasn't easy. Because the computer was unplugged when the nova hit the shield, he didn't have any data. Of course, it *was* the only part of the shield system that hadn't been slagged by the overload, so he had to take what he could get.

"How's it coming?" asked a voice over his shoulder. It was Scott. There was something about his tone that brought Eric's head up with a snap. The pilot slid into the room with Jessica right behind him.

"I don't know. Given another couple of months, maybe I'll get somewhere." He smiled grimly. "Of course, it's going to take us at least that long to get home, so . . ."

"Funny you should put it that way," said Jessica. "Scott and I have been doing some figuring of our own up front. We need to talk." Her voice was flat.

"I don't think I'm going to like this," replied Eric.

"Probably not," said Scott. "No matter how we ration, there isn't enough in the way of consumables to get three people home."

"I hadn't thought about that. I've been too busy with the reactor and the shield to think it through. What if we radio in as soon as Earth comes out from behind the sun? Could they send a ship to meet us?"

"No," said Jessica. "Consolidated won't have their asteroid miner done for at least another year, and there's nothing else that could do us any good given the possible launch windows. We're completely on our own."

"How bad is it?" asked Eric.

"We only have enough food and air to get one of us home, and that's if the other two check out within the next ten days."

Eric grunted as though he'd been punched in the stomach. "So, what do we do, draw straws?"

"No," said Jessica. "Scott and I have already decided that it's going to be you."

"What?"

"Look," said Jessica, "the *Phoenix* is NASA's last gasp. You know as well as I do that this mission was named in the hopes that we'd emulate legend and find something out here that would justify our existence. That's *Phoenix's* real mission." She paused for a second. "Your meteor shield, faster-than-light travel, is that something. If NASA can produce that, then there's still hope for the program. The only problem is that no one is going to believe it or give NASA proper credit without a living, breathing astronaut-hero pushing it all the way. That means one of us has to make it home with the news."

"Why me?" asked Eric. "Either of you would make a better hero than I would, Jess. You're both decorated military pilots. I'm just a physics geek. Hell, I can't even fly this bird."

"You're the man who knows the shield," said Scott. "Garten is dead. You might be the only person who can build another. As for piloting, that's all done. The *Phoenix* is aimed for lunar orbit. All you have to do is not touch anything. Look, this is NASA's last mission, and you're her last astronaut. After you left the academy, they closed the door. That's powerful symbolism. You can use it as a club on people like Thacker."

"I thought you said NASA was a dinosaur."

"I also said that she was my dinosaur. Sure, NASA's a flawed beast and I bitch and whine about her problems, but that doesn't mean I don't care about being shut down. I love the grand old dame, warts and all. Don't you see? This is a chance to do more than just keep her tottering along for another year or two. If this hyper-drive thing works out, you could bring back the glory days. I'd give everything I've got, my life included, to do that and call it a bargain."

Eric shook his head in denial. "I don't want the job."

"Too bad," said Scott, "you're elected."

Jessica nodded. "We already took our passports." She dropped a pair of empty syringes on the console. "We've got about fifteen minutes left." She leaned down and kissed his cheek. "I'm so sorry, Eric. We're leaving you the hard job."

He stared at the needles and the bottom dropped out of his heart. It didn't seem possible that something as simple as a needle could end something as complex as a human life, but there was no doubting the message of the syringes.

"I-I can't do this," Eric faltered. "It's going to take months to get home. I'll never make it. I'll crack."

"No," said Jessica. "You won't. If you do, it's all over. There won't be any more missions. I went through the same academy you did. I know what it takes to make an astronaut. You can't let it end with you, anymore than Scott or I could. That's why we're checking out now. I don't want to die. There's too much to live for. But there's only one way that the *Phoenix* can rise, and that's for the right person to make it home. If that person were me or Scott, I'd expect you to take the same route I'm taking now. But that's not how it worked. The job is yours, Eric. You have to finish the mission."

There was an expectancy in her voice and he knew what she needed to hear. He gave it to her, though it cost him most of his soul.

"I will."

•••

Eric took the syringe from its case. Carefully, almost lovingly, he attached a sterile needle. When that was done, he set it aside and withdrew a length of rubber tubing from the medical kit. Using his right hand and his teeth, he tied the tubing tightly around his left arm. After a few seconds the vein inside his elbow rose to the surface. It reminded him of a dolphin coming up for air. He grimaced.

"I can't do it, Jess, I just can't."

Picking up the syringe he jabbed the needle quickly into the vein. He covered the plunger with his thumb. He rubbed it back and forth. Back and forth. The moment passed. He stopped. Slowly, almost shaking with the effort, he removed the needle.

"Got to finish the mission," he whispered.

Blood welled up at the center of the prick. The bright red globule expanded and broke loose to float across the cabin. Eric stared at the hole it had come from. Beside the fresh wound there were more than a dozen others, running the gamut from a white scar six months old to a brown scab.

"Dammit, Jess, I never wanted this. I'm no hero."

He pressed a cotton ball into the hole and released the tubing. The needle went into a small container of bleach. He was still a long way from home. He might need it later.

•••

Eric leaned down and pushed the button that sent air pumping into the corridors of the academy dorms in Mare Imbrium. It had taken fifteen years for him to get there, fifteen years of hard work and political knife fighting, but Jessica had been right. The last astronaut carried a weight beyond all proportion. It was a weight that he'd thrown around with abandon in pursuit of his cause. Oh, there'd been sweet moments: watching Congressman Thacker go down to one of the worst defeats in electoral history, for example, and none so sweet as this. But it was a weight that he had to carry on his own back, and he was tired. Terribly, terribly tired.

After the ceremony, he walked across the barren lunar field to the *Phoenix*. It had been returned to Mare Imbrium and installed in a place of honor. Inside, in the place where the reactor had once been, were four coffins. Three cradled the remains of heroes, the fourth waited.

The air lock worked like new. The *Phoenix* was given the best possible care. Inside he stripped off his suit and went to look in on his old friends. He brushed his fingers across Jessica's casket.

"Well, Jess, the Federated Extra-Solar Development Agency isn't exactly NASA, but it's damn close." He laughed, a short, bitter sound. "You know what's ironic? They aren't calling them astronauts anymore, so I'm still the last and I always will be."

Eric lifted the lid of his coffin. Inside, on the pillow, was the hypodermic he'd carried next to his heart for the entire long trip home. It had taken thirteen months, many of them spent looking at sanity from the wrong side of the line, but he'd survived. He'd made a promise, and he'd kept it.

Eric reached into the coffin and pulled the syringe out of its case. He attached a new needle and brought it up to rest against the skin under his left elbow. Then, very deliberately, he pushed. There was a faint pop as the point broke the skin. The needle slid in. He could feel the cold steel embedded in the pulsing vein.

"I finished the mission," he said to the air, and placed his thumb on the plunger.

For ten minutes he stood there unmoving. Finally, he pulled the needle from his arm. The ampule was still full. In a ritual he'd performed a thousand times, he placed the syringe back in its case. It was not yet time. With a fresh hole in his arm, and another in his heart, he turned his back on his friends once again. He owed it to them.

For the last astronaut, the mission was never finished.

THE WRITER'S LIFE AND UNIQUENESS

Written by
Roger Zelazny

About the Author

One of the most interesting and individual stylists in the field, Roger Zelazny was a full-time writer for over three decades. By 1965, he was already recognized as a major SF force, winning Hugo and Nebula Awards for novels and shorter work; such creations as A Rose for Ecclesiastes *and* This Immortal *were then followed by the Amber chronicles as he settled into his career.*

His work was characterized by a "science-fantasy" touch—a blend of science fiction plots and fantasy images, so that he became noted as one of our great makers of legends. That orientation was the foremost of his many contributions as a judge of the Writers of the Future contest, a job which he performed most ably for twelve years, from the beginning of the contest to his untimely passing in 1995.

He contributed the essay that follows to the very first volume of L. Ron Hubbard Presents Writers of the Future, *and his message is as fresh and insightful today as it was when he wrote it. We are proud to include it here for a whole new generation of writers.*

A day or so after my first professional sale as a writer the activity in my pleasure center died down sufficiently to permit me to begin writing again. I sold sixteen more stories that year and I learned a lot of narrative tricks. The following year I stretched my efforts to novelette-length, to novella-length. I felt then that I had learned enough to try writing a novel. I did it and I sold it and the moment was golden.

I did not quit my job to write full time for another five years, however. I had seen others do this after an initial book sale—chuck everything and Be A Writer—with disastrous results. I realized that there was more to being a writer than the act of writing, that there were other lessons to be learned, that one could not rely on current sales for one's support, that one required an economic cushion and a plan for maintaining it. So I made my plans, I followed them and they worked.

There is no use in going into autobiographical detail about this. The times have changed, the markets are different. Only the principles stand. A writer still has to hustle in the beginning, and there seem to be as many different ways of going about it as there are writers. What I am saying is that the ones who succeeded and exhibited staying power had a plan. They followed it, they established themselves, they became secure. They sell everything they write now. They learned the extra-literary considerations as well as the writing reflexes necessary for the successful pursuit of the writer's trade. I counsel all of the new writers whose work is contained in this volume to begin learning about publishing, distribution, agenting, contracts, to talk with other writers and other people in the publishing business whenever possible, to learn how things work. The actual writing is in some ways the easiest part of this business once you've mastered certain essentials, and the business side is the hardest part of writing when you are getting started.

So much for the crass, commercial end of things. It deserves mention in a book of this sort, though, and if it causes even one beginning writer to think ahead to what it may be like to sell a book first and then have to write it and deliver it by a certain date, to wonder what it will be like to write on days when one doesn't feel like writing, to speculate as to the manner in which everything involved in one's occupation may be reflected on one's tax return and to consider the best ways of responding to interviewers, academic inquiries, crackpot callers and fan mail—and if the fruits of these cogitations help to make the difference between the writer's ultimate success or failure, then I am vindicated in prefacing my more general remarks with reference to the non-writing side of writing.

So I said it. Now I'll talk about writing.

In acting as a judge in the contests from which the stories in this volume emerged on top, I saw some good writing and some good ideas. Unfortunately, these were not always conjoined. When they came together in one tale it was great; it made my job easier. But in my place, which story would you choose? A story that is well written but light? A story with a good idea, a novel plot or a solid character but weak in the writing itself? This was my biggest problem. Usually the first-place story, as I saw it, stood well to notice, was possessed of several virtues. The second- or third-place stories were generally the ones where this problem loomed to devil me when it did appear. I generally resolved it by favoring originality over slickness, under the theory that narrative skills can be improved upon but interesting and unique viewpoints are harder to come by. The other judges may have proceeded differently—but that was my feeling, and I might as well state it here. I'll even tell you why.

I have taught at writers' conferences and I know a lot of editors, and I have become familiar with that species of narrative best called a "borderline story"—a piece suitably composed but not terribly compelling. I will have to give away a dark secret, also, in order to make this point. On several occasions I have been shown a borderline story and was asked, "What's wrong with this? Everyone's rejected it, and I don't think it's all that bad. I've seen worse in print." In each instance I've had to agree. It was okay. If I—or one of my established colleagues—had written it, it would have sold. But it was not strong enough for an initial sale. It would have been easy for me to point out some flaw or other (there is always *something* that can be improved upon) and suggest a rewrite to take care of it. But that wasn't what I was being asked. I decided to be blunt and honest on one occasion I can recall, and I said, "There isn't really anything wrong with it. Put it away and write some more. If you begin selling, dust it off and send it to the editor who's buying your stuff, even if that editor rejected it before." Two years later I received a copy of a magazine containing that story, unchanged. The author had had several stories appear in that magazine by then. This one was autographed, beneath the words "You were right." I have seen this sort of thing happen more than once. It is not perversity on the part of editors, but simply one of those Cold, Hard Facts of Life: While you'll need both in the long run, content usually has an edge over form.

With respect to science fiction and fantasy stories, I have often observed that they have all of the same requirements as a piece of general fiction with the added problem of stuffing in all of the extra background material dealing with an exotic setting or the functioning of the unusual concept which make the story a part of this genre—and to do it without losing the reader's interest. It pleases me to see that the authors of the stories in this volume have passed that hurdle and may be read for content without distraction by the stage machinery. They have learned certain basic reflexes and are ready to gain strength by focusing continuing attention on character and ideas. If this results in any borderline stories I counsel them to hang on to these for later study, to educate the ultimate editor—i.e., "the internal editor" every writer must develop, a benign species of schizophrenia permitting one to create and to look over one's own shoulder and kibitz at the same time.

I have always felt that anything is a valid subject for a science fiction story, that any idea can be run through the various "If this goes on . . ." and "What if?" machines to produce stimulating and sometimes profound results. I have also felt that when a person dies an entire universe passes, since no two of us seem to inhabit the same universe in terms of perceptions and values. It is this unique quality which, if one can put a handle on it and transport it into fiction, provides the reason for and value of all the world's literature. A story is a ticket to a new universe, and traveling in the worlds of science fiction and fantasy can be the glamour tour of the mental traveler.

It is a delight to a tourist such as myself to see the opening of new realms each time that someone learns the magic words and shows us the way. It is a sign, I feel, of the strength and attraction of this area of writing that so many new people have been moved to make the effort, and that some good things have been done as a result. For long-range success I can only counsel perseverance. After luck, I think it is one of the best things a writer can have. Good luck to everyone in this book. I hope to see you again.

LUCRETIA'S NOSE

Written by
Philip Lees

Illustrated by
Amanda Anderson Gannon

About the Author

Philip Lees was born and grew up in England, but has now spent more than half his life in Greece. His love of speculative fiction dates back to his childhood. He currently lives in a small resort town on the island of Crete, where he makes his living developing computer applications for healthcare.

About the Illustrator

Amanda Anderson Gannon was born in 1977 to wonderfully supportive, intelligent parents. Her mother and sister taught her to draw, and she has been writing and illustrating her own stories since she was five years old. She has never taken a formal art course. Much of her inspiration comes from the myth, art and history of various pre-Christian cultures. When she is not writing or painting, she can be found playing with her many beloved snakes.

Her wonderful and patient husband, Paul Batteiger, appeared in Volume XVI of L. Ron Hubbard's Writers of the Future *anthology, with his story "Like Iron Unicorns."*

Lucretia is thinking about Tycho Brahe. As an astronomer, she is as familiar with the name of Brahe as a painter would be with Picasso, a musician with Mozart, a philosopher with Russell. Brahe's meticulous observations of the heavens, using instruments of his own design, laid the foundations for Kepler's laws of planetary motion and the completion of the shift from the geocentric to the heliocentric view of the universe, a major change in thinking. Ironically, Brahe himself maintained to his death that the earth, not the sun, was the center. To imagine the earth moving would be too difficult, too complicated, he said.

But Lucretia is not thinking about Brahe's contribution to astronomy now: she is thinking about his nose. A sword severed some of it during a duel over the validity of a mathematical formula, and for the rest of his life he covered the deficiency with a copper-colored metal prosthesis.

Lucretia fingers her own nose, wondering how Tycho felt about his disfigurement. Wide brown eyes stare back at her from the mirror. Above them, a square forehead is framed by symmetrically cut brown hair that hangs to where her chin juts from a strong jaw. Her face is all planes and angles, sharp edges unsoftened by curves. There are lines from her nose to her mouth and at the corners of her eyes. She tries a smile and is satisfied by the result. Then she puckers her face at her own smugness.

Of course, she is not going to lose her nose, nor even a part of it. Modern medicine has advanced far beyond the primitive era when the only effective treatment for cancer was the surgical removal of the affected body part. Nowadays, a simple injection will do the trick: her own DNA, harvested while she was just a spoonful of cells within her mother's womb and preserved for just such a need. Of course, modifications have had to be made so that the scavenger DNA will be able to track down the melanoma, surround it and, eventually, digest it and excrete it as waste, leaving fresh new tissue in its place. The DNA culturing and programming takes a few days, which is why Lucretia has the time to rub her nose and think about how things might have been if she had lived in an earlier time.

Like a good citizen, conscientious about her health, Lucretia always rubs sunscreen over any exposed skin before going outdoors during daylight. How could she have missed even such a small spot? She shrugs at herself in the mirror, likes the way it looks, so she does it again. The discoloration is so slight as to be hardly noticeable. Only her routine three-monthly bioscan revealed the presence of the rogue cells, already growing and spreading their spores, like a fungus preparing to rot away a tree from the inside. Never mind. The treatment will take care of the tumor and all its children; Dr. Decker has assured her of that.

Her alarm implant chimes softly through her auditory nerve: it is time to go. She straightens her jacket, turns away from the mirror and heads for the door.

•••

One month later, Lucretia is in Dr. Decker's office, waiting for the results of her first post-treatment checkup.

The doctor is looking at his computer screen. He is frowning; he looks puzzled, perhaps even worried.

"What's the matter?" Lucretia asks. "Isn't it working?" But she's been feeling so good lately, so full of energy. In the mirror this morning she noticed that the lines of worry have gone from her face. Only her eyes seemed pale, but that was probably just her imagination.

"No, no. It's working all right." Dr. Decker is still focused on the monitor. She senses that he doesn't want to look at her. "The tumor is completely gone. Remarkable." *Well, that's good, isn't it? So what's the problem?*

"What is it then? What's wrong?"

"I'm not really sure. I've never seen a reaction like this before." He says it reluctantly, as if he were admitting to sexual impotence. "I'll have to run some more tests." He is stalling, she can tell; more tests won't help.

"Doctor, tell me what's going on." The voice she uses to discipline unruly students gets through to him and he stiffens. For the first time he looks in her direction, his watery eyes shrunken behind the lenses of his spectacles. Few people wear them nowadays; in his case she believes it is an affectation, maybe a defense. A wisp of gray hair lies across his forehead.

"Lucretia, as far as I can tell, the scavenger DNA didn't stop with the melanoma. It appears to have cleaned out a lot of other material as well." He taps the computer screen. "According to these readings, part of your body now has a genetic age of twenty-three. And the effect is spreading."

This is hard to take in. "You mean I'm getting younger?"

"It seems so. As you know, the scavenger DNA replaces cancerous tissue with healthy tissue, your own tissue, cloned from your own cells. Well, if these readings

Illustrated by Amanda Anderson Gannon

are correct, it seems to be doing the same thing for the rest of you. Old cells being replaced by new."

He tries a weak smile, perhaps intended to reassure her. "For a long time we've wondered whether there's any way to halt or reverse the aging process. Now it looks as if we might have found it."

She suddenly loses patience with his professorial ruminations. "And what's going to happen to me?" she snaps.

He looks hurt, as if disappointed that she is not more pleased by the news, more proud to be a scientific discovery: his discovery. "As I said, I'll need to run some more tests. But I don't think you should worry."

All right, then. She will not worry. After all, she feels fine. She tells him so.

"Good," he says. "By the way, did your mother have blue eyes?"

Blue eyes? "Yes, she did. Why?"

He looks uncomfortable again. "Well, I'm not certain, but I think that you're probably going to have blue eyes too."

•••

Lucretia is still trying to come to terms with the stranger's face that now looks back at her from the mirror. Or rather, not a stranger, but a new mix of the once familiar. It is like an intermediate stage in a morph transition between her mother's face and the one Lucretia used to wear just a few months before. It is the face of a twenty-year-old, unlined, unblemished: she has been given back her youth. Is that immoral? In her mind, she slips a *t* into the word, but will not pronounce the result, even to herself.

The eyes are the hardest to get used to. "The mirror of the soul," somebody once said. Has her soul changed color, then, from chestnut brown to this bright Mediterranean blue? Is she still really Lucretia, or has Lucretia's place been taken by the unblessed offspring of some scientific alchemy? The letter *t* is still trying to insinuate itself into her thoughts of immorality, but she will not let it settle there. Not yet.

Dr. Decker has asked her to come and stay at the center. He wants to monitor her condition, he says, take samples, run more tests. But she has had enough. She will be their guinea pig no longer; let them do what they like. She thinks of Tycho's advice: "When statesmen or others worry you too much, then you should leave with your possessions."

Lucretia has her bag packed and she is going to Mars. She has friends there; she has lectured at Lowell University. By the time Dr. Decker finds out, it will be too late. She takes one last look around her apartment, says goodbye to personal things too heavy to take on the ship. Perhaps she will return here one day, in a year, or five years (or fifty, or a hundred, says the voice in her mind, as she marvels at the concept). She slings the strap of her bag over her shoulder, steps out and pulls the door closed behind her, hearing the autolocks snap in as if her home, too, is saying goodbye.

• • •

For her birthday, Lucretia has decided she must do something really special. She is a hundred and fifty today, but still looks twenty, or thirty when tired. She has learned to be careless of cuts and abrasions, which heal within an hour or two. Broken bones take a few days.

She has not been ill, not even suffered the mildest infection, since those cells in her nose rebelled and had to be quieted.

She stopped working at the Lowell Observatory more than ten years ago. A century of saving made her independent, at least for a while. Also, Mars has been spoiled for astronomy now. She thinks back to before the terraforming started to show its effect, to when the atmosphere was thin enough for myriads of stars to penetrate the night sky with their light—hard and sharp as silver nails. She is probably the only one who can remember.

Still, the atmosphere is breathable nowadays, and dense enough for what she is about to do. Mars is now her home. Brahe again: "With a firm and steadfast mind one should hold under all conditions, that everywhere the earth is below and the sky above, and to the energetic man, every region is his fatherland." She feels the same, though this is probably not what Tycho had in mind. She sits in the passenger seat of the chartered gyrojet and reviews the last fifty years of her life, as part of the ritual on which she is embarking.

She has had many relationships, but none lasted long. After a year or so she always started to notice the signs that her partner was moving ahead of her on time's highway, leaving her behind, so she turned off to one side. None of them had ever commented on her own constancy, but Lucretia became very aware of those things.

She taught two generations of students, published two books. Her colleagues, of course, were aware of her condition, but respected her wishes by not talking about it outside the university. If any of them ever felt jealousy they never showed it. A friend from the observatory once suggested that she study history to get a better perspective. "There's plenty of it," he said. But Lucretia was no longer interested in history. The future that stretched before her seemed much vaster than any past that lay behind. Another reason she left was that she could not bear to stay on and watch her colleagues die one by one.

She never dared to try for children of her own. *Would her body accept pregnancy? Or would it reject the fetal cells, digest and excrete them, as it had the cancer? And if she could have a child, what would it be like?* She was not ready for that knowledge. Not yet.

So today, she has a choice to make. *The* choice. The choice between life and death. Tycho Brahe stayed too long at a banquet, stayed at the table until his bladder burst. She will not make the same mistake: she will not stay on too long. Fifty years ago today she chose life, for the first time. If she survives today, she will choose again fifty years from now. This she has sworn.

Ahead of her, she sees her destination; the gigantic cliff is like a red wall splitting the sky from the brown desert. Although it already looks high, she knows that most of it is still below the horizon. As the gyrojet skims along, the wall rises and grows clearer, until she can begin to make out the cloud of vapor at one point of its base, linked to the top by a silver line like a bolt of lightning. That is where she is going. That is where she will make her decision.

•••

Lucretia balances herself carefully, then lets go of the hawser that is her last connection to the gyrojet. The rock on which she is standing is part of a meteorite that streaked to Mars' surface eons ago and rammed itself deep into the ground, exploding into fragments, one of which was thrown for two miles before wedging itself into a crevice at the very top of this cliff. Because of its coppery color and the way it sticks out over the precipice, the early colonists named it "Tycho's Nose."

On either side of her, two torrents pour over the edge and plunge a thousand feet into the steaming bowl far below. Her hair is already wet from the spray. Lucretia is standing with her back to the drop and she gazes ahead along the line of the river, imagining herself following it all the way back to the melting southern icecap. It's a good thing I'm doing this now, she thinks. In another century, perhaps less, the rock will be so eroded that Tycho's Nose will slip loose and fall, leaving the river free to wash the wound it left.

The white noise of the water has faded in her perception, leaving her in a calm, quiet space of her own creation. The gyrojet is hovering nervously some distance away, its rotors slicing the silence like a chef's knife dancing across a chopping block. She wishes it would go away, but that was not part of the deal. It is time. She sets her alarm implant for start and stop, then counts the seconds, wondering what she will decide.

The alarm emits the first chime. Lucretia bends her knees in a crouch, then springs into the air, up and back, out over the cliff. Her body rotates slowly, and as soon as she is facing downward she extends her arms and legs in a star, just as she practiced in the simulator, balancing on the air, letting herself slide slowly back from the waterfall.

After a few seconds she can feel the wind rushing past her body. She watches the foaming cascade in front of her, judging her acceleration. The water is dropping more swiftly than she is, creating the illusion that she is being blown upward, rather than falling down. When this relative motion settles at a constant speed, she knows she will go no faster. Decision time is near. In spite of the weaker Martian gravity, she knows that if she hits the pool in her present posture the impact will do more damage than even her miraculous metabolism can repair. When the alarm chimes for the second time she must pull in her arms, let her head drop, make herself into a vertical arrow that can penetrate the water with the minimum of friction. That way, she can survive. She has deliberately set the alarm for the last possible second, so that her decision, when it comes, must be instantaneous and automatic. There is no margin for error.

Floating on the air, Lucretia plummets toward her destiny, swaying this way and that like a falling leaf. At the last moment she looks down, sees the boiling water rushing toward her. Then the alarm sounds. Without thinking, she twists, then straightens again. She is almost too late, but not quite; her angle is not perfect, but close enough. She enters the water in a dive that shocks her whole body like a thunderclap. Its icy caress takes her breath away as it tries to pull her hair out by the roots. She aches and smarts all over.

Then there is peace again. She feels no need to breathe, just lets herself float slowly toward the surface as the current carries her away from the cliff. When her head emerges, she opens her mouth wide and fills her lungs with the damp air, then coughs and splutters, as if it is the first breath she has ever taken. Now she can hear the gyrojet circling, coming to pick her up. This time, she has chosen life. Perhaps she has not earned the right to die. Not yet.

DREAMS AND BONES

Written by
Eric M. Witchey

Illustrated by
Yanko Yankov

About the Author

Eric Witchey developed a suspicious love of fiction while working as a door-to-door fire alarm salesman, a waterbed salesman, an art salesman and a motivational speaker. During lapses of creativity, he also worked as a forklift operator, a fabricator in a steel mill and a bicycle repairman. Tragically, the financial demands of college forced him into honest work as a dishwasher and a fire fighter. Then he surfaced as a teacher of expository writing at Colorado State University and then technical writing at Portland State University. Nowadays, he works as a computer consultant. What could be more ordinary?

About the Illustrator

Yanko Yankov is thirty-six, a teacher in middle school in Bulgaria. He has been doing illustrations for some time, but so far has not had one published. His entry in the Illustrators of the Future Contest *is his first success . . . but not his last, we'll wager.*

Say good night, Gracie." His first words felt right, familiar to his tongue and lips, remembered in the same way his hand remembered his *El Producto Corona*. He lifted the cigar to his lips.

His fingers touched his mouth. No cigar.

He was sure he'd been holding a cigar. It was as much a part of him as his sense of audience, the silent laughter rising and falling, attached to every thought like a meter marking the comedy value of each idea as it did a soft shoe across the stage in his skull. Dying, he thought, did odd things to the mind.

"Mr. Burns?"

That wasn't Gracie's line. It wasn't Gracie's voice. Too young. Too strong.

That's where the familiar words had come from. He'd said them to Gracie. He'd said them a million times.

"Mr. Burns, please wake up."

Gracie was dead. She died in 1964, thirty-two years ago. George opened his eyes. White glare made him blink and squint. He inhaled the clean sheet and chlorine cleanser reek of a hospital room.

He'd broken his hip. He'd had the flu. He remembered that he'd missed the booking for his hundredth birthday. Gracie would not approve.

He wiped away the tears in his eyes and looked up at the smooth cheeks and wrinkled forehead of a concerned woman of thirty or so. An old routine flashed through his mind. "Wake up, George. Wake up," Gracie said while slapping his face and pulling him upright. "What happened?" was his line. Then Gracie said, "You missed it, George! A man passed out."

Then he remembered that he was dead too, or at least he thought he was dying the last time he closed his eyes. He guessed the doctors had taken him to the hospital and brought him back.

"Mr. Burns?" The woman's voice was urgent. Her white one-piece coverall made her look more like a painter than a nurse. Her coverall had a hood that didn't quite cover the dark curls framing her face. Not a painter, he decided. The coverall was made of some kind of shimmer-and-shine stuff, odd looking. She seemed more like an actress from one of Rod Serling's sets.

Except Serling was dead too.

"Where's my cigar?" George asked, not really expecting the doctors to let him have one.

"We have a replica El Producto for you in makeup."

That made no sense. He tried to sit up, but a wave of dizziness overcame him.

She grasped his shoulders and lifted until he was sitting. "The resurrection will leave you weak and dizzy for a few moments."

He coughed a little. His throat was dry.

She offered him a straw. "This will help."

He sipped. It wasn't water. It was cool and sweet and much better than water. "What's this?"

"Vitamins, electrolytes, genofrenetic stabilizers. It's to help you get ready for your debut."

Cute girl. Kinda' wholesome and genuine. A *Carnation Evaporated Milk* girl, if ever he saw one.

Earnest enough, and her voice and manner were kind. "Look, kid," he rasped, warming to his role, "I did soft shoe with your grandmother. My debut was a long time ago."

"Maybe with my grandmother's great grandmother," she said. She pulled a strap free from his legs and tugged at him to get him to slide to the side of the bed. "We don't have much time, Mr. Burns."

"At my age, I don't have the energy to hurry, honey."

She tugged again.

He winced, anticipating the pain in his hip. But there was no pain in his hip. In fact, his hip felt great. His whole body felt great. "Whatever it was you gave me to drink, you should bottle it," he said.

His habit-trained hand slipped inside his suit coat, seeking his breast pocket and a cigar. His hand found his breast pocket at the same moment he realized he shouldn't have one.

He was fully clothed.

He lifted his arms and looked at the brown coat sleeves, then at the rest of his suit: long lapels, three buttons, no vest, white shirt, and wide, print tie. He hadn't worn such a thing since the fifties. "They don't make suits like this anymore," he said.

For a moment, her wrinkled forehead smoothed. She chuckled. "I knew you'd be authentic," she said. Then the wrinkles returned to her forehead. "But you're perfect. You're too real."

George blinked. The silent laughter in the back of his head quieted. Her wrinkled brow meant he'd lost his timing. He let a couple too many beats open up in the dialog. He recovered like the pro he was. "Look, kid. One of us is made of dreams. You better pinch me. If I pinch you, I'll either get arrested or have a coronary."

Illustrated by Yanko Yankov

She laughed full out, a high birdsong sound. It felt good to hear someone laugh. It was right. It warmed his bones and heart. He turned his feet out of the bed and stood up. *A dream*, he thought. *I've got my shoes on and shined.*

She steadied him. "Mr. Burns, I'm a big fan."

"You must be a historian," he quipped.

"Not exactly," she answered seriously. "I'm a memory reclamation technician. Media history's just a hobby."

He looked across the green-walled room at a mirror. His thirty-year-old face looked back. His knees went weak and he sat back down on the bed. "Good Lord!"

"Mr. Burns?"

"I'm young."

"Of course, Mr. Burns. Why would we make you old?"

"Make me? This is *my* dream."

"No." She bit her lip and frowned. "It's more like *our* dream. We constructed you from DNA maps made from exhumed bone shavings. Then we extracted data from media archives, medical records, and the memories of the few people who have been alive long enough to remember you."

George laughed. He loved dreams that went around corners and down long halls. "Your dreams. My bones," he said. He stood up and admired himself. "Not a bad combination. I like the way you see me."

"It's the hundredth anniversary of your death. We couldn't celebrate without the guest of honor and his wife."

"Gracie's here?"

"She was harder. We don't know as much about her."

"What's to know? Gracie was Gracie. Smart as Einstein and much funnier."

"Please, Mr. Burns. Listen to me. You and Gracie go on in ten."

"Take me to her."

Someone knocked.

The nurse shot a worried look at the door, then she gripped George's shoulders and put her face close to his. "When the show's over, run," she whispered. "You and Gracie have to run, Mr. Burns. The building is a museum replica of Radio City Music Hall, circa late 1950s. The stage exit is clear."

"Burns and Allen go on at Radio City in ten, and you want us to run?"

"Mr. Burns, you're a live replica. Our Population Control license only allows you one hour of life."

His nurse was pale and serious. George realized his dream was a nightmare. If it wasn't a nightmare, she was scared and maybe nuts; and if it wasn't a nightmare, Gracie was alive and he was almost two hundred years old.

The door behind her opened. A short man walked into the room. He wore a shining pin-striped suit George wouldn't have worn even as a costume. George pegged the man as a stage manager. He was overweight and his face was as red as vaudeville rouge. His hard heart showed on his face. His mouth and brow were pinched tight from years of being an ass.

"Is it ready?" The man said, ignoring George.

The nurse looked at George, her eyes watery and scared. "Are you steady, Mr. Burns?" she asked. "If you can stand, I'll take you through makeup and then to Gracie."

George stood. He felt strong and steady. He let the woman lead him past the stage manager to the door. The little tyrant held the door open. George noticed there was no knob on the inside. He glanced back at his bed. Straps dangled from shiny rails.

They walked from the hospital room onto backstage at Radio City. Dreams are like that, George thought. Or maybe heaven is like that.

•••

El Producto lit and in hand, suit smoothed, he straightened his hair and opened the door. Gracie stood at the mirror, poking at a curl on her temple. It was her, alive, young, as beautiful as the first day they'd stepped on the boards together. "Ya got some moxie, kid," he said.

She spun. Her tight-waisted taffeta dress twirled and rebounded. Soft curls bounced against her temples. Her shining eyes were real. Her smile was real. There was no pain in her face.

George's insides lit up to match that smile.

"Oh, George! Isn't it wonderful?" She ran to him and they held one another for a six-beat.

A bald dream-kid with a red spiral tattooed on his skull stuck his face into Gracie's dressing room. "Five to cue," he said.

George pointed over his shoulder with the cigar. "Son of Gregor, the tattooed man."

"Such a nice boy," Gracie said. "Takes after his mother. Of course, he doesn't have a beard yet."

George chuckled and rolled his cigar between thumb and finger. "Is this your dream or mine, Gracie?"

"George," she said, in her let-me-explain-things voice. "This is no time for philosophy. We're together and we're on in five."

"It doesn't bother you that you're dead?"

"I'm not dead, George." She took his hand. "I don't think I'd like being dead. I hate when you're sad and I'm not there to make you smile."

"I went on a long time without you, Gracie. A very long time."

"If it's a dream, it's a good dream, George. Radio City!"

"My nurse says we're replicas."

"Don't be silly, George. I'd know if I wasn't me, now wouldn't I?"

"She says we're built to look like us and think like us. Some kind of Frankenstein's monster."

"Boris Karloff won't like us playing his material." Gracie turned to her mirror, picked up a brush and pulled it through her hair a couple of times.

George checked Gracie's door. No knob on the inside. He checked her bed: straps and rails.

"This dream has some dark corners, Gracie."

She dropped the brush. "We're young, George. You and me, young, together, and going on in less than five." She pirouetted for him. "We're going on, George. That's all that matters."

The nasty stage manager opened the door and motioned for them to come out.

George took Gracie's hand and they walked to the wings to wait for their intro.

Gracie squeezed his hand, looked up at him and asked, "I got the funniest letter from my aunt?"

George took a pull on his cigar and smiled. "One of your best routines." But over her shoulder he saw two men dressed like painters wheeling a gurney out of a dressing room. The gurney had a shiny black bag the size of a man on it. The bag was full.

On the boards, an MC in black tails spread his arms. "Who on earth could follow a comic genius like Mr. Benny?"

"Oh, George, Jack is here!" Gracie said.

The MC pointed his top hat at George and Gracie. "Burns and Allen, in the flesh!"

George shot a glance into the wings. The men and the gurney were gone.

Hand in hand, Burns and Allen trotted out into the spotlight.

They faced front.

The theater was empty and silent.

Curved rows of velvet-backed seats with mahogany arms stretched away into shadows. The carpeted aisles looked like they'd never been walked on. The house was empty. *Dead*, George thought, *like a morgue or the mummy room of a closed museum.*

George glanced at Gracie. Her smile was fixed. She had her stage face on, but her eyes held confusion.

From backstage, a voice said, "It's like TV! Just go."

Gracie's eyes cleared and sparkled. She started laughing.

George took a long draw on his El Producto. "What's so funny, Gracie?" George asked.

"I got a letter from my Aunt Thelma. She has the funniest story."

"I could use a laugh. Go ahead and read it to me."

"Oh, okay. See, George, she writes, 'I have the funniest story to tell you, which I will the next time I see you.'" Gracie laughed, and her laugh was alive and warm and would have infected a thousand people had the house been full.

"How can you tell the story is so funny if she hasn't told you yet?" George spoke his line in gratitude to whatever god, dream, drug, or advance of science had given him one more moment on stage with a cigar and Gracie's laugh.

They were home. They fell into old rhythms and ran for a clean forty minutes. They took their bows. They trotted off stage.

In the wings, George laughed and hugged Gracie.

Gracie cried. "Oh, George, it was wonderful, just wonderful!"

The stage manager stood near the curtain ropes glaring at them. His suit reflected the stage lights.

"George Burns." George extended a hand.

"Uh-huh," the man said.

"You want to sign us for another night?"

"License expires in eight minutes." The little man turned away and headed for the dressing rooms. He obviously expected them to follow.

Gracie stepped after him.

George touched Gracie's arm. She looked at him. He frowned and winked.

Gracie stopped and put on her stage face.

"I don't have a license," Gracie said.

The stage manager turned. He was confused. They were off his script.

George smiled.

"I don't like to drive," Gracie explained. "If I had a license, I might drive more. The other day, a policeman pulled me over, and I told him—"

"The license expires in five. We need to inject you."

"What are you going to inject us into?"

"No," the man said. "I have to give you an injection."

"Well, if you think it's a good idea. But if I were you, I think I'd give it to a nurse. Don't they get trained for that kind of thing? I might hurt you—"

"The show's over." The stage manager's eyes threatened to explode from his crimson face. "We're done with you. You need a disposal shot."

George took Gracie's elbow, nodded to the stage manager, and urged her slowly toward the dressing room. The manager's eyes relaxed and his face lost some of its red.

"Oh, I don't drink, Mr. . . . I didn't get your name, but it doesn't matter since I'm not going to have a drink with you, but George . . ." She went on, keeping Mr. We're-done-with-you confused but not so confused that it might occur to him he could use some help.

While Gracie prattled and the stage manager tried to keep them moving, George smoked and shuffled Gracie back and forth a bit so he could get a good view of the floor, the backstage paths, and the catwalks. When he was sure the exits were where they should be, he squeezed Gracie's elbow and said, "Gracie, I think he wants us to take some medicine."

"Exactly!" Relief glowed on the manager's face.

"Well, I don't know why he didn't just say so. What was all that about drinking and shooting nurses? Why'd he go on . . ." She kept talking and George led her toward the dressing rooms.

The stage manager gratefully followed.

At the dressing room door, the stage manager hustled forward and opened the door for them.

Inside, two gurneys and two big men in painter suits waited for them.

Gracie stopped behind him.

"I'm not sick," she said. "I'm not even tired. I just got up from a nap an hour ago."

George put a hand on the stage manager's shoulder and winked conspiratorially. "Give me a minute with her," he said.

The flustered manager looked into the room as if considering George's request. Then his face got redder. His brow tightened and his lips pinched in.

Before the man could turn back from the open door, George shoved him. The little man stumbled across the threshold. He screamed in surprise. The definitely-not-painters leaped toward the door.

George slammed the door and flipped the deadbolt. The stage manager bellowed and pounded on the inside of the door where there should have been a handle. Two larger, deeper voices joined him.

"I don't think I like him very well, George," Gracie said.

George kissed her fast and hard. "I don't know if we're real or not," he said. "Dream, heaven, hell, or Tomorrowland, I'm betting if we go in that room, it's over." He squeezed her hands and winked. "Have another go with me, Gracie?"

Gracie blushed. "Oh, George. You know I'd never have a go with anybody else."

They bolted down a flight of steps, through the back-stage exit, and into fresh, night air.

MARKETPLACE OF SOULS

Written by
David Lowe

Illustrated by
Ane M. Galego

About the Author

David Lowe has abandoned a career as an aerospace engineer, having been given a case of ulcers by NASA. Now he keeps busy as a computer professional for a university library, which is a more relaxing way to fill his days. He is a lifelong reader of science fiction . . . and now he is a writer of science fiction, as well.

About the Illustrator

Ane M. Galego was born in Victoria, British Columbia, in 1968. From a very early age, Ane has had a great gift for illustration. Despite never taking an art lesson, she can produce stunningly lifelike renderings ranging from the innocent face of a child to the worst vision of a nightmare. The main body of Ane's work is graphite on paper, although inks and colors are sometimes used. In the future, she hopes to publish an illustrated book based on stories and characters she has personally developed over the years. To find out more, visit her at www.fantasygraphite.com.

When Esperanza was fifteen, she decided to sell her brain to the fat gringo.

Nine o'clock on a cold, gray San Francisco morning. Esperanza sat on the curb in front of the Mission Street homeless shelter and impersonated someone who didn't notice the greasy corn smell of tortillas on the grill of a pushcart. Last night they had caught Mama drinking again, so Mama couldn't go inside the shelter, not even to eat. And that included Esperanza, if she stayed with Mama. The social workers explained to Esperanza that she could give the foster-home scene another try or she could sleep on the streets with Mama.

Mama had gone off looking for something to drink. Esperanza thought about going to the library to spend another day reading magazines about real people, people with lives and homes, people with families to look after them. People who were not like Esperanza.

Instead she swore an oath. Esperanza swore by no god and no saint, and she swore with herself as the only witness. She swore that she would make herself into one of those people she read about, that today would be the last day that she would sit with her feet in a gutter and choose between begging and hunger.

Esperanza would never see Mama again.

All day she paced up and down Mission Street. No one paid any attention to the underweight Latina girl dressed in someone's discarded jeans, jeans too short to cover her ankles. She looked for a dealer in certain specialized products; at six o'clock in the evening she found him eating breakfast.

"Hey, Esperanza, you ready come pose for me? Old guys like pictures of skinny little girls. Pay extra." He wore a crimson jacket over a pale yellow-green sweater. A bright tropical bird lost in foggy northern California.

"Not that," Esperanza said as she snatched a piece of toast from his plate. "The other thing. The brainswap thing. Your fat gringo friend, he still pay to swap brains with me?"

Esperanza gobbled the toast and reached for another. She took the time to smear this one with margarine.

"Sure thing." The voice slowed, turned calculating. "Only not swap brains. Guy down South Bay, he can program all you know, all you remember, into another brain. It's like you swap your soul into someone's body, and his into yours."

"Can he for real make me rich?"

"You get two million dollars and a house in Sausalito. He gets to be a teenaged girl."

II

The man behind the wheel of the Mercedes spoke the purring, sputtering English of a Russian immigrant. He had a body as comically muscular as a boy's action figure, and he wore a sleeveless denim vest to show as much of it as possible.

Esperanza winced at the sight of his sun blisters.

She sat next to him on leather the color of coffee ice cream and stared out the window. The city disappeared behind them and the landscape turned into an exotic suburban world where lawns surrounded houses and the streets had no sidewalks. The Russian stopped the Mercedes beside an abandoned strip mall, and he led her through a parking lot spotted with dried weeds and discarded fast-food wrappers, through a battered door marked *Utility Access*, and into spotless hallways full of people in neat white uniforms and the scent of medical sterility.

A sweet-faced Filipina nurse took charge of Esperanza and injected her with some kind of tranquilizing drug. The nurse explained what they were going to do to her, but Esperanza couldn't concentrate on the voice that droned on about ISM meaning *induced synapse matrix* and FPI standing for *firing pattern induction*, and Esperanza was already starting to doze off when the nurse said something about MBU. All Esperanza understood was that she walked in one door as a thin, brown girl, and she staggered out another as a pot-bellied man with a pink bald patch on the back of his head and some serious confusion about urination.

III

Just when a man's body, a big man's body, began to feel normal, Esperanza lost weight. Twenty pounds, fifty pounds, eighty pounds. Now she was as skinny as when she had been a girl.

"You and I can remember when HIV was a death sentence," the doctor said. He didn't talk like the doctors Esperanza had known in the city. He smiled; he took the time to explain. Patients invited him to parties. He probably went.

Illustrated by Ane M. Galego

"So that's why he—," Esperanza began. "You can cure AIDS. Everybody knows that."

"Not cure," the doctor said, "treat." The precisely trimmed hair matched the gray eyes. A dignified gray. "We fight the virus by interfering with its reproduction. When it adjusts to one drug, we switch to another. But all the drugs have side effects, some of them pretty nasty." For a moment the smile became a frown, but the voice remained sympathetic. "But you'll be no worse off than a diabetic was when you were a young man."

Afterwards, Esperanza stepped to the receptionist's desk and stood there surrounded by soft seascape watercolors and other patients waiting their comfortable turn. She remembered being the girl who sat on a curb and swore to live in places like this, and she noticed that she was clenching her body's big hand into a fist. She was not right for this life, not yet. She thought of the gringo and she made herself another promise, a promise about revenge.

"Be careful crossing the street, sir," the receptionist told Esperanza. "Asian brainswaps hang out at the Indian restaurant. Most of them just got here, and they've inherited all these cars they haven't learned to drive." She wrinkled her perfect lip in disdain. "Just last week—"

"I could use some Indian food," Esperanza said.

A cold wind whipped across the sidewalk tables. Most of the customers dashed past her toward the inside warmth, but Esperanza sat outside where she could enjoy privacy in a public place.

Everything about the others clashed with their pale, middle-aged faces and expensive American clothes—their language all full of gentle rounded vowels and funny lisping D sounds, the fluttering motions of their hands when they talked, even their harsh-smelling unfiltered cigarettes.

Esperanza gave her order to the waiter and she took her telephone from her bag. She pressed the numbers that navigated her way through the menu system, and then she waited. Finally she spoke, "Reservations for Calcutta, *por favor.*"

Esperanza had a plan.

IV

Across the Hooghly River from central Calcutta sprawled the most densely packed slum in Asia. Esperanza walked across the neighborhood, through the multitudes that no longer amazed her. She wore a woman's body, an Indian body, slim and small and almost young.

Crammed together like the jostling frenzy under a rock concert stage in the States, the everyday crowd filtered past the open tables of an outdoor marketplace. Esperanza ignored the merchants' offerings—bruised, leather-skinned fruit, freshly ground peppers so hot they stung her eyes six feet downwind, two dozen goats' heads packed in ice. Diesel fumes and the smell of human dung followed her down an alleyway too narrow for the smallest car. She climbed a staircase stained with red betel-nut spittle.

A family of five lived under the staircase. Enough people lived outdoors in Calcutta to make their own great city.

Esperanza was not homeless—not quite. She rented a room the size of a large kitchen cabinet in a tenement where two hundred people shared a single dripping faucet. Esperanza had to live there because she was poor, because it had taken all the gringo's money to buy a brainswap after she'd told the expensive truth about her HIV. She had no regrets.

Soon she would have money again, she knew that, but first she had to study. Esperanza rushed upstairs to her daily lesson in Bengali, the language of Calcutta.

V

"You can't beat my rates," Esperanza told the couple from Iowa. "From me you get a healthy brainswap at the best price."

Her Indian body had grown substantial over the years. She wore a green sari and a simple gold chain around her neck.

The couple did not see the small comforts she had added to her office. They ignored the crocheted doilies, the electric fan, the fern in its hand-painted clay pot. They noticed only the bare light bulb dangling from the ceiling, the cheap furniture, and the flimsy partition that separated her operation from the jute wholesaler who shared her storefront. She noticed that they noticed.

"Look," she continued, "you're both over fifty, you've barely got half a million dollars and a house in some god-awful cold place. For that you don't get perfect teenaged bodies, not even in Calcutta. Take a look at Rabrindranath and Anrita." She called up images to her terminal and the couple leaned forward intently. "Early thirties, no health problems a dentist can't fix. Rabi's strong from pulling a rickshaw; Anrita's never had kids. Best I can do."

"But to have to stay in India," the wife began. Her eyes had that jet-lagged, unfocused stare, and she could have used another face-lift. Her auburn hair showed gray at the roots.

"Lots of American brainswaps in Calcutta. We have a club, lobbies the U.S. for recognition, or at least to grant us visas. We all want to go home eventually. 'Til then, I get you language lessons."

The husband studied the contract. "This says *medical exams*. We shouldn't take medical exams. We're the ones buying."

"My people trust me," Esperanza replied. "I won't stick them with cancer, anything like that." When Esperanza said *cancer*, their eyes flickered toward each other.

"Aren't you worried about the Fundamentalists?" the husband asked as the couple stood to leave. "I hear they believe you and your competitors interfere with reincarnation."

Esperanza didn't answer.

VI

Esperanza crouched on her storefront's rooftop in a worn and faded sari, a sari she hoped would let her pass for one of the ordinary poor. In one hand she clutched her escape bundle—a brown paper bag packed with an artfully manufactured passport, a change of clothes, and an account book from the Hong Kong and Shanghai Bank. She watched marchers, thousands, tens of thousands, strong, work their dusty way up Nehru Boulevard from the Temple. Two nervous rows of policemen blocked their path at the intersection. In the first row, the police held heavy bamboo clubs; in the second, they fixed absurdly long bayonets on ancient Enfield rifles. As the Sons of Kali approached the police lines, they took up chanting, angry and musical at the same time, and they surged forward. The police captain stood a few feet in front; he turned and shouted something at his men. The marchers reached him and he went down.

The police lines collapsed like grass huts beneath a tidal wave. The first wretched hint of nausea gas blew in her direction and Esperanza ducked down the ladder into her office.

She ran to the back room and threw her weight against a panel that didn't look like a door, and with an abrupt snapping sound, it swung open into an alley.

The marchers hadn't found the alley. Not yet. She dashed across to the rear entrance of a tiny grocery shop that faced the next street and jerked it open. A precariously overloaded shelf of canned goods toppled as she pushed her way inside, and hundreds of cans of tuna, fruit, and garishly labeled soup rolled and bounced their way across an aisle scarcely large enough for customers to slip by each other. A long-bearded Sikh tripped over a can and crashed into a counter covered with English crackers. The woman at the cash register shrieked something in a dialect she didn't understand, and Esperanza walked calmly out the front door.

Smoke and gas were blowing from the other block, and she could hear the gleeful shouts of men gone savage, but this street looked safe for the moment. Esperanza hailed a cab; "Dum Dum Airport," she told the driver.

VII

Six blocks south of campus, Telegraph Avenue changed.

Bookstores and street musicians and boxy little coffee shops gave way to offices and parking lots on an ordinary Berkeley street.

Esperanza, in the body of a red-haired male with a diseased complexion and an unsteady walk, stepped through a door labeled *East Bay Data Associates*.

The man waiting inside grinned when he saw Esperanza. He always grinned. He was broad-shouldered and tanned, with a robust mop of sun-bleached curls tumbling over his forehead. A hologram of Bugs Bunny rode a surfboard across his T-shirt, above the caption *Surf's up, Doc.* Others might see the very image of California indolence, but Esperanza knew better. She recognized the best of the rising generation of molecular physiologists.

"How did you ever find an American brain in Shanghai?" he asked.

"Heroin addict desperate for a clean body," Esperanza said. "First week hurt like hell."

The physiologist showed Esperanza charts and photographs of experiments with dogs and monkeys, and he introduced her to a baby chimp, which she cuddled while she watched a video of an older ape.

"When anyone can program himself into a clone baby, bodyswapping as we know it will be dead," he said and she nodded. "Immortality for everyone."

"Everyone with money, anyway," Esperanza said.

"That goes without saying."

"Where do the clone baby's memories go?" Esperanza asked.

"If a client has scruples, I keep the clone's brain from developing consciousness in the first place," the physiologist said. "For an extra fee, of course."

"Of course," Esperanza said, and handed over stacks of fresh, crisp Singapore dollars, held neatly in place by yellow rubber bands.

The physiologist grinned again.

"How much flesh do you need?" she asked.

"Just a few cells. One theoretically, but backups are handy."

"I can bring you a whole body," Esperanza said. "But it may take time to locate."

VIII

Esperanza found him in an unremarkable bar attached to a suburban motel. Her old body hadn't aged well. She had expected fat, like Mama, but instead she found jerky amphetamine eyes in a face like a shrink-wrapped skull.

The gringo—or was it *gringa* now—smiled when he saw Esperanza in a man's body. "Pretty boy, I'll go home with you anytime," the gringo said before she even asked.

The Markov 25 in her jacket held explosive bullets. Small, sleek, plastic. Maybe she should finish the job in her Porsche, right there in the parking lot. Only prudence made her hesitate, she told herself. Prudence and curiosity.

The gringo's apartment smelled of cat shit.

They tossed dirty laundry off an unmade bed and Esperanza caressed the Markov again before she hung her jacket across the open closet door.

Ten rough and sweaty minutes later, the man in Esperanza's body erupted in orgasm. Loud, long, and thoroughly counterfeit.

He faked it well, but not well enough to fool Esperanza. Then he opened his eyes—*her* eyes—and said, "You have it backwards, honey. The girl is the one supposed to scratch."

Esperanza noticed a sliver of her old skin underneath her new fingernail. She rose from the bed and reached for the jacket.

"Won't you stay the night?" asked the old gringo in his—*her*—wornout speed-freak voice.

"Things to do." Esperanza's finger curled around the trigger of the Markov, but she remembered the promise she made when she was a homeless girl sitting on a Mission Street curb. A promise about becoming a certain kind of person. She saw that he was crying.

Esperanza left the gun in her pocket.

IX

Marin County, California. The earth has natural gardens; one lies north of the Golden Gate Bridge. In the body of a five-year-old brown-haired girl, Esperanza sat in the morning chill, surrounded by her backyard riot of wildflowers. She lifted a dainty china cup and sipped cocoa, rich and sweet, but hot enough to burn her mouth. Esperanza blew cooling breath into the cup and inhaled the mellow steamy fragrance of chocolate.

The pale image of the freshly risen sun showed through a momentary thinning in the cloud cover. A scrub jay, like a midget strutting tyrannosaur, foraged under the columbines. In the distance, fog poured like syrup down the slopes of Mount Tamalpais. Esperanza took another sip of hot chocolate.

INTERRUPT VECTOR

Written by
Robert B. Schofield

Illustrated by
Andy B. Clarkson

About the Author

Robert Schofield has been writing fiction since 1990, when he was the first student to graduate from Indiana University's Cognitive Science program, with dual majors in computer science and philosophy. He is currently living in Cincinnati, where he takes classes at the Cincinnati Art Academy. During the day, he is a performance analyst and capacity planner for global computer systems at a large Cincinnati-based corporation.

I pulled the trigger and the BASHER detonated, one hundred and fifty million volts, ten times the power of a lightning bolt. I remembered that from the vid, a confiscated Taitano Corp research clip. It must have been a computer simulation. That was ironic. The vid showed the electromagnetic pulse ripping through intricate layers of silicon. It looked like a hurricane going through tissue paper.

The smoke cleared. Not really smoke, it was ozone, as thick as soup. The box still looked the same, square, blue, sitting in the middle of a white EC floor. Other boxes surrounded it: datastores, routers, redundant power supplies—but they weren't doing jack now, except burning nanoseconds in their little bitty computer brains. I pulled the BASHER in against my flak jacket. It felt warm, and heavy. Much heavier than my old degaussing rifle. The extra weight didn't bother me. It was worth it. One of a kind. Three months ago I got the gun, a quarter of a mill, and a prosthetic pinky when the EC—Environmental Controls—of that datacenter tried to put out the white phosphorus grenades Widget set off. The shit that got dumped from the ceiling caused the Willie-Pete to splatter. I don't miss the pinky. Could've been worse. Widget uses Thermite-2 now.

"Ready to cook!" Widget yelled from the access console where he'd been harvesting the "good stuff" from the datastores. Time to burn them down; down to liquid pools of glass and silver, where data congealed from holographic storage plates into a swirling blackened chrome river of technology.

"Do it." I braced myself for whatever undetected fire protection this datacenter had. Widget was at my side in a second, sliding a datacube into the custom-designed lead case in his hand. It had been his idea to collect the best intel from the corporation's main brains before giving them a lobotomy. Sort of a bonus for ourselves. We got paid to wipe the data, then we could sell the good stuff on the streets for added profit. Our employers never seemed to mind as long as we gave them first look. Small info, relatively speaking. Best of all, we didn't need to add a hackman to our team. We pulled the data from the service engineer's console, hardwired straight into the box, where software security was as easy as a Hydro-whore before Ration Day.

Widget triggered the thermite and sirens screamed. I aimed the BASHER at a pinhole grille in the wall and fired. The grille exploded as the speaker's magnet flew out of its socket at Mach-1. We waited. Nothing. Not even Halon. I pointed to my watch and Widget nodded. Redeye would be back from the disaster recovery vault any minute, having melted the holographic backup decks to slag. We were paid to be thorough. Sirens still wailed from the back of the datacenter and down the hall, out beyond the smoking double doors with the sign that said *Warning. Restricted Area. No Liquids! No Magnetic Fields!*

Widget and I were halfway down the hall when they rounded the corner. Six of them in black suits and masks, no hesitation in their stride. They walked around the corner like an onyx gate swinging shut.

Widget fell to the ground, fumbling at his pants pocket. I looked down at him and heard the hiss. Then the sniffer went off. It was the first time I'd heard it outside training and it took a split second for the shrill beep to register. When it did, adrenaline shot through my body like rounds through a Minigun. Nerve gas!

What were they doing? This was a datacenter in the basement of a corporate headquarters, not a battlefield.

Did I have my mask? Shit! I grabbed at my own pants pocket, ripping the buttons off as I tore the flap up and jammed my hand into the baggy pouch. No mask. The black suits were walking toward us in slow motion. I reached for the atropine injectors on my flak vest, realizing at the same time that their suits were more functional than just a design to impart maximum intimidation; they were activated charcoal.

Somehow I'd never been convinced that injecting myself with lethal poison was the best antidote for nerve gas. Once, when I was bored shitless on guard duty, I'd pushed the edge of an atropine injector up against the steel grate outside my guard shack. The inch-long needle shot out like a chrome viper and a stream of liquid squirted thirty feet across the microwave dishes.

Damn.

Supposed to clear your pockets. No time. The black suits were getting closer. Widget was already convulsing, even though I saw he was breathing through the honeycombed filter over his face. I gripped the thin tube and felt my biceps spasm. I slammed the injector down onto my thigh. There was a miniature explosion on my leg as the device began pumping its juice into my bloodstream. What a feeling. A swarm of locusts raced up and down my nervous system, biting, buzzing, overwhelming all in their path. I roared, the roar of a madman. My muscles

Illustrated by Andy B. Clarkson

knotted and bulged and I dropped the BASHER. Out of control. Then I saw them pause, wondering why I wasn't dying on the floor. And I saw Redeye come around the corner. Then I collapsed, kicking, screaming and pounding the air. I heard gunshots and bodies falling, and then my jaw locked and my eyes rolled up in their sockets and I lost consciousness.

• • •

I awoke in our van. Redeye's face two inches from mine was nearly enough to put me back in shock. I swear I could actually see red deep within his pupils. I forced my jaw apart and managed, "How?"

He smiled, baring inch-long fangs, gleaming white, as he backed away. He patted his rifle, then used it as a crutch to stand. It was his new toy. Electrosonic gun. It was like my BASHER, but worked on organics instead of silicon. I replayed the Taitano Corp vid in my mind, imagining human brain-matter instead of the insides of a computer being blown away.

"First live test," Redeye said, hefting the weapon.

"I guess it works."

He smiled again, licking his lips between his fangs. Then he turned, tossing his yellow-brown mane around. It fell over his shoulders, ending at a point in the small of his back.

"Hey, who's driving?"

"We're home," he said, turning back to me.

"How's Widget?"

"Better'n you. He's already inside wringing out the data. We didn't want to move you. You got a good whiff of that crap." Redeye wrinkled his nose.

"I don't feel too bad."

"That's cause you've got one helluva cocktail pumpin' through your veins. I pulled the recipe from Walter Reed Military. It's a derivative of Dehydroepian-drosterone, an adrenaline-based hormone; Hydro on the streets."

"Thanks." I knew what was coming next.

"'Course, with a little genetic work you could be immune from that stuff permanently."

"No, thanks."

Call me philosophical, but I still considered genetic alterations a degradation to basic humanity. Not that I didn't like Redeye. He'd saved my life more than once. But I knew him before he opted for the Lion-Hunter special, with infrared implant. I preferred drinking with him back then.

"So, did Widget find anything good so far?"

"Yeah. He'd better tell ya. I'll get him." Redeye popped the door, sprang down, landed in a crouch and froze. He looked like he was searching for prey, stray antelope roaming through our farm, maybe. How they'd ever get through the sonic minefield was beyond me.

I thought about Jamber while I waited. The juice in me made me jittery, just like I felt the first time I'd seen her at Retro Dejour. She was beautiful: thick, dark hair; walnut brown eyes; trim; not too tall. And she had a certain walk, a certain swing, that grabbed my eyes and yanked them, caused them to lock-on like a targeting grid. I'd said something stupid, and she'd smiled. My brain melted and I was a schoolboy with a crush. Somehow I'd managed a conversation that ended with a carefully written mail code on a napkin in my pocket.

Two weeks later, waking up next to her and looking at her sleek form under the sheets, I couldn't believe it. Crushes weren't supposed to work out. At least they never had for me. Maybe because I always fell for the beauties, women who could have any man they chose, like Saara last year, a friend of Widget's cousin. I think at one time I was one of six in her entourage. Or Daphne before that, who was always breaking up with her rock-star boyfriend and then getting back together whenever I asked her out.

Jamber was perfect—beautiful, passionate, warm and funny. She was also rich. And married. Her husband was a corporate management clone who treated her like a showpiece in his art collection. He'd skyrocketed fast up the corporate pyramid, but burned a few levels from the top and now he was on his way out.

There was a knock on the van door frame, and Widget poked his head in.

"Hey, buddy, how'ya feeling?"

"All right," I said, and meant it.

Widget looked fine. Short Afro on blotchy light-and-dark-skin, a wide nose, and thin lips. He could have changed it, picked either or. But he was secure in himself. I liked that about him.

"So, what'd you get?" I asked. "Military? It wouldn't surprise me to find Genetech designing goodies for our Tried and True."

Widget's face went all serious. "No," he said, looking at the ground. "Damn, Slater. You're a soldier and I'm no good at this, so I'm just gonna tell you. It was a setup, man. We were supposed to buy it back there."

"A setup? Who?" My mind started assembling a list of enemies. I didn't have much trouble. "The OSCT?

They hate us the most, but I doubted those flakes would have the guts to hire a nerve-gas-wielding death squad."

"No, man."

"Who?"

Widget looked up. His eyes drilled into me like bayonets. "She did, man. You knew it was too easy. Too good."

"Bullshit."

Widget reached up, held a printout in front of my face, and dropped it on my chest. "We'll be inside. Come in when you're ready. Don't take too long; we need to turn on the minefield."

I picked up the printout slowly. It was an org chart, standard quick sale intel. I scanned the gray striped page slowly, stopping a third of the way down. There it was: Mitchell Steward, Jamber's husband, Executive V.P., promoted last week.

• • •

I remembered the night Jamber laid out the plan to melt the datacenter. It was raining outside the hotel room. Neon smeared into a psychedelic rainbow, like an oil slick on the wall. Raindrops splattered dirt and grease on the narrow chrome window ledge eighty-seven floors from the trash-filled gutters below. She lay on top of me, running her long, silver fingernails through the hair behind my ear.

"It could be like this always," she said.

"Mmmm," I nodded.

"No, I mean me and you, together, without Mitch."

"You going to leave him?"

"Difficult right now." She cupped her hands around the top of my head and propped herself up. Her skin was warm and moist with sweat. Her legs slid around mine. "But I know a way," she continued. "I told you he's done at Genetech. It's possible he could find out about it ahead of time, try for revenge."

"How?"

"My little sweet soldier." She smiled and kissed me. "What do your employers hire you for?"

"For a competitive advantage. It takes weeks to reassemble the data we purge, sometimes months. Time *is* money to them."

"And you don't think it's ever for a 'less financial' objective?"

"Maybe."

"Suppose Genetech's datacenter gets hit by your team. I could make it look like Mitch had a hand in it, out of spite for the pink."

"What good would that do?"

"He'd be disgraced. Maybe even get prison time. A petty corporate crook. I'd have no problem leaving him then."

•••

Stupid, but it made sense at the time. I'd wanted it to make sense. So I'd done it. I'd talked Widget and Redeye into a freebie so Jamber and I could always be together. And now the printout on my chest read Asshole in huge bold letters. She wanted to end it? Okay. Like Widget said, it was too good to be true. She could have just said the word, but she had to involve the team. Mistake on her part. Redeye and Widget did not like to be played. I unplugged myself from the med-monitors, climbed out of the van, and went inside.

"Let's waste her, man," Widget said from his desk. He was running a Hyper-Smartscan on the data, a street program he'd supercharged with hardware. A pair of Z-Tech optical fibers snaked from the datacube to a circuit board clamped at the intersection of two neon-helium lasers. Text flashed by on his console so fast it looked like a fluid dynamic simulation.

I walked across the room and punched the code for the minefield, then went to the stool at my weapons bench and climbed onto it. A neat row of 7.62 mm rounds sat beside a pile of clip links. Two different length barrels with mounting hydraulics and shock distributors rested on the bench behind a microwelder, the third foam cradle was empty. I looked at Redeye. He was sitting cross-legged on his cushion, growling low and watching Widget.

"Let's just forget about it," I said. "Mark it down as a business loss."

"Hey, it's not like it's tax deductible, man."

"I know, but it's over now."

"You think it's over? Your honey wants you dead. Just because she didn't get you this time doesn't mean she'll stop. And I've got more intel for you." Widget punched his console and the scrolling text froze, then shrank. Another document popped up. "You're not the first of Mrs. Steward's co-marital love adventures." He pointed at the screen. "It was her husband's chauffeur last year and a plasma welder before that. The welder died in an accident on the job, and after the chauffeur was let go, he vanished." Widget swiveled in his chair, then shook his head slowly. "Sorry, man, looks like you hooked up with a black widow."

"Redeye, what about you?"

"We have an image. If word gets out, it could hurt business."

They were both looking at me, waiting for the unanimous vote so we could load up, and head out to kill the woman I'd destroyed fifty billion dollars' worth of data for. "I'm going to call her," I said. "Maybe there's another explanation."

"Aw, man," Widget said. Then, "Okay, fine. You wanna talk, we go see her. All of us." Redeye nodded.

We went prepared for action—full combat load, just like a data hit. Redeye gave me another swig of Hydro. "You're going to feel like your insides are trading places with your outsides through every pore in your skin when that wears off," he said. "You need full bio sterilization, not more action."

"Yeah, I know, but I gotta talk to her." His warning was frightening, though. Redeye was never so graphic, unless he spoke from experience.

Redeye parked half a klick from the Steward residence. It was a tidy little estate on a plateau near the top of the Reitran Slopes, north of the city. The house had only a single floor above ground, except for the domed art gallery, which had three, according to the satellite pics, floor plans, and defense schematics Widget snatched from his console. As we approached from the south, I was thinking the place looked like a miniature Taj Mahal. International flags spread across the lawn added to the feeling that it was some sort of tourist attraction, as long as you didn't know they were actually reinforced polyfiber helicopter impediment rods.

I'd never been to Jamber's house. We always met at a club, usually Retro Dejour. We'd talk and dance, and eventually party our way to one hotel or another. Once I asked her what she told her husband. "Oh, different excuses. Staying with Cindy who's just broken up with her latest boyfriend, or 'night out with the girls,' or a fabulous twenty-four-hour sale at the mall."

I admired her in a twisted way, able to juggle two men, keeping one completely in the dark. And this was at least her third time going through it all! That took some type of talent. I guess she eventually got tired of the juggling act. One relationship was always plenty for me. But, now that I thought about it, it wasn't much of a relationship. We simply used each other. I got my beauty. She got her excitement, or whatever it was she was after.

A hundred meters from the manicured lawn, Redeye charged. He pumped himself full of adrenaline until I could tell he was straining to contain a howl. Then he took off like a homing missile straight for the front door.

There are two ways for a small force to take a position: clandestine or full assault. You sneak around and try to circumvent or avoid as many defenses as possible until you're detected, at which time you go full out, or you do full force from the start. We judged time in and out to be critical, partly because Redeye said I had a few hours max before I'd start to feel like "shit on asphalt on a hot day," but also because we wanted to take action before Jamber got a second chance. Time was money in my business too.

As Redeye streaked across the fresh-cut smelling grass, I sighted on the auto-targeting machine-gun nest above the front door, my BASHER preset for the energy spectrum guaranteed to do the most damage to the targeting system's electronics. I acquired the machine gun in my scope, saw it swivel and track, then begin to lead Redeye all in the half-second before I pulled the trigger. There were no theatrics, no explosion; the machine gun just didn't fire. There was nothing left of the sophisticated computer's brains to tell the machine gun what to do. Then I switched frequencies and took out the security cameras. Finally, for good measure, I switched to broadest spectrum and clicked the high-energy radiator to maximum, blanketing the place with half- a-dozen shots, trying to keep Redeye out of my direct line of fire. The last shot killed the row of lights that ran along the driveway. Redeye slapped his package against the front door and rolled away. There was a double thump as the small shaped charge went off, leaving a smoking hole the size of a man's chest next to the doorknob.

Redeye had no way of knowing what was waiting for him on the other side of the door. He started running in a tight arc, crouched, then sprang through the ragged opening in the door. Three seconds later, what was left of the door swung in and Redeye waved the all-clear. Widget and I began to move. He took the west side, I took the east. We leap-frogged our way to the door.

The place sported the latest styles in furnishings, although I couldn't name any of the designers or explain the motif. There was a wall on our left. Three steps down to the right led to a sunken living room. A half-wall at two o'clock looked like it separated the front room from some kind of parlor, or den, with stairs that led up to the gallery. A closet in the wall to the left had already been cleared by Redeye. I recognized one of Jamber's fur jackets among the shredded pile on the floor. I dropped, then rolled down the stairs, ending up behind a footstool with the BASHER aimed at the half-wall. Widget backed into the corner and leveled his HK in the same direction. Redeye took three bounding steps, then cleared the half-wall with ease. We waited. Silence. Redeye finally stood and motioned us toward the stairs. I nodded, then waited for Widget to round the corner before following. Widget covered the hallway that went off to the left from the den further into the house, and I followed Redeye upstairs.

I was only a few steps up when she walked in. I didn't see her enter, just glanced down and saw Widget pulling the HK tight into his shoulder. Then I looked, and there was Jamber standing in the hallway raising her arm.

"Wait!" I yelled at the same time a short burp erupted from Widget's machine gun.

Blood doesn't really look like the greasy stuff they use in vids. It's much fuller, more vivid, like glistening drops of liquid neon. At least that's what I thought as Jamber's blood sprayed across the wall in peacock plumage. I shouted obscenities—at Widget, at Jamber, at myself, at the world—as I ran down the stairs and to her side. By the time I got there, she was gone. Not a dying word, not a flicker of life leaving her eyes, just dead. There was no weapon in her hand. A part of me heard Widget in the background.

"Thought she had a gun. Looked like a pocket greaser." She was holding a bloody, crumpled piece of gray, striped printout. I read it. It was a message detailing the special issue and use of nerve reagent Phosgene-VI for security guard staffing, Genetech Corporate Headquarters, last night, signed Mitchell Steward, V.P.

I shoved the paper in Widget's face. "Look. It was him, not her! I'm gonna kill the bastard with my bare hands." I stood up and raw energy poured through me. I felt like the BASHER must feel when I pulled the trigger and unleashed its power. I knew it was adrenaline mixing with the Hydro, and that triggered a vague reminder that I had a time limit, but I didn't care.

"No, man, no." Widget was saying. "He's corporate high brass, heavy shit. Let's leave it, like you said."

I didn't bother with a reply, didn't bother to remind him he was the one who wouldn't let it drop when I'd wanted to. I headed for the stairs.

Redeye met me at the bottom. He put a hand on my chest. "Careful," he said.

I nodded, then took the stairs three at a time. The gallery upstairs was open. There were paintings and sculptures and walls standing by themselves at odd angles, like a maze with half the walls missing. I didn't know if he was up there, didn't even know if he was home; but if he was, I was going to find him.

I started to hunt Mitchell Steward.

Widget and Redeye advanced behind me, but I moved by myself, coldly aware that it was the worst way to search a room like this. The BASHER was slung over my back. I held a chrome Sikes-Fairbairn, hilt backward, the blade against my right forearm, down along my side, with my left arm raised, fingers open. Ten minutes turned up nothing except ugly, abstract art and another stairway against the curved outside wall. I ascended slowly and found myself in a short hall ending at a door. The door was unlocked. I walked inside.

It was his office, tinted dome skylight above a circular desk with the center cut out so you could sit in the middle and swivel around to three hundred degrees of desktop space. Billowing curtains lined the walls, fluttering lightly from subtle ventilation. I hated curtains. They were rarely for decoration. A curtain to the left fluttered, separated, and Mitchell Steward stepped out.

"Jamber was a whore," he said. "Beautiful, and passionate, but a whore." He was immaculately groomed: slick, straight black hair; a loose white gauze shirt and business shorts; and perfect white teeth. He was tall and muscular, and he stood with his head high. I raised the knife, flipping it around so I could throw it, then paused.

"Then why stay with her?" I asked slowly.

"Because I loved her. I promised to always love her, and she promised to always love me." He took a step away from the curtains, held out his hands. "What now, Mr. Slater, will you kill me?"

"You had the others killed," I said. A twinge of nausea swept briefly over me. I didn't know if it was from the drugs, or the thought of "the others," or from Jamber's death, so fresh in my mind.

"Yes, I had the others killed, and I would have had you killed too, but now there is no need."

"How did you know about our mission?" I asked.

"A vice president knows many things."

"But she thought you were on your way out."

"I arranged that."

"This was all your idea?"

"I planted the seeds, with help. She followed through. I knew my wife well, Mr. Slater. Better than she thought." He started walking slowly toward his desk. I sheathed the Sikes-Fairbairn and unslung the BASHER, planting the muzzle in the soft carpet and leaning on it to relieve the sudden knotting in my stomach. "I neglected Jamber for my career," he continued. "By the time I realized my mistake and began to get things straight between us, she had already fallen out of love with me. I spent the last years trying to change that. Now things are different. She is gone. I suggest we both get on with our lives." He sighed.

"Something still bothers me," I said. It did, but I couldn't put my finger on it. Something was still missing. I believed his story, I believed he loved her. But he did not seem sad enough about her death. His sigh seemed like a sigh of relief, relief that it was all over, that he was finally out of a situation he could not control.

"You're a smart man," I said. "You had to realize you might never be able to change Jamber." I remembered Widget pulling up the data about the chauffeur and the welder. If Widget could get it, so could others. "You couldn't keep killing her lovers forever. Maybe this time you decided to kill her instead. Which would mean . . ."

Mitchell Steward stared with a steady gaze, and the curtains behind him parted. "It's been a big Interrupt Vector, man," Widget said, stepping into the open. "You know what that is, Slate? It's a hardware intercept. Something that can't be changed. The software runs along, thinking it's in charge of the world, until bam! A Non-Maskable Interrupt Vector kicks in from the hardware, takes control, does what it wants. When it's finished, and only when it's finished, it gives control back to the software. That's you, Slate. You and Jamber, you're software. We're hardware, Steward and me."

"Widget?" I said. "The team."

"Screw the team. Like Mr. Steward said, now things are different."

"Yeah, now I know what was bothering me. Back at the hit, when they used the gas. You had your mask on before the sniffers went off. So, Widget, you're his personal dog. How long do you think that will last? Only as long as it's convenient for him, then he'll get rid of you too."

"Until that time, bro." Widget began unslinging his HK.

I snapped the BASHER up first, aiming through Mitch Steward at Widget's head. Widget raised his eyebrows and smiled. He was right, the BASHER's electromagnetic pulse probably wouldn't be fatal.

The underslung 7.62 mm recoilless would be though. It was a recent mod. I guess Widget hadn't known about it, or else he would have been faster acting. Both he and Mitchell Steward knew about it, though, when I dropped my hand and pulled the trigger. Red liquid neon sprayed across the wall in peacock plumage.

GETTING "LUCKY"

Written by
Sergey Poyarkov

About the Author

Sergey is the buoyant, enthusiastic winner of the 1991 L. Ron Hubbard Illustrators of the Future Gold Award. He arrived in Los Angeles to receive his award, directly from his home in the Ukraine, as Communism fell in his homeland.

Sergey has since gone on to a successful artistic career as an illustrator and made a career transition to fine artist, with his works displayed in museums in Russia, Europe and the United States. He has now published his own book, Balance of Contradictions, printed and bound in the Ukraine, in which he conveys not only his art but his own philosophy of art, bringing an expression of pride in his roots and appreciation of his new friends in other countries.

He exemplifies much of what the L. Ron Hubbard Writers of the Future Contest is all about, and what Mr. Hubbard said of artists: "A culture is as rich and as capable of surviving as it has imaginative artists. The artist is looked upon to start things. The artist injects the spirit of life into a culture."

Luck and happiness. These qualities are what I wish to share because I believe they can be created just as you create any work of art. And, in turn, they increase artistic production and success.

Neither "luck" nor "happiness" are things that "just happen" to an artist. They also don't come to you by not sharing with others what you know. Obviously, others can accept or reject what you tell them, just as you have that choice in what I tell you here. But because I have gained some success, I have a responsibility to tell you what I believe made that success possible.

I was a university student when I won the L. Ron Hubbard Illustrators of the Future Contest, and almost simultaneously I got work for magazines, and the world around me changed as Communism fell. That was 1991.

You could say that I was lucky. I was. But people are lucky all of the time, in many locations. The problem is, they aren't ready for their big chance. I was ready. I had spent my life drawing, studying art and in maintaining my personal integrity.

In Russia, it was a common practice for children to be at home while parents worked. So, when I was three, my mom went to work and left me a lot of colored pencils and paper. I didn't start reading until I was four, so I started to draw. I liked it so much, I kept doing it. In high school, it was a problem because they wanted me to study mathematics and physics. But I only wanted to draw. My parents wanted me to go into the Army, like my father and grandfather, but I said, "No, I only want to draw."

Even from kindergarten, I said that I will never have a "9-to-5 job," I will not drink alcohol, I will marry late in life. And everyone thought this was very funny, especially in high school.

So, I made myself ready. The important things were persistence towards my goal, being myself and working hard. And in my work I always try to give a communication.

When the chance came, I was ready. I won the L. Ron Hubbard Illustrators of the Future Contest, which really helped launch my professional career; and I got work for Ukrainian magazines; and Communism's restrictions became dust. It was a fascinating time. I worked hard before that moment, and so I was "lucky."

The other thing about that moment was a willingness to see the change and accept it. For example, those first days after the Fall were horrible. There was confusion and I was on the list of people considered to be trouble because I had been involved in anti-Communist activities, and there I was, out of Russia, a very suspicious thing. It is kind of humorous now, but I had to recognize that when the Communists are gone, your career as an anti-Communist is over. There are other activities to pursue and greater things to contribute to your country and the world.

Another important thing is the friendships you form in preparing for your professional work and then in pursuing it. It is another element of luck. Your communication with the wonderful people around you every day. People who wish you well and will help you. I have had my friends through the years, and there are the people at Author Services who run the contests, and today I continue to meet many wonderful people. I have also learned that there are those who do not wish you well, and those are not friends. They must be treated differently, though hate is certainly not part of it.

In terms of the hard work element of luck, it is not a matter of whether you are abstractionalist or conceptualist. It is the energy you use in work. There is severe competition in this market, but competition is a very good thing. The Soviet Union collapsed because competition was suppressed. Competition allows one to blossom. It is a natural thing for people. It is a natural way to build your career.

I learned a lot in America that I was able to take back with me. And as a result, I was also able to help build the pride of my own country. I think the diversity coming to America is also what makes her great.

The great lesson I learned in America and from L. Ron Hubbard, that relates to my success, is tolerance. I grew up in an intolerant society where there was aggressive pushing to make people believe certain ideas. I am also grateful to those who have given me information politely and calmly and left it up to me to decide. I carry that on in my artwork today. It is a great message to allow another to learn and see and decide for himself. It is the artist's role to provide new things for others to see.

I take every moment to learn skills that will help me. I always have the small Russian-to-English dictionary in my pocket that I pull out to learn a new word when I am waiting. And so it is with your art. Every day you get new information, every day. And every day you should know that the next day, there is something you have to learn. Never stop. This is a first for any success.

I've had people tell me they tried ten times and failed. And they say, "Look, you have had eight successes. How can you be so lucky?" Well, that's right, I am lucky, but what you didn't see was that I tried two hundred times. You are seeing the eight but not the two hundred failures.

But I think the eight successes and the people I met and the joy of doing what I want in life were worth it.

I do not assert that my position is better than the other ones. No, it simply is my position, my philosophy. Once, I heard a story about a rabbi, Dzussi. He said: "When I die, God will not ask me why I was not Aristotle; he will ask why I was not Dzussi." I want to be myself and consider that such a desire is the most important for any artist. I wish you luck and happiness and realization of yourself in your artwork and communication.

TEN GALLONS
A WHORE

Written by
Anna D. Allen

Illustrated by
Dwayne Harris

About the Author

*Born in 1968, in the Midwest, Anna D.
Allen grew up in Europe until the age of
fifteen. She went to school in the Deep South for a while, then
moved to Baltimore, picking up and discarding accents along
the way. Now living in western Michigan, she has to fight the
urge to sound like a character in Fargo. When not writing,
Anna has several obsessions: ancient Egypt, sixteenth century
England, the works of Hans Holbein the Younger and the films
of Ridley Scott. She is also a great cook.*

Chapter One

No one knew much about the stranger. He lived in the mountains beyond the Wasteland, apparently alone. He answered to the name Kincaid, liked his water straight, and never spent more than an afternoon in town.

He rode out of the Wasteland just before noon on a dusty September day. A packhorse loaded with old plastic milk jugs filled with water followed behind him. He came to town a couple of times a year to trade water for supplies—the purest water anyone had ever tasted, better than the filtered and recycled water the towns-people lived on. No one knew how he did it. Either he had come up with the best filtering system known to man or he had a natural source. But a natural source was impossible. The toxins and contaminants in the earth made all water deadly, the effects not always immediate. Even the stream running through the town, the source of all their water, was deadly, since it flowed from the Wasteland. Without the filtration systems, the town couldn't survive.

Making his way along the familiar trail that led into town, Kincaid passed the gardens which fed the towns-people. The food they grew supplemented the flour they brought in from faraway places like Kansas and Ohio where grain could be grown again. The combination of the two was just enough to survive. In every garden there was a contraption, like a still, built from odd parts, in order to filter water for the plants. If not for the long-term drought, it wouldn't be necessary, but it rained so rarely now.

As Kincaid passed the garden behind the town saloon, he saw a young woman with brown hair working on a water filter. Wearing a red dress, she stood barefoot in the middle of the garden, surrounded by lush green plants—tomatoes, beans, squash, cucumbers, peppers, onions, potatoes, and herbs—all well watered and cared for without a trace of blight. He'd never seen her in town before, and while he didn't spend a lot of time there, he thought he knew everyone. She seemed to be having problems with the filter and kept checking the various hoses and filters to make sure each was connected properly. Yet despite her efforts, the filter was not working.

"It's the battery," Kincaid said, stopping briefly.

"What?" she replied, looking up at him as she squinted in the sunlight.

"One of the connecting wires has probably come loose."

The woman checked the battery and discovered Kincaid was right. As soon as she reconnected the wire, the filter began to hum and water began to trickle out of it.

"Thanks," she said, but Kincaid had already moved on, heading toward the bank.

"Girl!" Kincaid heard someone yelling at the woman from the saloon, "Get in here. You're supposed to be starting lunch. What the hell you doing out there?" Kincaid glanced back and saw Evans, the saloon owner, fussing at the woman, raising his hands and motioning her inside, his corpulent body dwarfing the woman.

•••

Mr. Biddle, the banker, as well as the town's blacksmith, dealt in four currencies—metals, gems, gasoline, and water. Most folks came in with bits of metal they'd found and wanted to change it for water, sometimes gasoline. Kincaid was one of those rare customers who always brought in water, and he never wanted anything except town credits to purchase supplies and the occasional splurge on something frivolous—a computer game, an old CD, a book.

"No, no, no," Biddle yelled at someone just inside the doorway of the blacksmith shop, "You don't store gasoline near a fire, you idiot. Take it out back." Biddle shook his head.

"Northerners," he said to Kincaid. "All that inbreeding."

Kincaid didn't say anything in response. He just looked at the banker.

"Well, how much you got today?" Biddle asked, standing on the front porch of the bank and taking off his leather apron. He ran his fingers through his greasy black hair, rolled down his once-white sleeves, and buttoned the cuffs.

"Ten gallons," Kincaid replied, dismounting.

"Loomis," Biddle hollered over his shoulder toward the blacksmith shop. A teenage boy covered in dirt and dust along with bits of straw appeared in the open doorway—apparently the person Biddle had yelled at just a moment before.

"Wuh, M'Bidl?" he mumbled, sticking his finger in his ear and scratching it. Taking it out, he looked at his finger and then wiped it on his shirt. Kincaid had no

FREE

Send in this card and you'll receive a FREE POSTER while supplies
last. No order required for this special offer! Mail in your card today!
❏ Please send me a FREE poster.
❏ Please send me information about other books by L. Ron Hubbard.

ORDERS SHIPPED WITHIN 24 HRS. OF RECEIPT

___ L. RON HUBBARD PRESENTS WRITERS OF THE FUTURE® volumes:(paperback)
   ❏ vol I $7.99 ❏ vol II $7.99   ❏ vol III $7.99
   ❏ vol IV $7.99 ❏ vol V $7.99   ❏ vol VI $7.99
   ❏ vol VII $7.99 ❏ vol VIII $7.99 ❏ vol IX $7.99
   ❏ vol X $7.99 ❏ vol XI $7.99   ❏ vol XII $7.99
   ❏ vol XIII $7.99 ❏ vol XIV $7.99 ❏ vol XV $7.99
   ❏ vol XVI $7.99   _____
___ L. RON HUBBARD PRESENTS THE BEST OF WRITERS OF THE FUTURE:
   (trade paperback) $14.95 _____

COLLECTOR'S ITEM (while supplies last)
___ Battlefield Earth 1st edition hardcover $75.00 _____

OTHER BOOKS BY L. RON HUBBARD
   MISSION EARTH® series (set of 10 volumes) $67.86 _____
   ❏ vol 1 $6.99   ❏ vol 2 $6.99 ❏ vol 3 $4.95
   ❏ vol 4 $6.99   ❏ vol 5 $6.99 ❏ vol 6 $6.99
   ❏ vol 7 $6.99   ❏ vol 8 $6.99 ❏ vol 9 $6.99
   ❏ vol 10 $6.99   _____
___ audio (specify volumes:_____)(each)$15.95 _____
___ Ail Pedritol—When Intelligence Goes Wrong $25.00 _____
___ A Very Strange Trip $25.00 _____
___ Battlefield Earth® paperback $7.99 _____
___ Battlefield Earth 8-hour audio $29.95 _____
___ Final Blackout paperback $6.99 _____
___ Final Blackout audio $11.95 _____
___ Fear paperback $6.99 _____
___ Fear audio $9.95 _____
___ Slaves of Sleep & The Masters of Sleep hardcover $9.98 _____

CHECK AS APPLICABLE: **TAX*:** _____
  ❏ Check/money order enclosed. **TOTAL:** _____
    (Use an envelope please)
  ❏ American Express ❏ Visa ❏ Master Card ❏ Discover
★ California residents add 8.25% sales tax.

Card#:_____

Exp. Date:_____Signature:_____

Credit Card Billing Address Zip Code:_____

NAME:_____

ADDRESS:_____

CITY:_____ STATE:_____ ZIP:_____

PHONE#:(   )_____ E-MAIL: _____

Call us now with your order 1-800-722-1733
www.bridgepub.com

Illustrated by Dwayne Harris

idea what the boy said, but Biddle seemed to have no problem understanding him.

"Help unload this water," Biddle said, "and then take care of the horses."

The boy didn't reply but went right to work helping Kincaid unload the jugs of water from the horse and carrying them into the bank. As Kincaid brought the last jug into the bank, Biddle was already opening the first jug. With an eyedropper, Biddle took a sample of the water. He let one drop fall into a hole in the tester—a palm-size electrical device that gave an instant analysis of the water. Biddle smiled seeing the results.

"Perfect," he said.

"As always," Kincaid said, taking off his hat and shaking the dust off it.

"How much you want for it? The usual? Fifty credits a gallon?"

"I don't know," Kincaid replied, turning and looking through the iron bars and out the window. "Does Evans still have all those books by Dickens?"

"Yeah, the complete works."

"I may need a little extra, especially with winter coming. I might not make it back into town until spring."

"I'm sure we can work something out," Biddle grinned.

Kincaid looked back at the banker.

"I'm sure we can." Kincaid returned his gaze to the window and saw the woman from the garden going into the saloon.

"Who's the woman?" he asked.

Biddle glanced out the window.

"That's Maggie."

"I've never seen her before."

"Evans just bought her," Biddle explained.

"I thought that was illegal."

"Well, let's see those bureaucrats in Washington come out here and try to put a stop to it," Biddle continued. "He bought her over in Warwick. Wanted her to act as hostess, entertaining certain paying customers, if you know what I mean. But if you intend to be one of those customers, you're wasting your money."

"What do you mean?"

"The customers have a habit of passing out before they get what they paid for. Evans is fit to be tied over it."

"Well, I just need supplies, nothing else," Kincaid said. "I'm going over to the mercantile, get what I need, and then we'll see what's left."

"It'll be waiting for you when you get back."

Kincaid headed across the dusty street toward the mercantile on the edge of town. He cut down an alley and was about to pass the kitchen porch of the saloon when he heard voices. He stopped and looked. Maggie stood on the back porch with a small boy.

"For every pound," she said to the boy, "I'll give a quarter unit of water. That's the best I can offer."

"A quarter unit of pure water, not that recycled crap?"

"Of course, and mind your mouth."

"A quarter unit of pure water plus you fry me up a mess."

"Getting greedy now," she said, "but I suppose I can do that. As long as they're clean. If they're contaminated, the deal's off. Understood?"

"Yes, ma'am, I understand," the boy said, smiling, and he took off running down the alley.

Maggie went back into the kitchen, and Kincaid continued on his way to get his supplies.

●●●

Having placed his large order with Mr. Peters, the mercantile owner, Kincaid looked around the cluttered store for anything else he might need. He selected a pair of leather boots and added them to the order. But other than that, there was nothing out of the ordinary about the supplies. He'd ordered all he'd need to get through the winter—flour, sugar, coffee, oil, rice, beans, dried fruit, and some canned goods. He'd negotiated a fair price, and there would be just enough credits for him to buy a few luxury items, such as the books, without having to delve into his reserves.

As Kincaid looked through a box of old CDs, Evans walked into the store. Despite his roundness, he was not very tall, only of average height, with an oily complexion and large pores.

"Damn that girl of mine," were the first words out of his mouth.

"What she do this time?" Peters asked, boxing up part of Kincaid's order at the counter.

"Oh, it's just more of the same," Evans said, leaning on the counter. "Won't do this. Insists on doing that. From the way she acts, you'd never know I owned her." Evans looked over at Kincaid.

"Kincaid!" he said, coming over to him and shaking his hand as if he were an old friend. "Coming by the saloon for lunch?"

"As always."

"Good, good. God only knows what that girl's fixing. Course, she's a better cook than my wife."

"I was sorry to hear about your wife."

"Yeah, it's a shame," he shook his head. "If I'd known she was really that bad off, I'd have taken her to the doctor in Warwick. She just said her stomach hurt. I figured it was one of them women's problems. But, what can you do?"

Kincaid just nodded his head—not in agreement, but after a statement like that, what was there he could say?

"Peters tell you about the girl I bought? I got her after my wife died 'cause I figured she could do everything my wife did—and some things she wouldn't do—and I could even charge customers . . . well, you know. Anyway, she does something to the customers. They never get a chance. They just pass out. I tried to do her myself, but there I was, undoing my pants, and the next thing I know, I'm waking up in my own bed. If you want, you can give her a try. Who knows? You might be the lucky guy who gets the prize. Of course, you'll probably need a rope." He laughed, his double chins shaking.

"I'd much prefer your set of Dickens," Kincaid said.

"Dickens? Oh yeah, those books I got. Sure. We'll talk after lunch. I'm heading over to the Malcolm place. He died, you know, so I'm going to offer my condolences to his old lady. Left her three acres, freshly purified, too. Nice. I'll see you later."

With that, Evans left.

"Have everything ready and I'll be back in a little while to pick it up," Kincaid said to Peters as he walked out of the mercantile. With the talk of lunch, Kincaid realized he was hungry, and he decided to head for the saloon.

The saloon was really part bar, part diner, a place to get a drink or a meal, to play a game of poker, to negotiate a deal, or a chance to sit with strangers as if they were old friends. The chalkboard on the saloon porch that normally told the day's lunch simply read

"Grub." Kincaid had always found the food to be decent, but when he saw Maggie working behind the bar, he wasn't so sure how it would be this time.

The place was busy, most of the tables full, but there was space at the bar, so Kincaid sat next to the boy he'd seen talking to Maggie earlier. He looked around to see what everyone was eating. Some had bowls of some kind of stew with dumplings, but most of the customers were still waiting.

"What's good, kid?" Kincaid asked.

"The grub," the kid smiled in anticipation.

"Now, Brian Maguire," Maggie half-scolded half-teased the boy, "everything on my menu is good. Don't just hawk your own contributions." Maggie turned to Kincaid. "What'll you have?"

"What's on the menu?"

"Crow and dumplings, . . ." she began.

"You raise them yourself?"

"Oh, yeah, I've got a crow coop out back. Didn't you see it as you rode in?" Maggie said. "Old man Harper shot them in his cornfield."

"How do you know they're clean, then?"

"I do know how to use a scanner. Besides, I irradiated them. Kills all the bugs, nice and clean."

"What else do you have?"

"Fried green tomato sandwiches—"

"Just get the fried grub," Brian interrupted.

". . . and fried grub," Maggie said, glancing at the boy.

Brian smiled and looked past Maggie at the counter opposite the bar where she did all the cooking. Kincaid followed his gaze and saw on the counter what the boy so eagerly awaited—a large bowl of white grubs, each the size of his thumb, all writhing and wiggling in a dredge of flour and seasoning. Next to the bowl was a deep fat fryer ready for use, the stillness of the oil belying its scorching heat.

"You needn't worry," Maggie said, "they checked out perfectly clean."

"I'll have the crow."

"Oh, I'm sorry," she said to Kincaid, then glanced at Brian, a mischievous gleam in her eye, "I just served up the last bowl. But don't worry, the grub is an excellent choice." And without another word, Maggie went back to work preparing the grub for the waiting customers, never even asking Kincaid if he'd prefer the fried green tomato sandwich.

Kincaid couldn't help but watch as Maggie threw a handful of the grubs into the hot fat, a rush of oily bubbles consuming the creatures. He half expected to hear a dozen tiny screams, but only heard the sizzling and spattering of the grease. Maggie turned back to the bar as the grubs cooked.

"What'll you have to drink?" she asked Kincaid.

"Water, straight," he answered without thinking, "the real stuff, not recycled. And half a glass of the same for my friend." He motioned to Brian.

"Put it with the rest of mine," Brian quickly said to Maggie. "I'll have the recycled crap . . . I mean, stuff."

"You have to forgive the boy. He's saving up," Maggie explained, pouring a glass of water.

"What are you saving up for?" Kincaid asked.

"A passage to Africa for my grandfather and me."

"Africa?"

"Where the water runs pure."

"And the streets are paved with gold, no doubt."

"I hadn't heard about that. All I know is there are no toxins and you can eat fried grub every day."

"Well, then," Kincaid said, raising his glass of water to Brian, "to Africa and to grubs every day."

Brian raised his glass of recycled water to Kincaid and said, "By Saint Elvis and the Memphis Mob, Amen."

"Amen," Maggie said, her back to them as she dished up plates of fried grubs accompanied by tomato salads and corn bread for waiting customers. Balancing the plates in her arms, she scurried around the saloon, and delivered the plates to the tables. Returning to the counter, she threw another batch of floured grubs into the hot oil. At last, she set a plate of grubs, tomatoes, and corn bread down before Brian and then another before Kincaid.

Brian immediately grabbed one of the fried grubs on his plate and shoved it in his mouth, the grub crunching and popping as he chewed. Kincaid looked at his own plate, picked up his fork and cautiously stabbed it into one of the grubs. Bringing it up to his mouth, he stopped and took a sniff of the grub on the end of the fork. It smelled like any other fried food—like grease and salt. He glanced up to see Maggie staring at him, her hand hiding a smile. He took a bite. It wasn't slimy or mushy. The texture was firmer than he'd expected. And it tasted like . . .

"Nothing like chicken," Maggie said, "is it?"

It was more like shrimp, sorta, well, not really. And something about it reminded Kincaid of popcorn. It could've been the crunch in his mouth. After a moment, Kincaid shrugged.

"Not bad," he said and tried another.

"Thanks."

"Where'd you get the idea for this?"

Maggie's smile faded.

"You'll eat anything when you're hungry." And she turned around and went back to work preparing lunch for all the customers.

Brian finished well before Kincaid. Pushing his plate back, the boy stood up.

"Time to pay up, Maggie," he said.

"Four pounds at a quarter unit of water per pound, right?"

"Plus half a glass," Brian reminded her, pointing at Kincaid.

"Well, you've done quite well for yourself today," Maggie said, as she poured pure water into a small plastic jug for the boy. The amount of water didn't even fill it up, and there was less than a pint.

"Thanks, Maggie," Brian said, taking the small jug from her.

"Anytime, Brian."

"See ya," Brian said to Kincaid and started to leave. Yet as Kincaid raised his hand in farewell, he saw Evans come in through the kitchen. Evans saw Brian, and his face turned red—not surprising considering how over-weight he was—and he appeared as if he were about to burst a primary organ.

"What the hell you doing, girl?" he yelled at Maggie while pointing at Brian. Everyone turned and stared at Evans.

"Oh, crap," Brian said, holding his water close to his chest, and quickly ran out of the saloon before Evans could stop him.

"I told you not to give that boy any more water," Evans yelled at Maggie.

"I didn't give it to him," Maggie tried to explain, "I bought the makings for lunch from him."

"I'll be damned if I'll let you give away my hard-earned water," Evans continued, picking up Brian's empty plate and throwing it at Maggie. Maggie ducked just in time, the plate shattering against the wall.

"Come here," Evans said, grabbing her arm and pulling her close, despite her effort to stay away from him. The look on her face wasn't fear. It was anger. It was defiance.

"You're not so high and mighty," Evans continued. "You may think you're just like everyone else, but you're not. I own you. That means you do what I say when I say and how I say. When I say fix lunch, you fix lunch. When I say don't give my water to that urchin, you don't give my water away. When I tell you to go into the back and spread your legs for a customer, that's what you're gonna do."

Maggie jerked her arm away from him and, without warning, spit in his face.

"You bitch," Evans yelled, and smacked her across the face, sending her falling to the floor.

"That's it," he continued to yell, pointing his fore-finger at her as she held her check. "Tomorrow I'm taking you to Warwick. I'm sure we can find someone stupid enough to buy you. I'm sure the whorehouse will take you. You think you have it bad here. Wait 'til payday at the refinery."

At last he stopped yelling, and all was silent. Evans looked around at all the customers.

"What are you looking at?" he yelled at them.

One of the customers made the mistake of speaking.

"Evans, what are you doing?" the man asked. "She's just serving up lunch. There's no need—"

"This is my place and I can do whatever I damn well please. It's my place, I'm in charge, I'm the one in control, not her." He was getting flustered. "Oh, to hell with all of you. Get out. All of you get out."

Evans pointed at the door as the customers slowly got up and made their way out the door, some leaving their half-eaten lunches unpaid on the tables while others dumped the fried grub into their cloth napkins to take with them.

"And if you've got a problem with how I run my place, don't come back," he yelled.

As the last straggler reached the door, Evans turned to Kincaid still sitting at the bar, his lunch before him.

"You deaf?" Evans yelled. "I said get out."

"How much?" Kincaid quietly asked.

"What?"

"The woman?"

"What are you talking about?" Evans seemed to calm a bit.

"You said you were selling the woman tomorrow," Kincaid said, standing up and facing Evans. "How much?"

The side of Evans's mouth turned up in a half-grin and he looked down at Maggie.

"He wants to buy you," he said, laughing. "I told you we'd find someone stupid enough to buy you. I just never figured it'd be you, Kincaid."

"How much?"

Evans was quiet for a moment, apparently thinking it over. He looked down at Maggie then back at Kincaid.

"We talking water, credits, or what?" he asked.

"Which do you prefer?"

"Well, water, of course."

"Water it is, then."

Evans was quiet again.

"Two hundred units."

"I've only got gallons."

"Then twenty-five gallons. Pure."

"Five."

Evans laughed.

"That's little over forty units. I'll get a lot more for her in Warwick."

"Sure you will," Kincaid said, "but think of the water you'll waste on the trip and back. Then you have to find someone to buy her. That might take most of the day. You might have to stay overnight. You'll need food, shelter, feed for the horses. That's more water. I'll take her now for eight gallons."

"Fifteen."

"Ten. That's eighty units. I take her with me when I leave, and your life can get back to normal."

Evans seemed to mull it over.

"Ten, you say?"

"It's right over in the bank. Biddle's already checked it out. Purest water he's ever seen. You can go ask him yourself."

He thought about it a moment more.

"All right, then, you have a deal," he said, "provided I check it out with Biddle. She's yours. Watch that she doesn't slit your throat." And he grinned. Looking down at Maggie, Evans said, "Get all your stuff out of here, and when I get back, you better be gone."

And Evans walked out of the saloon, leaving Maggie and Kincaid alone. Both were quiet for a moment, then Kincaid walked over to where Maggie still sat on the floor. He held down his hand to her.

"Come on," he said, "let's get you out of here before he comes back." Maggie looked up at him, then at his hand, and after a moment of hesitation, she took his hand and he pulled her up off the floor.

"It'll take me a little while to get all my stuff together," Maggie quietly said, then headed for the back. Kincaid followed her down a short hallway and into a room, her room, dark and dusty, with only one window, the curtains keeping out most of the light.

"Do you have a wagon?" Maggie asked, getting down on her knees and pulling a carpetbag out from under the double bed.

"No," he replied, staring at the bed, an old brass bed with a sagging mattress. Maggie looked up at him.

"What?" she said, a flash of anger in her eyes. "Thinking you'll give me a try?"

"No," Kincaid said, his face turning slightly red. "I was just wondering how you made . . . all those . . . men . . . pass out."

"You'll never know."

Both were quiet as Maggie opened drawers, took out her few items of clothing and other belongings, and stuffed them into the carpetbag.

"Look," Kincaid said as she finished with her clothes, "you don't have to go with me. You can go wherever you want. You can go back to Warwick or wherever you come from."

"Thanks," she said, "but I can't go back there. There wasn't enough food or water to go around, and I'm sure they've long since spent what they got for me. If I went back, they'd just sell me again."

"You could go somewhere else then."

"No, I couldn't. I have nothing. I wouldn't get far. I suspect I'm better off with you. Unless . . ." she hesitated for a moment, "unless you don't want me."

"No, no, it's not that," Kincaid said. "It's just that . . . Well, I just spent all my water on you, and I don't know if I have enough for the supplies I ordered. Without them, we'll never make it through the winter."

Maggie sat down on the bed.

"How much do you have?" she asked.

Kincaid reached into his pocket, pulled out a small pouch, and tossed it on the bed. Maggie opened it up and dumped the contents into her hand—silver. Tiny bits of chains, rings, trinkets, and beads.

"This is a fortune," Maggie said.

"No, it's not. It'll buy about half of what we need to survive. I don't suppose you have anything of value?"

"No, nothing." But then Maggie's face brightened. "Evans does. He keeps a small stash under the floorboard in the kitchen." Before Kincaid could respond, she rushed out of the room. Kincaid followed her back into the saloon and into the kitchen.

"Maggie," he said, trying to stop her as she pried up a loose floorboard, "I'm not stealing. Even from Evans."

She looked up at him.

"You're not stealing," she said, "I am. Besides, it's not really stealing. It's payback." She reached into the hole in the floor and pulled up a small wooden box. She opened it, revealing a dozen little bits of metal, mostly silver, some gold.

Kincaid shook his head. "It's still not enough."

"How can it not be enough?" Maggie stood up. "With what you have and this . . ."

"You don't understand. We can't come back to town until spring. And when the snows come . . ."

He saw the look on her face as he said the word, her eyes widening and her mouth opening slightly.

"Snow?"

Kincaid realized too late what he'd said. He'd revealed the secret source of his water.

"It snows where you live?"

"Yes."

"It's not toxic?"

"No. It only becomes toxic after melting and flowing through the Wasteland. It's the source of the stream."

"Does it rain?"

"Yes."

"Then how come it doesn't make it here?"

"It rains itself out in the mountains. I don't understand the science of it."

"And the land? Is it clean?"

"Yes. The rains washed away what few toxins there were decades ago."

Maggie stood there silently, the wooden box open in her hands. Kincaid took it from her.

"I won't steal," he said, closing it and putting it back in its hiding place.

"But we still need the supplies," Maggie said, "and we still have to find a way to survive across the Wasteland."

"Oh, that's easy. Just don't drink the water."

"Well, that's great," she said sarcastically. "That means we still need water."

"Recycled water will do. It's just a couple of days across."

"So we need recycled water and supplies for the winter," Maggie said, then looked around the kitchen and out the window, ". . . and a wagon."

"We don't need a wagon."

"Yes, we do. Don't argue with me on this one."

"Fine," Kincaid said, "but we still need a way to pay for it."

"I think I know where we can get some water."

"Where?"

"Brian."

"Brian?"

"We can repay him in the spring."

Kincaid didn't like the idea of borrowing from the kid, but he saw no other option.

"Oh, all right."

"Good. You go find him and convince him to loan us his water and I'll finish up here."

"We're not stealing Evans's silver."

"Don't worry. I'm not taking the silver."

"Okay then. I'll be back in a little while. I'll try to find you a wagon."

"I'll get one from Mr. Biddle. You just pay for it."

"Right."

And he left to go find Brian.

• • •

It took him a while, but after asking around, Kincaid finally found the shack down by the stream where Brian lived. It was a quiet spot just outside the town limits, with only the sound of the water rushing by. Kincaid knocked on the rough wooden door.

"Brian," Kincaid called out, then slowly pushed the door open. "Brian," he said more softly.

There, through the sunlight beaming down between the rafters, Kincaid saw Brian sitting alone on the dirt floor, a few tattered comic books scattered about him.

"Kincaid," Brian said, standing up, "I didn't know your voice. I thought you might be someone trying to mess with me."

"You have a problem with people bothering you?"

"Not usually," Brian said, "but sometimes when I get some water, people think I might be keeping it here, and they come out to try and steal it."

"Where's your grandfather?"

"He's gone," Brian said, looking down at the dirt floor. "He went out looking for food last winter and he never came back."

Kincaid looked around the shack. There was hardly anything in it—an old stained mattress on a homemade frame, a couple of wooden crates used as a table and chair, some warped pots and pans, but no food.

"You live here by yourself?"

"Yeah. It's not so bad, except in the spring when it sometimes floods. But Maggie said I could stay in the garden shed next spring . . ." His face dropped. "Oh, I forgot. You bought Maggie."

"Where'd you hear about that?"

"Down at the mercantile. Evans is telling everyone all about it—he didn't see me. I was hiding under the porch. Says you're the biggest idiot he's ever known . . . No offense."

"None taken."

"Well, I'm glad you bought her. She'll be better off."

"Look, Brian, I've got a problem. When I bought Maggie, I spent all the water I brought to town. I have some silver, but it's not enough for the supplies we'll need to get through the winter. Maggie thought you might be willing to help out. Loan me your water and I'll pay you back double come spring. The purest water you've ever tasted."

"Spring? That's not until next year. I was going to Africa. Soon, too. I almost have enough . . . well, enough to get to the ocean, but they hire boys to work on the boats, and I know they would hire me."

"I'm sorry, Brian. I know you have your heart set on Africa, but I wouldn't ask if we didn't need it."

"I know. Maggie would never ask for anything, especially water, unless she really needed it."

Brian was silent for a moment, then he said, "I've got forty-three and three-quarter units. It's down at the bank. You can have it all. For Maggie."

Kincaid stood there, stunned by Brian's offer. Forty-three units. That, along with his silver, would buy everything they needed—including the wagon—and then some. He looked at the boy standing in the middle of the shack, the dirt floor beneath his bare feet, the cracks in the wall, and no Maggie to fix him grubs or anything else come winter.

"Brian, why don't you come with us?" Kincaid suddenly asked. "It's not Africa, but the water's pure. There are no grubs, but I've got chickens and pigs, and they're pretty good eating, too. And there are no toxins."

"No toxins?"

"I'm sure Maggie would be happy to have you there."

"You think?"

"Yeah, I do. And you can always go to Africa next year. After all, you'll have all that water."

Brian smiled. "Okay."

"Come on, then," Kincaid said, "let's get going before it gets too late."

And they both headed off to the bank to make the arrangements.

• • •

Kincaid quickly learned from Biddle that Maggie had already been around to get the wagon as well as his horses. While he went ahead making the arrangements to obtain credits for Brian's water to pay for the supplies as well as the wagon, Kincaid sent Brian on over to the saloon to help Maggie. Then he headed to the mercantile to pay for his order. Yet once again, he discovered Maggie had already been there and picked up the order, telling the storeowner that Kincaid would be along shortly to pay for it. With everything taken care of, Kincaid headed back to the saloon so they could get moving before it got too late.

Walking into the empty saloon, Kincaid immediately knew something was amiss. The place had been cleaned up, the chairs put up on the tables, the floors swept, the counter washed.

"Maggie?" he called out. "Brian?"

There was no response. He walked back to Maggie's room. The bed had been stripped of the quilt, blankets, sheets, and pillows, and the curtains had been torn down from the window. Kincaid hurried to the kitchen, only to discover every speck of food missing. He headed out the back door, out into the garden, and found Maggie and Brian hard at work, quickly harvesting the garden. As a result, it looked completely ransacked. Most of the plants had been dug up, roots and all, while others had been chopped and cut down. Little remained for other people to harvest. The horses and wagon were nearby, the supplies only taking up half the wagon, the other half being all the produce from the garden in canvas sacks. Brian was busy picking every tomato, red and green alike, regardless of size, while Maggie pulled up the potatoes, both with canvas sacks.

"What are you doing?" Kincaid asked.

"What's it look like we're doing?" Maggie replied.

"You're stealing."

"No, I'm not," she said, never looking up from her work. "Evans's saloon. My garden. I planted it. I'm taking it with me. You about done, Brian?"

"Yep," Brian said, putting the last of the tomatoes into the wagon.

"I can't believe you're doing this," Kincaid said, looking into the wagon as Maggie dumped in a sack full of potatoes. Everything they needed was there. Water for the trip across the Wasteland, feed for the horses, all the food from the kitchen, plates, pots, pans, glasses, a spice box, bundles of herbs, even bottles of wine and liquor from the bar, and all, surprisingly enough, neatly packed. Maggie had even made a space with her pillows and blankets for Brian in the back of the wagon.

"That's about it," she said.

"I think that *is* it," Kincaid said, looking over the destroyed garden.

"Nope," she said, "I forgot one thing." And she walked over to the water purifier, disconnected the battery, and placed it in the wagon.

"Now, *that* is it," she said and smiled, "You ready?"

Kincaid stood there for a moment, a little stunned.

"Yeah, I guess," he said, then picked up Brian and put him in the back of the wagon. Maggie climbed up onto the seat. Kincaid followed, taking up the reins and snapping them. Yet, as they started toward the Wasteland, Kincaid heard the back door of the saloon open as Evans came running out into the ruined garden. With his mouth wide open, he stood there looking at the wrecked plants, then noticed the wagon heading off into the Wasteland.

"You bitch!" he yelled after them. "I'll kill you. I'll make you regret the day you were born. I'll do things to you . . ." He started to run after them, but his weight got the better of him and he stopped as they drove on into the Wasteland, still screaming obscenities at Maggie. But she just laughed, pointing at him as he gasped for breath at the edge of the Wasteland.

"You know, he'll starve," Kincaid pointed out to her.

"Evans?" Maggie laughed. "Never. But he will have to sell all his precious water. The water you bought me with. Don't you think that's hilarious?"

"Well, maybe a bit ironic," Kincaid said, shifting his foot and accidentally kicking something hard. "What is this?" He motioned to a covered box next to his foot. Maggie moved the canvas cloth, revealing books.

"Dickens." Kincaid's face lit up.

"And Joyce and King."

"How'd you know?"

"Biddle told me. I don't think Evans will notice, what with everything else missing. But I didn't take the silver."

"Thanks."

"You're welcome. And thank you for taking us with you, Kincaid," Maggie said, then asked, "What is your first name?"

"Nicholas."

"Nick," she smiled, "I like that."

MAGPIE

Written by
Meredith Simmons

Illustrated by
Amanda Anderson Gannon

About the Author

Meredith Simmons was close to fifty when she discovered the delights of speculative fiction, having taught at the high school and college levels for fifteen years and sold real estate for seventeen. She attended James Gunn's Writers' Workshop, where Frederik Pohl urged her to enter L. Ron Hubbard's Writers of the Future Contest. After two previous honorable mentions, she took First Place in the Fourth Quarter. She has long been married to Bob. They have one grown son and an incredible grandson.

They came in the dark of the moon—eight horsemen, faceless behind visors. Their great steeds met no resistance but hemlock and hawthorn and hillocks of dried grass. They thundered into the glade and pounded down the door of the hut.

The old woman within was deaf to their approach, so intent was she upon her conjuring. But she knew she had waited too long when the draft from the broken door blew the flames back into the chimney, leaving the lump on the hearth unformed and smoldering. She raised her eyes to the faceless men and her cry was one of rage, not fear. Rage that she had deluded herself into trading power for peace. Rage that she had ignored for so long the horrors seen in her scrying glass. Rage that she had delayed her own return to the darkness and that the potential for her revenge still lay unfinished before her.

They slew the old woman where she sat by the fire. An easy task for eight armed men. They hacked her into bits of bone and sinew and flesh. Their swords, red and slippery, flayed the body until there was nothing recognizable as human, for the men feared that she had never been such.

But they found the smoldering lump frightening beyond their power to strike. A black miasma of power and evil steamed from its unformed shape. Each in turn approached it, and each found his arm lacked the strength to raise his sword. Finally, one thought to use a booted foot to kick the lump into the flames. The fire licked it greedily, flaring red and gold and blue, shooting gouts of flame across the room.

The men scrambled away through the broken door. They had done what they'd been paid to do and would do no more. The thing in the flames was beyond their ken. They had been warded against the old hag, but the smoke from this conjured lump slid through their defenses, piercing them with doubt and fear, a slender knife that found the seams in their armor and let madness seep in.

They fell upon one another, there in the glade in the dark of the moon. They stabbed at each other in unreasoning anger and fear; insanity ruled their minds. The battle raged long, for they were all well matched, but in the end, eight bodies littered the glade.

With dawn came the first faint birdsong. The great war horses wandered, snatching clumps of grass from the hillocks until they dispersed through the wood.

Then came the magpies, carrion birds whose gaudy plumage belied their nature as eaters of the dead. They pecked at the men in the glade, finding the eyes within the helms and bits of flesh near the great wounds, but they were frustrated by the armor that held them from their feast. Following the scent of new blood, some found their way into the hut. Here food was easily obtained. Soon, all were within, gorging themselves.

The lump cracked as it cooled, thin slices of iridescent red and green and blue sloughing off the darkened shape. The sated birds found the gaudy colors irresistible. One magpie snatched a bright streamer and flew with it to a nearby hawthorn. This one was followed by another, bearing a glittering wafer. Over the next hours, the magpies wove bits of bright and shiny strips into the bush until they had knitted together a human form. And then the wind rose, flapping the tatters and frightening the birds away from their creation.

That night as the moon set, the bright pieces moved against the wind instead of with it. The form awakened, stretched, looked about the glade with uncomprehending eyes. The form was a woman, clad in bright tatters with raven dark hair heavily streaked with white. She followed the track of the browsing horses, away from the glade and into the world beyond.

By morning, she had reached a small village, just a few huts scattered at the edge of a stream. She heard children's laughter and was drawn to it. The children ran from her, shrieking, but more from pretend than actual fear. Their parents, however, were truly afraid of this odd stranger with the strangely streaked hair. They chased her away with sticks and rocks. Unharmed, she came back to perch on a boulder at the edge of the village. This pattern was repeated time and again, until one of the village women took pity on the stranger and brought her some bread. Having no words, the bright, tattered woman nodded her thanks.

And so, over time, the villagers became accustomed to seeing the silent woman near the edge of the woods and they left her offerings of food and shiny things. Because of her silent, quick movements and black-and-white hair, they called her Magpie and treated her as such.

By harvest, the woman had found her voice. She pulled almost-remembered words from her mind and thanked the villagers, which caused confusion since they had long thought her mute.

And then she was gone.

Illustrated by Amanda Anderson Gannon

The villagers still left food on rocks for her to find, but only birds came to the feast.

•••

The tattered woman moved north along the main road, a rutted track that wove between straggling villages. She was driven by a compulsion she did not understand, but which beat at her with a wordless urgency. She felt as if she were a sapling, stretched to the ground as part of a hunter's snare, a sapling whose whole being wished to loose itself from its tether and spring free. This quivering tension sent her ever northward.

The weather grew colder, the sky now more gray than blue. She begged in the villages and gleaned in the harvested fields. Her nights were spent curled under a haycock or beneath leaves in the woods. She learned to tell a tale of widowhood or abandonment, stories pieced together from lives of the villagers she'd observed, sparkling bits of detail that would bring her a meal. She called herself Maggie and met with little resistance as she made her way north, always north, following a route almost remembered, driven by a necessity she did not comprehend.

The land slowly changed. Fields gave way to large tracts of brooding forests. Villages disappeared, replaced by scattered smallholdings. And the people changed with the land. They became mistrustful and suspicious, their faces as shuttered as the huts they defended with staffs and snarling dogs.

One evening, as a biting mist began to settle, she came upon a trail leading off into the forest and recognized it, as one does a half-remembered song whose tune remains elusive. She followed the scant path through hemlock and hawthorn until she came to a tumbledown hut in a clearing. The thatch sagged, the door slouched, the clay chimney tilted.

"That's not right," Maggie said, filled with a fearful certainty. She squinted her eyes, envisioning a snug little cottage with smoke flowing from its chimney, a refuge from the damp and cold. And suddenly it was so.

Maggie blinked rapidly, but the scene didn't change. Before her stood a well-tended cottage, beckoning with light and warmth. Maggie felt both confusion and confidence. Her words had made things as they should be, had fulfilled a potential trembling on the edge of reality, but *how* she'd done it defied her understanding. With the hut's transformation, however, her awful compulsion to travel north lifted and Maggie was filled with peace. She approached the door without hesitation and walked in.

The cottage was exactly as she knew it would be, compact and neat. Firelight revealed a sand-rubbed table, a stool, and a small trundle bed. She knew that up the ladder was a storage attic with herbs hanging from the rafters, and sacks of grain warded against mice leaning on the walls .

Here she could winter, or perhaps had wintered, in safety and comfort. A smile creased her face, the expression unaccustomed but comfortable, as she went unerringly to the small cupboard that held a pot for porridge.

The next morning she awoke to a world strewn with silver. Each sprig of dry grass, each naked branch, and each needle on the towering pines glistened with sparkling ice. Her delight bubbled forth as a laugh, at first a rusty sound that strengthened with use and soon filled the glade.

The snows came in earnest after that, piling up against the door so she had to shovel it away to get outside, for the world in all its glittering white glory called to her and filled her with discovery. Each morning she awakened fearing the familiar compulsion would exert itself, but the need to move northward seemed as frozen as the world around her.

At night she tried her magics. Some worked and some didn't. She tried to find the reason for her success or failure. To light a candle with a thought was easy; to make this same flame flare upon a pot, impossible. A dormant branch could be willed into bloom, but no flower would grow from the legs of her stool. It slowly came to her that her spells, if they were indeed such, only worked if the object she desired to change was endowed with the potential for this change. And so as the wind moaned in the chimney, Maggie experimented and learned and grew.

One morning, in the deep hush of heavy snow, Maggie heard a haunting call. The sound, hurt and lost, resonated in the winter stillness and found an echoing chord within her. Throwing a cloak about her, she followed the call until she came upon a scene of carnage. Some farmer's cur lay torn asunder. Blood soaked the snow, staining it a dismal pink. Wolf tracks circling the carcass told of a battle fought and lost. And the call, which had seemed so loud, now became a mewing—the plaintive cry of an abandoned pup. Maggie scooped the pup up from where it crouched under a hawthorn and felt its frantic heartbeat through her hands. She looked for littermates, but if there had been any, they had disappeared down the gullet of a wolf.

Maggie took the surviving pup back to the hut and fed it gruel through a cone of fabric. She searched her almost-memories, but could find no helpful information about dogs. To her surprise, the pup flourished. He soon accompanied her outdoors, stalking any movement in the snow-covered world, tumbling over too-large feet in his exuberance to catch a blowing twig, a fleeting shadow. His coat grew thick and shaggy, a bluish gray studded all over with black specks and splashes of white. He seemed to be wearing a motley of smoke and soot. For his coloring and his antics, she called him Fool. He brightened her days and warmed her feet at night, filling a hole in her life that she hadn't known existed.

Slowly the days warmed. Water dripped from the eaves in sunlight and froze into tapering icicles over night. Maggie marveled at this magic that did not require her aid. In the late afternoon of one of these melting days, Maggie was drawn out of the house by Fool's frantic barking. The dog bounded back and forth in front of the woodpile, sooty tail wagging, his barking more playful than fearful.

"Fool," the woman called, her voice a mixture of amusement and irritation. "Stop that noise. Whatever small creature has hidden there is now beyond your reach. Admit defeat."

But the dog ignored her and continued to bounce and bark. Maggie crossed the yard to pull Fool away and allow whatever squirrel or rabbit had hidden in the woodpile time to make its escape. Then she saw the footprints, plainly delineated in the slushy snow— small, human prints, the edges streaked with pink.

She grabbed the dog by his ruff and pulled him back. "Sit," she said, her voice now filled with command. Fool went to his haunches, whining and quivering, but he didn't move.

"It's safe to come out now," she said and watched the pile for movement. Nothing happened. "Come out."

Nothing moved. She followed the tracks to the side of the pile and pulled away a few logs. Huddled among the wood was a boy—a coltish boy, all knees and elbows and spindly bones. The mud that coated him could not obscure the cuts and scratches on his limbs, the raw and bleeding abrasions on his feet. Shaggy brown hair fell over a narrow face made lopsided by a darkening bruise and swollen eye. He trembled and the look he gave her was the same that she had seen on Fool as a pup, hiding from the wolves under a hawthorn.

"You're safe," Maggie said gently. "No one here will hurt you." She reached a hand to touch him and he bolted, but toward her, not away. He grabbed her around her waist, his thin arms encircling her like bands. His human touch thrummed through her, a note reverberating in her heart. The boy wouldn't release his hold, so she edged him toward the cottage, murmuring soothing words that promised safety and food and warmth.

Maggie seated him by the fire and wrapped a quilt around his shivering form. She continued to speak softly as she washed his torn feet and spread a healing salve on them. The boy never answered, but followed her movements with wide and wary eyes. When she gave him some soup, he slurped it down quickly, the heat of it bringing tears to his eyes. She gave him a second bowl, telling him to let this one cool some before eating, but it was as quickly gone. Maggie cut him a large chunk of bread, but when she turned to give it to him, the boy had curled up in the quilt and was fast asleep, his fingers still grasping the now empty bowl.

"It seems that I've collected another fool," she said softly to herself. But the dog heard his name and cocked his head. Maggie smiled and absently scratched his ears. "No, you're my only Fool," she told the dog. "I expect the boy has a different name."

The logs shifted in the fire and the boy slept on.

The gloom of dusk had settled when the two men entered the glade. Maggie saw them coming toward the cottage and walked outside, pulling the door closed behind her.

Both men were big and bearded. The foremost swung a heavy cudgel as he walked. Maggie felt her pulse quicken. Her first impulse was to flee into the hut and bar the door. But somewhere a memory whispered that there was no safety in this. To her surprise, the men stopped some distance from her, heads lifted like deer ready to bolt.

"Witch woman," called the leader, "just give us the boy and we'll be gone."

Maggie smiled without humor. Witch woman, they had named her and there was about them the smell of fear. She stood straighter, her own dread draining away. "What boy do you seek? The one I found battered and bleeding in my woodpile? No father should treat a son so, regardless of the transgression. I'll give over no boy to such a man."

The leader now smiled a humorless smile. "I'm no father to that whelp. He's a slave, bought and paid for two years ago. And a poor bargain I made with that one, since he's fought me every day I've had him. But he's my possession to do with as I will. So turn over what is mine."

Maggie tasted the unknown word *slave*. It was bitter on her tongue. To think of another person as a possession was beyond her understanding. In the villages to the south she'd seen poor people and frightened people and people without hope, but she had never seen one who in the end did not belong to himself. She had assumed that this was the normal human condition.

"How can you own another person?" she asked, her curiosity genuine.

The bearded man now barked a laugh. "We are all owned. Everyone belongs to someone more powerful. We hold our land from Sir Garrick, and should he put us off, we would be nothing. Sir Garrick holds his land from Lady Elise, and for all his bright armor and huge horse, Sir Garrick would forfeit his life to the Lady if he displeased her. The slave boy is just the lowest on the chain, sold by his family who needed food more than another mouth."

"And to whom does this Lady Elise belong?" Maggie asked.

The man suddenly looked less confident. His companion shifted from foot to foot. "She sold herself to Evil and has been owned by the Darkness since my grandfather's time. But then, you'd know all about that, being one of her kind."

Maggie tried to keep the confusion from her face. One of her kind? Owned by the Darkness? Maggie, pondering on her lack of clear memory, had often wondered where she fit in this world. She knew she was someone who drank in experiences to fill a void she felt in herself. Was this desire for knowledge, this thirst for new experience, the Evil that controlled even the most powerful? Maggie didn't recall selling herself to the Darkness. Her earliest memory was of children's laughter. But the two large men seemed wary of her and she realized that she could use their suspicions to her advantage.

"You have guessed my purpose," she said. "All this long winter I've been sequestered here, honing my skills and bargaining with the Darkness for more power. My dog was once a woodcutter whose infernal chopping irritated me. The boy you chased into my snare will make a fine horse, long-legged and swift. And in you I see mice. Yes, I think a nice brace of mice." She flung her hands toward them, imagining the dirty snow at their feet as water, and, with the thought, the men were standing on wet, boggy ground.

Both men yelped as if struck. The companion jumped back with a squeak that was distinctly mouse-like, and took to his heels. The leader stood his ground for a second longer, then either could not or would not face her alone. He quickly followed in his friend's footsteps, the cudgel, which had appeared so lethal, now bumping into his own legs and hampering his flight.

With a laugh, Maggie opened the door to find the boy was awake, standing with his back to the fire and brandishing a stout log. His face, where it was not bruised, was the color of new snow. He breathed heavily through his mouth.

"Put that down," she said gently. "The men are gone. You're safe."

The boy relaxed his hold on the wood but did not put it down. "Did you kill them?" he asked. "Did you magic them in some way like they say a witch can?" The eye not swollen shut was bright with hope.

"Aye, I changed them into mice. But that wasn't difficult, for mice they've always been. Mice who are much owned and fearful. But even a mouse may feel powerful when playing with a cricket. They were not so bold when faced with a wolf in front of her den. And so they are gone."

The boy looked at the woman with confusion, but he put down the log. "You magicked yourself into a wolf?"

"Only for the moment," she said with a smile. "I'll keep my human form when around you, my Cricket."

"My name is Cedric," he said.

"That's a strong name," she replied. But she continued to call him Cricket.

•••

The melting days came closer together until the snow was completely gone. Tiny flowers peeped from the grass. Trees put forth buds that slowly unfolded into leaves. The pines shook in the blustery winds and sent golden pollen adrift on the air. In this world awash in gold, Maggie again felt the necessity to travel north. At first, the compulsion was just the rustle of the wind in the thatch, but this soon became the sound of trapped birds, beating their wings, attempting to answer the irresistible urge to migrate. Maggie's heart pounded with every imagined, frantic wing-stroke.

But now this compulsion had a name: Lady Elise. The name was whispered in the dark pines, heard in the croak of frogs at sunset. Elise, a name that filled Maggie with dread and a certainty of confrontation. The end of her road had always been Elise.

Maggie fought against the pull of the north, reluctant to surrender the joy of watching Fool dash about the yard, the delight of answering Cricket's perpetual "why's." But, in the end, the call was irresistible and she found herself preparing bundles for the journey.

When all was readied, Maggie saw that the cottage was ordered and the fire was quenched. Then she led the way down the narrow path to the road, Cricket following and Fool bounding through the brush at their side. She steeled herself to not turn back for a last view of the only home she'd known.

They traveled north for many days. The few people they met were poor and subdued. Never was there a smiling face. Maggie was thankful for Cricket's incessant questions and for Fool's antics. She and her companions seemed the only creatures truly alive in the bleak landscape they traversed.

Journey's end arrived unexpectedly.

They were trudging through a fine mist when the forest suddenly opened onto a desolate plain that bordered a pewter sea. Thrusting from a steep cliff above the water was a keep, stark and severe, its dull black stones drinking in the available light.

Maggie felt a shock of recognition. As with the cottage, she knew what she was seeing wasn't as it should be. She had an almost-memory of the same plain filled with fertile fields, a white keep rising above sparkling waves. "That's not right," she said, waiting for the magic to begin. But this time nothing changed. All remained dark and sere.

Dread engulfed her, but the compulsion was stronger than ever. The pull of the black keep was now a physical sensation. Cricket tugged at her arm, "Maggie, let us go from here." His voice was high and unsteady.

"But this is the place I seek," she replied, turning to face the pale boy and cowering dog. "You're right, though. This isn't the place for you or Fool. You should . . ." She stopped, unsure of what advice to give. All options seemed equally poor. Her impulse was to tell the boy to flee this unwholesome place, but flee to where? Maggie felt a wave of protectiveness, the desire to clutch Cricket to her and never let him go. "You should stay by the edge of the woods and wait for me. If I don't return by sundown, then go south for many days. Go until you hear laughter. There you can stay in safety."

The boy's hands encircled her arm. "I don't want to leave you. Come south too. Let's go back to the cottage."

"I can't go anywhere until I've finished what I've been called here to do."

"What must you do?" he asked plaintively.

"I don't know," Maggie said, resignation falling on her shoulders with the weight of a winter cloak. "Go."

She shook free of his grasp and strode toward the keep. But she heard the boy behind her and felt Fool brush her legs. She turned in anger to chase them away and saw the knights slowly sweeping toward them—eight horsemen, faceless behind visors, herding them toward the keep. And Maggie realized that she had waited too long to get the boy and dog to safety. She felt the dull ache of regret, put her arm around Cricket's shoulders, and led him to the bailey gate.

Inside the bailey, heaps of rags covered the ground. Maggie had to step over and around them as she made her way to the stairs. Nudging one of them as she walked, Maggie drew back in horror as the rotting rags fell back to expose the desiccated form of a human beneath. The skin stuck tight to the bones, a husk as an insect might shed on a tree. She shuddered as she realized what each bundle in the bailey yard represented. Cricket made a stifled cry beside her and she gripped him more closely as they made their way up the steps and into the keep.

The echoing room was almost as she remembered, imaged, it would be. She recognized every beam of the ceiling and every stone in the walls, but they were somehow darker, duller.

"So you come," said the woman on the dais, rising to her feet in a ripple of purple silk. And the woman, too, was expected, familiar. She looked much like Maggie, only drawn with a finer quill. Her hair was a lustrous black that fell nearly to her knees. Her smooth skin had never been roughened by the wind or chill of winter. Her movements were graceful and sure. Maggie had never seen a more beautiful woman.

"You are the Lady Elise," Maggie said.

The woman nodded, a slight smile on her face. "And you are the Magpies' leavings. My sister's magic must have been strong, though, to so influence the carrion birds. You look much like my sister when she left. It's a good thing to know that she hadn't totally forsaken her use of the Power."

Maggie stood mute and the woman must have read her confusion. "Ah, you don't know what I'm talking about, do you? You really don't know why you've come." Elise's laughter was a tinkling chime. "You're the revenge of my sister, Margaret, come to depose me and set the world to rights." Again the laughter rang like a bell. "And you had no idea. Margaret was always the fool. She thought she'd escaped, but guilt ate at her all her life. She was too weak to confront me herself, so she tried a great conjuring, as if I wouldn't know. As her weapon, you're a small thing indeed.

"But then, Margaret always did delude herself. She conveniently forgot that at one time she too had been happy to sell a miserable human existence for all the Darkness could offer. She made the bargain and then fretted over soft and silly things. When it became apparent that we could only retain our Power and our youth by pulling the life force from our miserable peasants, she left. Left for a life as a mortal. Gave up the

Power for the pleasure of aging and farting and scratching at fleas. Yes, Margaret was always the fool.'

Maggie searched her memory and found only blankness. Nowhere could she find a trace of Margaret, a woman who had rejected power and youth drawn from the death of others. "I don't remember my mother," Maggie said. "I don't know anything of her planned revenge."

The belling laughter clanged more loudly. "You are so amusing. I'm glad I let you come instead of having you killed on the road. Margaret wasn't your mother. You're a *made* thing, conjured in the dark of the moon. You're nothing but a smoking lump of Darkness. But you are entertaining. I've watched you in my scrying glass. I've enjoyed the drama of your stumbling through simple spells. I've laughed at your attempt to knit together a family from your foundlings. You've been playing at being human. Such futility. In the end you were compelled to come here, to try to usurp my place. Of course, Margaret's fond hope won't come to fruition. You were unfinished. Your core may be dark, but who knows what else the Magpies wove into you. You haven't the ability to do what you were created to do. You have the potential, but your training is lacking. Under my tutelage you'll grow into the dark form you were meant to be."

"No!" The word echoed around the barren walls of the hall, echoed the loathing that welled up in Maggie. She had often wondered at her own lack of memories, but never had she thought she was a conjured thing of smoke and dust. Maggie stood frozen, a bird before a snake, conscious of her doom but powerless to prevent it.

"I see in your eyes that you finally recognize yourself for what you are," Elise said, her smile one of triumph.

"Come, I'll show you the wonders that you can be heir to—the fine and glorious things that my stupid sister would have had you destroy."

Elise held out her hand and Maggie walked slowly toward her, suddenly wanting with all her being to take that hand, to see what Power could be hers. If she were destined for evil, she would embrace it and glory in the Power.

Elise looked over Maggie's head. "Take the boy. Kill the beast."

And Maggie stopped in mid-step. She realized the knights had entered the hall. She and Cricket and Fool were caught between faceless hostility and seductive evil. "No," she said again, but this time low and with control. "No. There is no need to harm a boy and a dog. They're only a Cricket and a Fool, no threat to anyone."

"No threat now," Elise said with her ringing laugh. "But you're forgetting about the potential. Even you should have come to realize that all of the future is about shaping potential. Where do your magics come from? Haven't you ever pondered on that?"

Yes, thought Maggie. *Yes. All magic is about shaping potential.* She was here with a dog she'd called Fool for his antics and his coloring. But a real Fool could entertain best when his humor walked the narrow edge of discomfort. Many were the monarchs who used their Fools to tell truths that could otherwise only be whispered. A Fool could be as sharp as glistening fangs, as lethal as a wolf. She could imagine the potential within her Fool; she had just kept it hidden with her vision of him as a silly pup playing in the yard. Now she saw him as a war dog, bigger, stronger, more vicious. She felt him grow by her side; his growl now reverberated in the hall.

And Cricket, her Cricket, whom she had made small with a name. Really Cedric, a boy edging toward manhood, a boy who had overcome much and now stood at her back ready to fight. He had the makings of a good man, a strong man, an honorable knight whose like is seldom seen. Then she heard a man's deep laugh and the rustle of mail behind her. "Sir Cedric," she whispered, and she knew it was so.

And for herself, for the Maggie who had been conjured from Darkness, what had been her shaping? She had seen humans at their worst and seen glimmerings of their best. She remembered a frightened woman who gave bread to a mute stranger. She recognized the feelings she had for Fool and Cricket to be human love. These and the sound of children's innocent laughter, and the sparkle of bright sunlight on ice, and the glow of pollen-filled air had all been part of her shaping. To wallow in the unconscious mire of Darkness did not seem to be her only potential. She was the Magpies' leavings. *Who knows what else the Magpies wove into you,* Elise had said. From somewhere deep in her mind came the sound of rustling feathers. And the sound grew and grew until it had blanked out the siren call of Elise's Power.

Now Maggie turned her attention to the woman on the dais, no longer laughing and smiling. No longer beautiful. Instead Maggie saw a dark form, shimmering with corruption. There was about Elise the smell of rotting flesh that Maggie suddenly found irresistible. Something within her cracked and broke. And as was her nature, the Magpie rushed toward the carrion so swiftly she flew.

Elise tried to scream a curse, but no sound came from her mouth, for the dead are silent and the Magpie knew this lump of flesh was long dead. Dead to the beauty of the world. Dead to the sufferings of the people around her. Dead to feelings of love and friendship by which humans know they're alive. And so, amid the clashing of swords and the cries of battle, the Magpie tore at putrid flesh with her talons and pecked at the decaying face and running eyes. Gore covered bright feathers as the Magpie feasted.

Then there was silence in the hall, only the labored breath of one man and the panting of a dog. Maggie came back to herself, surprised at the blood on her hands, the torn lump of flesh at her feet. But she remembered it all, remembered the joy of her feeding even as the gorge rose in her throat. She looked up to see Cedric leaning on his bloody sword, with Fool, crimson, muzzled, sitting at his feet.

"What have I done?" she cried.

"The necessary," said Sir Cedric, removing his helm. "The unfortunate necessary."

The man walked to the dais followed by the huge dog. "My lady, I await your commands," he said, kneeling before her.

A bone-deep exhaustion settled over Maggie. "No, Cricket, I'm not your lady. Elise was right about one thing. I was playing at being human. We see here in this blood and chaos what I really am. A thing made of Darkness."

Sir Cedric raised his head to look directly at her. He was a handsome man, clean featured with a mouth that wanted to smile. But he was still Cricket; compassion and understanding glowed from his eyes. "You are Maggie, who has always done the kind thing."

"Where is the kindness here?" she asked, opening her hands to include the butchery in the hall. "I have taken your innocence and made a killer of you. I have stolen your boyhood."

Cedric chuckled. "There has never been a boy who did not want to be a man. I am satisfied with this change. And as for my innocence, it was gone long before I ever came to you. If I have killed, it was to defend something that I hold important. I killed to protect you and to destroy the evil that surrounded us."

"And what of Fool?"

The man fondled the big dog's ears. "Fool is still Fool. He was always thus. Did you think the rabbits and squirrels jumped into his mouth? You have just made him more of what he already was." Cedric looked down for a moment and when he looked back, his eyes were filled with tears. "As you have made me more than I ever hoped to be."

Maggie felt the tiredness begin to lift. "Then it is settled. You will hold this land and make it bloom. It won't be easy to wean a whole people away from wickedness and fear, but I see in you the strength to accomplish this thing."

"I would aid you in this task," the big knight said, "but the power of the ruler should be yours."

"Ah, Cricket, you still don't see. I'll not be here. I don't *want* to be here. You are what you should be. Fool is what he should be. I, too, must be what I am."

"You are my lady," he said with a surprising stubbornness.

"No, I am the Magpie, eater of the dead. I am that which cleans the world of rot and corruption. That is my place. I see it clearly. To cage me here would be the worst type of slavery. Your need was the chain that bound me, but you need me no more."

"I will always need you." The knight's heavy mailed fist gripped her arm. And for a brief moment, he was

Cricket again, tugging at her arm, eyes filled with questions. Then the man's hands relaxed and fell to his sides. "But I would not enslave you. Fly free."

She felt the shock of release, the joy of her true form. The Magpie shook her feathers and took to wing. She flew out the door of the hall, sailing high above the keep. The land stretched below her, a quilt of dark forest and plowed fields encompassed by the shining sea. The Magpie made a chortling cry of delight and flew on, until the bright keep became a speck and then was lost from sight.

GOD LOVES
THE INFANTRY

Written by
Greg Siewert

Illustrated by
Andy Justiniano

About the Author

Greg Siewert graduated from the University of Wisconsin, became interested in wine-making through friends, and now works in the wineries of the Napa Valley. Although this is an activity he finds relentlessly interesting, it has never detracted from his first love, writing fiction. Greg started his first novel, "Tall People From Outer Space," in 1994, and it is now ready for submission. Meanwhile, he has tried his hand at novellas and short stories, working them in between the writing of a film documentary on Seattle's Andrew Wood, front man for early grunge-era bands.

About the Illustrator

Andy Justiniano has lived a various and still short life, including being a Gulf War veteran. His artwork is his inspiration and guiding precept for his emergence into civilian life. Through it, he has begun a serious art career that is already showing great promise. With each book he reads, and each picture he draws, another step forward is taken. We wish him the very best.

The soldier looked over the shrubby hills and saw the beetlelike craft moving slowly through the air with its array of scanners flashing beams onto the ground like a great disco ball in the sky. He carried his weapon as he would a suitcase, and he hoisted it to his shoulder. When he depressed a release catch on the massive rifle, a monopod telescoped to the ground from a protrusion under the barrel. He worked the bolt, and a round that was almost as thick as a can of tennis balls locked itself into the chamber.

Two lenses, as big and thick as ashtrays, functioned as his sights, and he peered through them, aligning the information on the first with the information on the second. Crude, red LED displays showed him the range of the craft—2.8 kilometers—and its speed—34 knots. As he centered the craft in his sights, sprays of gunfire emanated from its belly toward some unseen target. The computer on his rifle wasn't completely accurate, but he'd fired this weapon every day for almost eighteen years, and he barely glanced at the information anyway.

By his calculations, the physical strain of combat, the injuries he received, and the debilitating effects of working 19.5 hours a day forever would disable him as a functioning soldier in 4.2 years. If he were still alive in 4.2 years, they would cart his body—eight feet and two inches tall—deeper into free country so that he could sit in a classroom and teach weapons and tactics, until these weapons and tactics became obsolete. Then he could sit in his apartment, drinking beer and watching football.

The dense barrel was a massive section of hardened steel pipe. When the gun went off, the shock that wasn't absorbed by the gas dampener shot into his shoulder and made him wince. There was a time when his huge frame barely registered the impact, but repetition over time was taking its toll. His experiment with shooting from the other shoulder had been a failure.

When his round reached the flying target, he was busy loading another one, so he just had to assume he had hit it. When he leveled the rifle again, he could see an insignificant-looking flame in the shell of the aircraft. He fired a second time and saw the disco lights searching for him. He'd removed the flash suppressor from his weapon to improve accuracy, so he knew he'd be spotted quickly. When he fired his third and final round, he could already see incoming munitions. The aim was way off, but it was time to go. He continued to sight through the weapon until the third one hit. That was the one that usually mattered. Three solid hits would result in a kill almost 82 percent of the time. The flying machines were inherently unstable, and their flight control systems were easily disrupted by anything that could get through the armor.

He retracted the monopod and realized he'd forgotten to set the mine. Hearing rounds tearing through the bush twenty yards uphill, he almost decided to skip it. But his training was powerful, so he pulled the cylinder from his backpack and unfolded the corkscrew that now extended from the back of it. He cranked it into the ground and armed it. The incoming fire ceased and he looked up to see the aircraft trying desperately to gain speed. It listed to one side and vanished behind the brush that obstructed his view. A few moments later he heard the crunch.

He grabbed his rifle, lowered his face shield, and ran downhill at a sprint. Branches, brush, prickers, logs, and trees flew at him, pounding on his plastic armor as he picked up speed. His suit made him impervious to the effects of light brush, but if he got moving full tilt and hit a tree trunk or a boulder, it would sometimes knock him out cold and he would have to regain consciousness and remember where he was before setting off again downhill. The search craft would make mechanical assumptions about the amount of distance one man could cover in any given terrain, in any given time. The game was to exceed that rate.

He didn't see the access road coming as he streaked through the brush. When he hit it, the suddenly level ground was like hitting an obstacle. He lost his balance and careened off the other side of the road into a pile of dead branches. He made the mistake of trying to stay on his feet, and his leg was leveraged into the V-shaped crook of a log, breaking his leg at the shin. He was aware of the sensation, but he was in a state of shock and didn't perceive any real pain. Pushing himself backward with his hands, he removed his leg from the wooden trap and nestled himself into the woodpile as far as he could. He removed two canisters from his backpack and pulled the tab on the first one, holding the thing over his legs. Brown foam issued from the nozzle, and like clowns from a little car, the stuff kept oozing out in nearly magical quantities. Remembering his weapon, he grabbed it from where it fell and tucked it to his side. The brown secretion now coated him to the waist. It

Illustrated by Andy Justiniano

sputtered to a stop and he removed an oxygen tube from his equipment and put it in his mouth. With the remaining can, he began to cover the rest of his body until he had the thing resting on his chest, spilling out its contents like a science project volcano. When the hissing stopped, he lay still.

In a period of time that was alarmingly brief, he became aware of the pain in his leg. The actual pain was amplified by two psychological factors. Number one: he hadn't seen the injury, and therefore his imagination was free to invent images so gruesome that no real scene could match it. Number two: he would have to lie there for another seven hours and fifty-eight minutes, so any part of his brain that wasn't busy drawing pictures of bloody bone fragments was speculating on how much worse the pain would become.

Ten minutes after the accident, he could hear the thumping whoosh of a large rotorcraft in flight above him. It sounded very far away, but the foam had a muffling effect on sound and he knew it must be close. He wondered if it would find him and kill him. The thought was not disturbing. He was neither fatalistic nor suicidal, but the intense exhaustion of his daily life made him anxious for a change.

The foam did its job, shielding his body heat, bioelectricity, and brain waves from the overflying search craft. He could almost predict the instant that it would explode. The mine—a form of mortar—was an amazingly simple instrument. An infrared sensor was mounted to the tip of the explosive shell deep inside the barrel. In this way, the infrared searchlights of the aircraft would only trigger it when directly in the path of the weapon. The helicopters never seemed to stop traveling directly to the site of the soldier's muzzle flash.

With surprising regularity, they would scan the area until they were in the path of the mortar, and their own sensors would pull the trigger.

The sky was quiet now, and as he pondered his pain something wonderful happened—he fell asleep. If he'd slept for eight hours, it would have been the longest stretch he'd had in six months. He slept for eighteen hours, inhaling and exhaling, rhythmically and slowly. He might well have kept on going, but something poked him with a stick. The thing that periodically pierced the foam to jab at his ribs, or push up the skin of his cheeks, did manage to awaken him, but he wasn't terribly worried. Even in his semiconscious state, he knew that nothing he feared would poke something with a stick. He sat up and heard the thing scramble away. His leg throbbed, but he wasn't interested. The foam had solidified to the consistency of meringue, and it fell away from him in chunks as he pulled the tube from his mouth and took a breath of air.

The girl wasn't tough to spot. Despite the abundance of suitable hiding spots, she peered at him from behind a rock the size of a basketball. Realizing she was caught, she scrambled several feet away and took cover behind a tree trunk. He hadn't seen children in a long time, but guessed that she was about eight. He watched with fascination as she peeked from behind her shelter and then quickly ducked from his sight. He imagined that he was in the presence of an incompetent elf. "What's your name?" was all he could think of to say.

He began to think she wouldn't answer and then: "May."

"Hi, May. Are you a grape?" He regretted the question immediately and her voice, defensive and wounded, replied, "I have a mom and a dad."

He worried that the offended child would leave him, but after some shuffling about, she approached him and presented him with two wrinkled pictures, both of which seemed to have been clipped from magazines. The woman's outrageous necklace suggested a jewelry ad, and he recognized the man immediately. "That's Nathan Wood," he said.

Her face exploded with astonishment and joy. "You know my dad?"

"Not personally," he replied, "I've seen him on TV. He's a receiver for the Hawks."

"Wow!" she said, snatching back the picture and holding it with reverence. "My dad's a football player!"

He felt uncomfortable at her deluded joy, but something about her smile and the delicacy of her face, made it unthinkable for him to take away something that made her happy. "Yeah, I guess."

She was obviously a clone. Her features suggested that she wasn't bred for work or organs, so most likely she had been grown in one of the northern farms that raised girls in batches of 75 or 100. They were raised until sixteen or seventeen, then shipped to other countries as brides and mistresses. Occasionally, a political grudge or a shift in policy would occasion a police raid that would temporarily shut down the farm. Lacking any alternative plan for the crops, the girls would filter into society as beggars and orphans. The grapes (grown in bunches) were curiously easy to spot, though they looked completely normal.

She held the picture of her father with both hands, rubbing it gently with her thumbs. Her face made alternately serious and pleasant expressions as her brain updated her father's mental picture with the new information that he was an accomplished professional football player. She was engrossed in her thoughts while he brushed off the rest of the foam, and she gasped when she saw the leg bone jutting through the skin of the man's leg. She twisted the cuffs of her brown work-shirt and looked away, grimacing in sympathetic agony.

The foam was antiseptic and nonporous when dry, so the wound was relatively clean and free of infection. It had essentially formed a new skin while he slept. As soon as the stiff brown cakes were pushed away from the break, it began to bleed and the soldier smothered it with a gauze pad he had ready. Pushing against the errant bone with his fingers caused pain so intense that it made his ears ring. He understood by its resistance that it had begun to heal in its askew position. He secured a heavy stick, broke off the spare branches and wrapped the thick end in gauze for padding. Then he removed a marble-sized balloon from a pocket in his pants. The tiny red balloon was fastened to a T-shaped metal piece. The thin rod that protruded away from the balloon had a plastic cap that he removed, revealing a surgical needle. The two crossbars were short and thick and he used them as finger grips, pushing the needle into his leg. When it seemed in place, he depressed a small dimple in the recess of the intersection of the three bars. The valve opened and the balloon began to shrink slightly as the anesthetic was pushed into his leg. Suddenly, as the soldier was fiddling with a bandage, the needle popped out of his skin.

The squirting liquid created a jet action that made the ball skip about as he groped for it, this being his last one. It fell out of view to his side and he felt about for it in the dirt until something sharp stabbed his wrist. He lifted his arm quickly, but as he fumbled to remove the needle, the balloon emptied the last of its contents into his left wrist. The girl watched with open-mouthed amazement.

He yanked the thing out of his wrist and threw it aside, but it was too late. His skin felt numb where the needle had punctured and the sensation was spreading. The broken bone was in his left leg and it was jutting out to the side and somewhat backwards, making it impossible to get an angle on it with his right arm. He grabbed his padded club with his left hand and could already feel his fingers tingling and losing sensation. Assuming he only had one chance to rebreak the bone before he lost the use of his arm, he swung the club hard at the jutting whiteness.

The pain that radiated from the impact, three inches up from the break, indicated that very little of the anesthetic had entered his leg before the balloon sprang free. He tried for one more blow, but the club tumbled slowly away from a hand that no longer sent and received signals from the brain. It hung limp at the end of his arm, like the hand of a corpse. May still watched, partially covering her eyes, but peeking through her fingers so that she could shut off the image at any second.

"May? Could you come here? I want you to do something for me." With her hands still over her eyes she shook her head back and forth. "Come on, kid, I need your help." She removed her hands from her face and looked at the soldier.

"Can you help me find my mom and dad?"

He looked away. "I wouldn't know where to find them."

"But can you try? I just want you to try, and if my dad's a famous football player, it should be really easy."

"I don't know."

"Please!"

He forced himself to face her and saw her pleading blue eyes. What a weird power she seemed to have, he thought to himself. "I guess I'll see what I can do," he said guiltily and unlocked his eyes from hers.

She approached him cautiously and for the first time seemed to get a full sense of how large he was. She looked up and down at him in amazement. "Are you a clone?" she asked.

"No, but my parents messed around with my code a little bit. They wanted an athlete." He handed her the makeshift club and rolled slightly to his side so that the protruding bone was more exposed. He heard her drop the club and suck in a gasp of air. "Do you see the bone?"

"Yes," she squeaked.

"I want you to take the stick and hit it really hard."

"No."

"You have to."

"No."

"May, I'm hurt pretty bad. This will help me get better. Please, May."

He looked over his shoulder and saw the skinny arms grab the club. She took a position, but her thin blonde hair fell in her face, so she set down the club and pinned her hair back with some barrettes she had in her pocket. Then she retrieved the large stick. "Hard?"

"As hard as you can."

That was harder than he would have imagined. The blow fell a few inches off, missing the protruding bone. It connected solidly, but didn't loosen the calcified deposits that were gluing his leg together in the wrong place. He grimaced and could hear her drop the club and dance about in horror. "Again," he said, when he regained his composure.

"No."

"May . . ."

"Okay." She picked up the club, sighted the bone and concentrated so hard that her tongue protruded from her ruby lips. The blow was dead on and he could feel the bone shift inside his leg. He gripped a handful of dirt.

"Good," he croaked.

With some trepidation, she helped him dress his wound. He used the fingers of his right hand to reach under his leg and push the bone into place while she doused the area in antiseptic spray. She pulled off the tape strips and fastened them while he held the bandage, and then helped him gather wood for the splint. She muttered to herself almost constantly, and had taken to saying, "Ho, ho, ho. Fee, fi, fo, fum, ho, ho, ho." In her active imagination, she was in the presence of a magical giant.

They lacked the proper padding for the splint, and she said she'd get some from her house. Without another word, she vanished into the forest. May ran through the brush for about five minutes, stopping now and then to look for coyotes and snakes. Her house was a discarded refrigerator that someone dumped from the access road above. It had tumbled down the hill and landed conveniently against the trunk of a tree with its door open, making a kind of lean-to. Branches were piled all around the refrigerator and fastened together with multicolored yarn. A few toys and dolls littered the area around her house, and crayon pictures on construction paper were tacked to the tree. In the rotted-out crook of the trunk, there were several cans of food and a half-full gallon of water.

She quickly removed the pictures—most of them were renditions of her parents riding ponies—and placed them between the pages of a pop-up book about kittens that drove cars. The book went into a small blue duffel bag along with a few toys and knickknacks. Finally, she took a blanket, sweater, and sweatshirt for use as padding. She left the water and food, except for a small package of cookies that she stuffed into the pocket of her dungarees.

By the time May returned, he was satisfied that his break was as set as it was going to get without proper medical treatment. He had regained some sensation in the tips of his left fingers, but could not yet use the arm.

She wore the duffel like a backpack, and when she found the soldier again, she wriggled out of the tight straps so that she could present him with the padding. She folded the blanket and clothing carefully before wrapping it around his leg while he removed a spool of thin nylon cord from his bag. After a few failed efforts at one-handed knot tying, he abandoned the effort. Holding his hunting knife, he had her cut off three-foot-long lengths from the spool. A shoelace knot was the only one she knew, and soon his leg was bound with little bows.

During May's visit home, he'd taken the time to snap apart a thick branch near its V-shaped crook. Left with something resembling a large slingshot, he inserted the handle end into the barrel of his rifle and twisted it until it was firmly lodged in place. This way, he could use his rifle as a crutch without the barrel getting plugged with dirt.

He dragged himself a few feet to a fallen tree, and used the sturdy wood to pull and push himself to his feet with his good arm. He teetered on his right leg, and looked down to see May craning her neck up at him, skittering around him like a lumberjack unsure of which way a tree was going to fall.

"Fee fi fo fum, ho ho ho. Fee fi fo fum, ho ho ho," she was saying under her breath, possibly unaware that she was talking at all.

"May?" he said, interrupting her at "fum," while she stared at him with her head thrown back. "May, I need my gun." In the process of pulling himself to his feet he'd left it on the ground. She looked at the huge weapon dubiously, but went to it and grabbed the barrel. Both of her hands wouldn't fit completely around it. The rifle was more than twice as tall as she was, and much heavier. With a powerful second effort, she dragged the thing to where he was, falling once when her foot went out from under her leg. She dusted herself off and started over immediately without pause.

He was leaning against a branch from the fallen tree and his splinted leg would not let him bend far enough to reach the rifle on the ground. She grabbed the end of the barrel once more and hefted it off the ground like a power lifter, complete with facial contortions. Moving her shoulder underneath it, she tilted the weapon up on its stock and wedged her body underneath it until the weight vanished from her shoulder. She staggered with the exertion and could see the giant flipping the weapon upside down with his good hand so that he could insert the stock under his left shoulder.

Walking was difficult for him, even with the crutch, because he had to hold the rifle butt under his left armpit using his right hand. He methodically planted the forked end of the barrel plug into the ground, teetered his weight onto it, lurched forward, and repeated the procedure. In fifteen minutes his left arm would be functional, but he didn't want to wait. Patrols were common in the area, both in the air and on the road.

May was terribly excited and she walked right at his side, staring up at him and muttering her giant's song. She wore a blue sweatband on her right wrist, and her left thumb was thrust beneath it, rubbing fiercely at her skin. She did this out of habit and wasn't really aware of it anymore. Every five minutes or so, she would pull back the sweatband and look at her skin. She checked her wrist in this fashion as they moved along the dirt road. The mark was still there. "17C," it said. She didn't know what the thin black tattoo meant, and she didn't remember receiving it, but she hated it so much that the skin around it was raw and inflamed from the ineffectual rubbing.

She didn't hear the approaching vehicle. She'd forgotten about her wrist for a moment, and was pulling the barrettes out of her hair and combing out the snarls with her fingers. By the time she realized the man wasn't next to her, and turned around to look, he had the barrel plug twisted from his weapon, the monopod extended, and was sighting down the road behind them while he chambered a round.

She sprinted off the side of the road and scrambled into the roots of a large bush. Plugging her ears with trembling fingers, she waited for the explosions. None came. She squinted through the thick branches of the bush and saw the truck approach the man. He lowered his weapon. It sounded like a happy reunion, and as the two men with the car loaded him carefully in back, May started to wriggle her way out of the bush. The duffel bag snagged a branch, and while she struggled to free it, she heard the voices turn argumentative, though she couldn't hear what they were saying. She reached her hand behind her, probing for the unseen snare, then she heard the engine rev and fall into gear. She tore herself free as she listened to the crackling noise of heavy-treaded tires rolling away over dirt and gravel. When she reached the road, the truck was disappearing around a bend. She ran after it for a bit, but it was gone. She stood alone on the empty road.

In a state of confusion and dismay, she walked up the road, kicked some rocks, looked around, and walked back. When he returned for her, she didn't want to be far from where he left her. Otherwise, he might miss her altogether. May figured that the best thing to do was to wait for the giant to come back and take her to her parents.

She decided that the road wasn't safe and tried out a cluster of boulders uphill. They were an excellent vantage point, but if something came along the road she would have to escape uphill. She looked around on the downhill side of the road and found a tree with a split trunk. She could sit in the crook of the limbs and have a decent view of anything that came or went on the road.

As the sky darkened above her, the road seemed to become more and more silent. She was hungry, but it was her thirst that was almost unbearable. As she sat in the tree, shifting uncomfortably, she decided that she would have to risk a trip back to her house. When she swallowed, her throat felt like tissue paper.

She hiked parallel to the road and stopped every twenty or thirty yards to listen for traffic. She moved slowly until she was too far to hear a vehicle arriving at the rendezvous. Out of this range, she ran back to her house. Terrified that he would come looking for her while she was gone, she scrambled around bushes and over logs. When she arrived at her house, she pulled the cap off the water and carefully drank. It was a relief to her parched body, but she still felt a panicked urge to get back to the meeting point. Her plan was to take one can of food and the water, but she remembered the giant's injury and realized he might be delayed. She grabbed all the food she had, the water, a metal pot to use as a bowl, another picture of her parents riding a pony, and two cans of orange soda. She stuffed these things into her duffel, pulled the straps over her shoulders, and ran. She ran all the way back to the meeting spot and then stopped and held her breath while she listened and looked about for signs of life. It was as silent as before. She brushed her hair away from her ears. Nothing. The best thing to do was to wait for the giant to come back.

She resumed sitting in her spot as night fell. She napped in the crook of the tree, but the curving limbs that seemed almost luxurious at first became progressively less comfortable until her back ached from its distortions. Day came, and she wondered if he'd missed her because she was sleeping. She spent the day waiting ten yards downhill from the road, throwing rocks and stealing catnaps in the sunshine.

Night came, and he'd still not returned. She wanted to retreat to her house and sleep, but she couldn't dare to be away from the meeting spot. The thought of being on the unprotected ground at night was more than she could take; she kept imagining coyotes sitting over her while she slept. She spent another tormented night, resting in the crook of the tree. Day came, and still no sign of the giant. He was injured, and it might take him a while.

She hadn't had a real rest in the tree and she looked forward to napping once again in the sunshine, but the weather was uncooperative. Soon the sky was gray and the first tiny drops of rain were falling. Rain was not totally uncommon in the area at this time of year, and she had a black plastic garbage bag with a hole to stick

her head through. Even as the rain became more insis-
tent, she remained at her post, creeping forward a bi
because the noise of the rain might make it hard to hea
approaching trucks.

Her ears were sharply attuned to the noise of motors
but the din of the rain masked the noise of the
approaching tank. She saw it before she heard it. She'c
been digging in the mud with a stick, and when she
looked up she saw it rolling silently down the road
small, rusty orange, and covered with spots of green. I
didn't appear to have seen her, and she planned to stay
where she was. As it rolled closer, she realized she
couldn't bear to watch it approach. It would be righ
next to her. The thing motored down the road, seem
ingly straight at her, and finally she couldn't take i
anymore. Aware of how unprotected she was, she
turned and bolted down the hill. She hadn't had a
chance to look where she was going and immediately
the brush began to claw at her. She didn't hear the sound
of the firing gun, but she was aware of a twinkling pres
ence around her, as if the leaves sparkled with evil and
death. She ran headlong into a bush and it was too thick
to fight her way through it.

She grappled with the branches and suddenly some
thing hit her from behind. The impact blasted her
through the bush, with the branches ripping at her body
She was propelled through the air and hit the ground
face first. Her arms were too weak to keep her from skid
ding along the muddy gravel when she hit the surface
She lay still, in shock, in terror. In her mouth she coulc
taste dirt and blood, and she wondered if the thing was
still watching her. She wondered if she was dying. She'c
been shot, and her back throbbed in slow, heavy waves. A
cold wetness spread across the back of her shirt.

With her body rigid and dirty water pooling in her lips, she imagined the tank sitting right behind her, waiting for her to move so that it could shoot her. She lay still as minutes passed, and she could taste her own blood in the muddy puddle.

All at once, she turned her head to look behind her before she could lose her nerve, steeling herself to see the rusty orange tank. Instead she saw nothing but a drenched forest with rivulets running this way and that through the mud. She pushed herself off the ground, wondering what body parts were left. Her small fingers were still there, and seemed to move normally, but the ones on her right hand were numb. Her back ached and her face, stomach, and chest screamed from skidding on the rocky soil.

She removed what was left of her garbage bag rain-coat and walked mechanically back to her house. She didn't want to return to the hovel she'd twice departed—thinking it would be for good both times—but it was all she had. Scared to death of the tank, it took her cold, aching body an hour and a half to make the journey. Her shirt and sweatshirt were torn apart by sharp, muddy gravel and she pulled the torn fabric around her like a cheap robe. When she arrived once again at her refrigerator, she lay down on the discarded ironing board she used as a bed and realized she had no blanket, having given it to the soldier.

Lacking this basic comfort, she stood up and exam-ined herself in the mirror. It was a skillet she'd found that had a chromelike nonstick finish. Her reflection showed a pale face covered with dried blood, and clothes torn down the middle, revealing a chest and belly striped with bleeding scratches that could have been made by a wildcat. She pulled off her duffel and her torn shirt and twisted herself to look at her back, sure that she would see a scene as gory as the giant's leg, full of blood and bone and exposed body parts. There was nothing but a dark blue bruise that spread over most of her back. She cautiously put her hand to the wetness on the wound and, to her surprise, it wasn't blood. It seemed to be orange soda. Her duffel had a tear in the side and she unzipped it. Looking through the contents, she found the exploded soda can and saw that the pot had a big circular hole in the bottom. She turned the punctured pot over in her hand. The bullet must have passed under her armpit. She remembered sliding across the ground on her face and hunched herself over at the memory, suddenly feeling the cold wet air on her skin.

The recollection of having a blue sweater in the crisper seemed too good to be true, and when she yanked open the plastic drawer and saw it, it seemed like an oversight by whatever machine or committee had been designated to torment her.

She pulled it on immediately. It wasn't thick, but the warmth was instantaneous. Her torn sweatshirt could be used as a blanket, but she knew that if she used it right away it would wet her dry sweater, so she patiently fastened it to the door of the freezer with a clothespin. Then she curled up on the ironing board, shivering lightly; too cold to sleep. Sometimes on cold nights, she imagined that the refrigerator was still working just a little bit, showering her with chilled air as she lay on her bed.

In the late morning, when the full rays of the sun hit the forest and her body warmed to a reasonable temperature, the change was like a sleeping pill. She fell into a deep sleep and did not awaken until the sun began to fade. The rain had stopped, but the forest was still alive with the sound of leaves shedding their wetness to the ground below.

The sweatshirt was dry and she wrapped it around her shoulders like a shawl before she set off for the point where the giant had left her two days earlier. She worried that he'd come back while she was sleeping, but there was nothing to be done about that.

She took a cautious route to the spot, and listened for approaching traffic before stepping onto the road to inspect the ground. There didn't seem to be any recent tracks. The rain had washed the road smooth. She returned to her post and waited a few more hours. The giant had not returned. His injuries must be severe, she figured, or he'd returned for her while she was sleeping. The prospect was too awful to think about, but she had to be practical. Her food and water were almost gone, and anything she owned that might be needed on a journey was with her. There was a town one day away where she begged for money and food, but the giant had gone in the other direction. Shouldering her duffel, she set out on her way.

Crawling through the woods quickly wore on her patience, so she hiked tentatively on the edge of the road, stopping periodically to listen for traffic, poised to leap into the brush. She didn't know precisely where she was headed, but she knew that the giant's army used a system of tunnels and caves, so she kept a close watch on the hillside for entrances. She didn't see any that evening and spent the night huddled under a bush. In the morning, she resumed her journey and occasionally heard the noises of traffic. She would dart into the brush and hide until it passed. She was unable to tell if most of the vehicles were friend or foe, so she feared that she and the giant might be unwittingly crossing each other's path during their mutual search.

Later that day, she came across a grassy road that jutted off from the one she followed. She froze when she heard voices, and as she watched from behind a tree she saw two men and a woman wearing the same kind of uniform the giant had. It was an olive-drab color, streaked with random lines of brown arranged like electrical sparks darting this way and that. It was meant to simulate sparse brush.

"I'm trying to find an army man," she said. The startled soldiers grabbed at their weapons reflexively before relaxing at the sight of the little girl in the blue sweater. "He's really tall. Much taller than you."

"What's his name?" asked a man with a mustache and a shotgun.

"I don't know."

"Why are you looking for him?"

"He knows where my parents are," she said.

"Really, you're looking for your parents?"

"Yes."

"Where'd you lose them?"

May looked around, then back at the soldier who was addressing her. He was a white man of medium build, with skin stretched tightly across his bony face. His mustache protruded like vegetation.

"I haven't seen them since I was . . . really little."

The man smiled with amused sympathy. The two other soldiers, a man and a woman who'd both been tinkering with the engine of a truck that was pushed into the brush, didn't say anything. They wouldn't look at May. "Come here, kid," said May's questioner.

She didn't say anything and wondered if she should run. Impatient, he walked over to her. She wanted to run, but she was too tired. He scooped her blonde hair into a bundle and lifted it up so that he could see the back of her neck. He dropped her hair and pushed up the sleeve of her sweater and looked at the inside of her thin arm. Seeing the sweatband on her other wrist, he pushed it away and found what he was looking for.

"17C. Is that your name?"

"My name is May."

The man smirked. "Did you have lots of friends that looked just like you?"

"They didn't look that much like me," said May defensively.

"Were there many boys where you grew up?"

"They didn't allow boys in the foster home."

"Foster home?" said the man with a laugh.

She was wounded at his attitude. "My dad's a football player. He's really good. He plays the receiver."

"A football player. I'm impressed."

Hearing his skepticism, she dove into her bag for the evidence she had stashed in the pop-up book.

When he saw the picture of Nathan Wood, he could no longer contain himself and started laughing out loud. He grabbed her wrist and held it up. "This number means you don't have a dad."

May pulled her hand away as if she'd been burned and rubbed at the black tattoo. She looked around, wanting to get away from the man, and realized she was about to cry. She tried to hold it in, but her face contorted and she lifted one hand to her face to cover her eyes while her other hand retrieved the picture.

The man didn't say anything, but walked away stifling a fake snicker. The woman who was working on the engine intercepted May, who was headed back into the woods. "What happened to your face, Sweetheart?"

May didn't answer, but stopped and let the woman brush away her tears. "Are you hurt anywhere else?" asked the woman.

May lifted her sweater to show her the lacerations on her stomach.

"Just sit right there. We'll take you to the infirmary as soon as the truck's fixed. The woman retrieved a thick blanket from the truck and wrapped the girl in it. May was chilled to the bone, and soon after she nested into the big blanket, the man's mean words seemed distant. She listened to the engine start on a few short test runs. The third time it didn't shut off and it revved angrily. The woman walked her quickly to the truck— they'd been in the area much too long—and the four of them shot away down the road.

The gravel churned beneath the tires and May stared tiredly out the open back end of the truck as the country rolled away. She was happy to let the woman be nice to her, and accepted the warm cup of instant cocoa that was offered, but the lady seemed strangely unnerved. The way she smiled was like a waitress, though May had only ever seen waitresses on TV.

The hard plastic back of her seat prodded her at irregular intervals, and the passengers jostled about like jello. Her view was uninterrupted until the moment it went black. The transition to the darkness of the cave was like the sudden onset of a violent and gripping sleep. The walls of dirt were dashed with green light fixtures that strobed across May's vision. Her recent life had been that of a traveler, and now more than ever she felt the lonely sting of being lost without a clear idea of destination.

The truck stopped and May was handed off to a nurse, who checked her wrist and led her down the dirt and concrete hallway. May was tired to the bone, but she kept her feet moving as she stared at the ground and struggled to keep pace with the tall nurse.

At last she was shown to a room. The nurse led her inside before shutting the door. May stood just inside with her pack clutched in front of her like a teddy bear. There were six other girls in the room, with her exact facial features, who looked at her with varying degrees of indifference. She turned around and twisted the knob on the door. It turned freely, but wouldn't open. Her sisters all stared at her. Some bit their knuckles absent-mindedly or looked on with wide eyes from the upper bunks. One girl was pouting. May walked silently between the bunks looking for a place to put her bag. A hand gripped her elbow and led her to a thin mattress in the corner. May thanked the girl, who was peering at her intermittently. Returning the eye contact, she recognized her best friend immediately, even though the girl looked identical to all the others save for her hair, which had recently been cropped to just below the ears with the precision of an industrial accident.

"April?"

"May!" answered her friend and they hugged fiercely. The two sisters threw themselves down on the mattress in the corner and took turns explaining what had happened to each of them after their foster home was raided. "I'm looking for my parents," said April.

"Me too," replied May, but some of the conviction was gone from her voice. They showed each other the worn pictures they carried of their missing loved ones. April's picture consisted of a tall, smiling, dark-haired man pushing a woman on a swing. May took the picture and held it carefully. They'd showed each other these pictures a thousand times in the foster home, but she looked at it now as if it were the first time. The casual confidence of the couple made May think that they must be very good parents. She glanced between April and the glossy picture, and the similarity restored some of her faith that the taunts of the soldier were nothing but cruelty and lies.

"I think there's a man who knows my dad," said May. April threw her hands to her mouth in astonishment and envy.

"Where?"

"In the army."

"Which one?"

May shrugged. "He's a giant." May then relayed the whole story of her encounter with the infantryman, faithful in all details except that she had the man marching about saying, "Fee fi fo fum, ho ho ho!"

April listened carefully to the story, her mind whirring with possibilities. Maybe the giant knew her parents too, or, if not, then at least maybe she could live with May and her mom and dad.

The fact that the two sisters obviously shared genetic heritage was not something that April could consider. For either of them to acknowledge that their physical similarity was the result of being twins would be to question everything they'd ever been told about where they came from, and who was waiting to be reunited with them.

As they pondered their pictures, May watched a girl sneak a blue plastic bottle from under her bunk. She went to each of the girls in turn, poured a little of the liquid into their waiting cups, then topped it from a water bottle she carried. April grabbed her aluminum cup and held it out for the girl.

"Can I have some?" asked May.

"You don't need any," replied April. "You're all beaten up."

May couldn't understand the logic of the remark, and she was stunned when she saw that the bottle was labeled as some kind of industrial lubricant. The liquid that poured into April's cup was a thin gray oil. May watched as April closed her eyes and gulped the concoction as fast as she could before dropping the cup in revulsion. From across the room, May heard a girl vomiting violently, and it snapped her out of her daze so that she grabbed her friend. "What are you doing? Why did you drink that?"

April was doubled over and fighting not to wretch. "This is a hospital," she said. "You can't stay if you're not sick." May wrung her hands in despair as she tried to comfort her friend who lay on the mattress in heaving convulsions. She held April's head and wiped at her mouth with the sleeve of her sweater.

The girls had their timing perfected and it wasn't long before a nurse opened the door. She had a clipboard in her hand and read from it. "15C, 17C, and 57C," she said. May covered her wrist reflexively. Two other girls stood up dutifully and walked to the door clutching their bellies. The nurse looked at their wrists. "17C," she said again.

"You have to go see the doctor," said April, whose face was sweating. May stood up quietly and followed the other girls.

She was led through a tangle of corridors and shown into a small room littered with surgical instruments. She sat on the examination table as the nurse instructed, and waited for the doctor. She waited and waited until she knew every detail of the sterile room. She began fidgeting with the surgical instruments and found a razor-sharp scalpel. Holding the blade at a steep angle to her wrist, she scraped carefully at the tattoo like a man would shave with a straight razor. The blade frightened her, but she scraped with ever increasing pressure, stopping occasionally to see if she'd made any difference. She was so absorbed in the activity that the noise of the door opening startled her, and before she knew it, she'd slipped the blade guiltily into her pocket. It went in handle first and the blade jutted out dangerously from the front of her jeans.

The doctor was a short, powerful man who breathed through a sanitary mask. He didn't say a word; he simply looked at some papers he had and started examining May's wounds. He rubbed a paste into the deep scratches, pushed painfully into her ribs to feel for broken bones and then left. She didn't know what to do, so she pulled on her sweater and sat on the table feeling cold. The nurse finally returned and had her take some antibiotic pills before leading her back to the room.

The whole experience left her feeling unpleasant, and she was preoccupied with the way the hairy-armed doctor did his job without ever appearing to see her. Her melancholy faded when she saw April, then vanished when she saw what kept the girls drinking doses of all-weather military transmission fluid.

May's body had adapted to being hungry all the time, but when she smelled the cafeteria her mouth watered so that she had to swallow repeatedly. Following April's lead, she held out her plastic tray and received a roll with butter, tomato soup, a ham and cheese sandwich, a glass of juice, and a cookie. She ate without a word, hunched over her food as if afraid that someone would see it and take it away. When she was done, April said, "You can get more." In disbelief, May returned to the line for more juice and another sandwich. She ate it carefully, without the panic of her first course, and felt the satisfaction of being full for the first time since she left the foster home.

The girls went back to the room, and when they filed inside they were not alone. May's doctor—with his mask unstrapped, revealing a plain face and a stern demeanor—was talking to a staff sergeant and holding the bottle of transmission fluid. Finishing their conversation, they left without so much as a glance at the despairing faces scattered below them. The nurse, wearing a strained smile, quietly shut the door and locked them in. Some of the girls cried, but they were essentially resigned to their fate. May alone was frantic. With only one hot meal in her belly, and not so much as a single night on the warm mattress, the thought of abandoning the haven was maddening. She pleaded with April to tell her that they would find a way to stay, but April, knowing the workings of the hospital better than May, was not optimistic. She was packing her bag. "It's okay. We'll just go find our parents."

The door to their room never opened that night, and despite May's anxieties, she slept soundly on the mattress next to her rediscovered friend. In the morning, they were taken to breakfast, which kindled a hope in May that they were being allowed to stay. The nurse came to their table and explained that because of the war, there were many needy children, and space would have to be made for kids that were really sick.

The girls were allowed to collect their things, and then they were loaded on a truck that shuttled them to the bus stop at a small outpost city nearby. Each girl was

given a voucher for a one-way bus ticket. Having
nowhere to go, they sold their vouchers to travelers and
vanished into the streets to beg for money and find
shelter from the chill of the night air. The two sisters—
who wouldn't dare admit they were sisters—stayed in
the warm bus stop until they were kicked out by the
staff. They used their money to purchase chili dogs from
a vendor and ate them while they wandered. As evening
approached, their search for a place to spend the night
became more urgent. With the newspapers they had
gathered, they could weather the chill but as the sun
went down the good people went home, and the population of the city became a fearful thing for the two girls
to behold. May noticed a gap at the bottom of a fence and
they scrambled under it on their bellies. This opened
some of the cuts in May's stomach, but she was starting
to get scared of the men she saw in the street, so
she pushed herself quickly through. The sisters were in
the parking area of an office building, and were soon re-
warded for their effort. Behind some bushes there was a
steam vent that poured heat through a grate on the
ground.

They huddled together on the vent and the churning
noise of the building's machinery was comforting.
Making a nest from their newspapers, they passed the
time discussing their parents and dreaming aloud about
the lives they would lead after being reunited with their
loved ones. They began to doze and were both asleep
when the noise of the machinery lessened abruptly and
the flow of warm air underneath them slowed to a
trickle. They awoke when the chill reached their bones,
and they were unable to regain sleep no matter how
tightly they clung together or how well they layered
themselves with newspaper. Every time one of them
was close to drifting off, the gnawing cold would prod

them awake. At the height of their misery, a wailing alarm ripped over the city indicating a missile attack. There was nowhere to take cover, so they squashed themselves against the building and covered their ears against the noise of nearby explosions that shook the ground beneath them like an earthquake. When it was over they were unharmed, but tears rolled down April's cheeks. May wiped them away, and they watched the glow of fires and the racing pumper trucks until the light of burning buildings was replaced by the light of morning.

It was about that time that May found the scalpel. She was searching for a piece of candy that she knew she'd eaten but was hoping to find anyway, and felt her fingers touch the smooth cold steel of the blade. Miraculously, she didn't cut herself. She showed the prize to April and they played with the instrument, slicing newspaper and carving twigs. Bored with this, May used it to scrape at her tattoo as she had in the hospital. A half-hour of effort made no visible change in the number, but left her skin red and swollen. She was exhausted to the bottom of her heart. She felt like a cold, dead battery. Wordlessly, numb from lack of sleep, she handed April the blade and pinched the tattoo between the thumb and forefinger of her other hand. "Cut it off," she said quietly.

April didn't say anything. She looked May in the eyes and saw herself reflected in them. Carefully, she took her friend's hand and put the scalpel to the pinch of skin. Then she sliced it off and sat back stupefied. May shoved the piece of skin through the grate like it was a gross bug. She felt no pain and accepted the scalpel. She was suffused by a peculiar sense of total detachment, a complete disassociation from her body, and it was only after she duplicated the surgery on April that she came to understand she was wounded. The spell was broken and it felt like someone was holding a match under her wrist. She dropped the scalpel and it clattered through the vent.

April, too, seemed to awaken from the dream. She stared at her wrist in horror as thick red blood emerged from the wound like dish soap oozing from a sponge. The girls stopped the bleeding with newspaper that they gripped tightly with their free hands. They grimaced in pain, but also felt a saturating sense of euphoria and freedom, as if they'd gotten away with something grand; playing a trick on a world that was trying to bury them.

●●●

The soldier did not want to open fire on the helicopter. Underneath the gunship was the familiar bulge of a Laurence Engineering 40 mm electric cannon. As he watched the helicopter fire into the city, the quiet gun was barely audible, and a cloud of Freon hissing from the red-hot barrel was the only visual indication that the weapon was shooting one hundred and fifty propellant-free tungsten rounds per second at a target that the soldier could not see, but had most likely just been shredded with the rapidity of a snowball in a lawnmower.

He opened the chamber on his gun and removed the standard high-explosive round. From his pack he pulled three shells; two went into belt loops and the third he examined carefully. They were ceramic-shelled, active penetration munitions, in every way superior to his regular ordnance except that they were very expensive. He blew the dust off it, wiped it with his shirt, then slid it carefully into the open breech, giving it a gentle twist to make sure it was seated properly. He locked the breech, opened his sights and peered over the wall he was using for cover. The six-foot-tall concrete slab was about two feet thick and seemed to represent an abandoned effort at a hillside home. Rebar still spiked from the top of it at regular intervals. The structure was great cover, but it was the only cover on an otherwise barren hill. This was what made him hesitate: the idea of being pinned down in the open by the flying cannon. In the end, he decided that he was a soldier, and if he didn't fire on the helicopter, then he was just some idiot sitting on a hill with a rifle.

The wall made a perfect benchrest for the soldier's oversized frame, and he rested the weapon on it, held his breath, slowly squeezed the trigger as he sighted down his target, and missed. The instant after he felt the recoil he had the weapon open and the empty brass shell fell smoking to the ground. He worked quickly and smoothly loaded the new round, but his heart was crunching about in his chest. The gunship would register the passing round and would be looking for him on the next shot. The soldier was already locking his breech when he heard the noise of his first round impacting somewhere in the distance. He rested his weapon on the wall once more and sighted the helicopter, which had stopped firing and was moving upward and to his left.

The aircraft—nearly two kilometers away—did not seem to have located him yet and he held his breath and watched the readout indicating the ship's speed and direction. He adjusted the crosshairs and pulled the trigger as gently and carefully as he could. As soon as the stock kicked into his shoulder he wanted to grab the round out of the air and stuff it back in the barrel. His target had changed its rate of turn, and he knew the shot would be off its mark by several feet.

Crouching behind the wall once more, he loaded his weapon for the third time and waited for the gunfire that would be coming at any moment. His face felt like soft wax, and he couldn't have made a facial expression even if he'd had occasion to. The target's engine was growing louder. His logic was being melted by fear, and what he really wanted to do was to press himself into the ground and blend in like a chameleon. The only portion of his brain that would still make decisions was the part chiseled from endless days doing his endless job. The gunship hadn't opened fire because—understanding its advantage—it wouldn't want to waste ammunition until it visually acquired its target. It seemed as if the craft was still a kilometer away, meaning that its ammunition would take a half-second to reach him, which, added to its reaction time, would give him a full second to squeeze off one more shot. He centered his sights, leveled his rifle while still in the crouched position, and rose quickly with the rifle against his shoulder. He fought against the instinct to jerk the trigger, and waited until his weapon was steady and the gunship was in his sights. As it went off, he saw the cloud of Freon steaming from the cannon. The gas cooled the friction-induced heat of hundreds of projectiles that were streaking directly at him. He saw the flash of an explosion even as he ducked behind the cover of the wall with bullets tearing into the hillside above him. Something terrible was computing in his mind. The flash had come too early, and the sound that accompanied it came too early as well. With a sense of wonder, he realized that his round had impacted one of the gunship's projectiles in the air.

With every one of his senses, he was aware of the incoming fire approaching him and moving around him like the breath of an angry god. When their full force hit the wall behind him, it felt like fifty workmen were attacking it with jackhammers at the same time. He lay down and took cover as head-sized chunks of concrete sprang from the wall like popcorn. It began raining rocks, then a slab of concrete flaked away from the vibration and landed on him. His nose was pressed into the dirt from a weight that steadily increased as chunks and slabs melted from the wall in a dusty shower and pinned him to the earth.

The helicopter moved into a position above him, and when it poured the last of its ammo into the rock pile it felt to the soldier like a massage by a tormenting demon. The crushing weight pulsed on him ferociously until he was completely numb, unaware of sound or feeling yet still cognizant of the force above him and the idea that it was causing him harm.

For some time, his thoughts were as numb as his body. He didn't think anything. He was neither happy nor sad, neither worried nor comforted; he only lay still. He was suffering from the effects of hundreds of separate concussions inflicted upon him in the space of five seconds.

Out of his state of suspended animation an interruption arrived in the form of a vivid dream; all the more bright and surprising set as it was in the midst of his mental darkness.

The little elf reappeared. The one he had searched for in the brush of no man's land. She had reappeared and was tucking him into bed. Like a trained nurse, she fluffed a pillow and shoved it under his head. Then she pulled a sheet and blanket over him and folded the sheet a few inches back over the blanket. Finally, she tucked the linens carefully around the mattress, securing them at the ends with hospital corners. When she was finished with the bed, she sprinkled him with sparkles and bits of colored yarn. The colors and patterns seemed important to her, and when she was done, she kissed him on the cheek and vanished as quickly as she'd arrived. With her gone, the soldier felt suddenly tired, and sleep began to smother him. When it had him fully it felt glorious, as if it were meant to recover him from twenty-two years of meaningless toil.

A new dream awoke him, but he couldn't remember what it was. He was confused and couldn't feel his body. Not knowing where he was, and seeing only darkness, he thought he was lying motionless in a grave, when actually his unfeeling body was twisting and thrashing with panic at the bottom of a large pile of concrete. Dread consumed his mind at the idea that he could be dead and still aware. Superstitions of an eternity with only his thoughts fueled the movements of limbs that he didn't even know were moving.

At the first ray of light, he struggled forward. It felt to him as if he were floating, weightless, toward an unearthly glow. He reached it and broke through, with his heart exploding at the possibilities of what lay on the other side. It was dusty rocks and a shrubby hillside.

He fell on his knees and looked down at himself. His vest was torn to shreds and he was a living, breathing bruise. His rifle was clenched in his left hand. The soldier was completely deaf, and he marveled at the lack of sensation when he pushed his thumb into his left biceps, which was purple and bloody like the rest of him. His memory of the battle came to his mind as a foggy and inconsequential recollection. He removed a round from a pocket in his trousers and loaded his weapon. The sights had been torn off in his struggle with the rocks.

His initial attempts at marching met with failure. Lacking all sense of balance, he felt as if he were on the surface of a stormy ocean, and occasionally the ground would rise up and swat him. Eventually, he found a method of holding his rifle in front of him like a tightrope walker's pole and staring at the ground in front of his feet. In this way, he kept his stumbles to an acceptable minimum, and made his way across the hillside where he found the trail that turned into a gravel path. This primitive road swerved its way down the side of the hill until it flattened out into a clearing where a cargo tank was loading ammunition into the side of the gunship.

In his deafness, he couldn't hear the idling of the engine, the soft whoosh of the spinning rotor, or the rumble of the conveyor, and when he saw the scene in front of him it seemed peaceful and surreal. It was the same helicopter—he never forgot markings—but he'd assumed that he was under the rocks for days. He fell to the ground on one knee, tried his best to stabilize his swaying weapon, and yanked the trigger when it pointed at the seam between body and turret of the cargo tank. The shell penetrated the armor and detonated, blowing the rooftop hatchway into the sky and leaving an opening that poured brown smoke. He loaded his last shell while he laboriously stood up and moved closer. At a range of twenty yards, he fired the shell through the open door of the gunship. Unimpeded by armor, it slammed through the back of the cabin and went off as it crushed into the engine, ripping apart machinery and seizing the rotor shaft so quickly that the craft lurched over on its side from the sudden torque. The soldier watched in wonder as the events unfolded in silence.

Two personnel spilled from the front cockpit of the large helicopter, scrambling away from their burning ship. He felt he was in no position to take prisoners, so he drew his side arm and shot them. Three hundred yards later, he passed out on the road from exhaustion and blood loss.

•••

When the doctor removed the soldier's identification tag from the chain around his neck, he was surprised to find a wealth of information within. The square rubber sheet, laminated and folded into the tag, was ten inches by ten inches and covered on both sides with small printing. The first side was chiefly a medical history that catalogued the extensive damage inflicted on the huge body. With fascination, the doctor read the abbreviated details of an eighteen-year string of combat wounds.

The reverse side of the thin rubber sheet was entitled "Directions for Traumatic Injury." The doctor guessed that this dissertation was written by the patient because the details were specific, and the grammar atrocious. The writing described the painkillers and antibiotics that reacted most beneficially with the man's system. It directed the reader to avoid amputation, even in seemingly hopeless conditions. Finally, and most interestingly to the doctor, it outlined a complex array of dietary supplements and injections. Most of the herbs would have to be sent for, but some of the vitamins were readily available, such as the massive doses of liquid calcium.

"In case of coma," read the instructions, "administer diet for seven days, then raise body temperature to 105 degrees Fahrenheit." Ordinarily, such an array of medical advice coming from a layman would have seemed absurd. The doctor presumed, however, that if the man had lived through the list of horrors that were compiled into his medical history, then he must have a certain expertise in the matter. The frequently misspelled instructions were followed to the letter.

Seven days later, with most of the medical staff watching with curiosity, the soldier's body temperature was elevated with heating blankets until it reached the feverish level of 105 degrees. His eyes opened.

The recovery was a dark nightmare. He felt as if he were spinning slowly—but constantly—end over end. Twenty-four hours a day this sensation tormented his brain. With his eyes closed, he felt himself forever turning and if he opened his eyes, the stationary room around him wracked his mind with vertigo and intensified his nausea. The result was a feeling of perpetual seasickness worsened by the disorienting effects of his medicine. This torture was with him for days, and then he saw the elf again.

He opened his eyes when he felt something tugging at his bed sheet, but there didn't seem to be anyone there. Eventually, through his drugged haze, he saw a small hand grip the rail on his bed. With some difficulty, the small girl hauled herself up onto the bed with her skinny arms straining. There was a bandage on her wrist. She was so focused on the climb that when she saw the soldier looking at her, she let out a gasp.

He smiled, and somewhere in the back of his mind the vision he'd had beneath the rocks crept back to him. He wondered, passively, whether or not he was conscious. As May smiled broadly and gazed in wonder, the bed continued to jiggle—then it stopped as something fell to the floor; then once again the motion resumed until April poked her head over the side of the metal rails. Never having seen him before, she was truly astonished at the size of the man, and panned her head toward his toes as if she were staring out over the horizon. The soldier looked with amusement at the girl who was identical to May right down to the bandage on her wrist, except for her hair, which appeared to have been partially ripped off by an engine fan.

"Hi," said May.

"Hey," said the giant.

"Hi," said April.

"Howdy," said the giant.

"What's your name?" asked April. It had never occurred to May to ask.

"Ament," he said. "What are you doing here?" He directed the question at May. Although it could have easily been she who cut her hair, he could tell May from her sister at one glance.

May held up her bandaged wrist. "We cut ourselves," She said. "The cuts have been better for a month, but they're keeping us here because we're depressed."

At this point, April leaned over so close to the soldier that he thought she might bite his ear. "Not really!" she said in a hoarse, conspiratorial whisper.

"Are you okay?" asked May. Ament's hearing was better, but it still sounded like she was talking to him through a bad radio. He nodded affirmatively.

"Who's this?" he asked.

"April," said the other girl, with wide eyes. He smiled to himself. Naming grapes was not always a very creative process. He supposed that somewhere in the city July, August, and February were looking for food and a place to stay. The door opened. May and April scattered like field mice. In the days and weeks that followed, their absence felt to Ament like a dull pain behind his temples.

His body grew steadily stronger. It was trained and conditioned to recover from trauma, and before long he was out of his bed. His inquiries after May and April yielded nothing but shrugs. The constant movement of orphaned clones in and out of the hospital was very difficult to track, and no one really bothered.

When the soldier was well enough, he made rounds of the hospital looking for them. He saw a few of their sisters once, but not for a second did he confuse any of them with the girl who had set his leg in the forest. When he was granted outpatient status, he extended his search into town, wandering through alleyways and shelters. He performed his search in an unhurried way, as if it were of little importance to him, but the truth was that he felt almost desperate to talk to May and her sister. During his recovery, he was plagued by a disturbing and recurring sensation that he no longer wanted to be a soldier. This idea in turn caused the revelation that he had nothing else in life. He was immensely respected—actually, he was something of a legend—but he had no real friends. He'd never had the time. His family was a fragmentary and vanishing entity with no ties of any real meaning. Only the thought of May, of protecting her and providing safe harbor from the dirty storm of urban war, lit his heart with any hope or sense of future. This, too, appeared to be gone. Reluctantly, he resumed his training.

One problem with using unguided artillery in an urban setting is that if the weapon is off by even a little bit, it hits completely different target. Ament sighted in his rifle over and over, but no matter how many times he adjusted his sights, burnished the barrel, or shifted the wind correct, his shells fell wide of the practice targets. *Stationary* practice targets at no more than medium range. He fired his rifle for hours at a time over the course of many days, but his skills would not return. Some infinitesimal level of precision in his balance and coordination was gone. He disassembled his weapon, cleaned it, and set the parts carefully into a plastic case that had been under his bunk, untouched, for eighteen years. The dust on it was like a gray woolen blanket. He signed the weapon into the supply sergeant.

The depression that struck him was so intense that he first suspected it was an aftereffect of his medication. He wandered the city feeling hollow and gloomy. At night he drank in the bars, but without friends it was a joyless task. For eighteen years he'd either been in combat or in the hospital. Being a soldier had consumed his life, and now there was nothing else.

His shoulder hurt so badly that he wondered if it might be broken. In the past week he'd fired thousands of pounds of lead ammo as he waited for his aim to return. For this reason, he drank the vodka with his left hand while his right arm lay motionless on the bar. He thought about the way the girls had appeared to him in his drugged haze and he wondered if it had been real. As he daydreamed—staring with fascination at his useless arm lying on the bar—he thought about the bandages he'd seen on their wrists. He wondered if the girls were really suicidal, or if they just cut themselves to get into the hospital. It dawned on him that those bandages were right where their ID markings would have been. All at once, he understood what had happened as clearly as if he'd been there and watched them as they carved away their pasts.

• • •

May and April were starving when they saw the man with the beard. It was a hunger so acute that nothing seemed to exist but their aching bellies. The man with the beard and balding head was a face from the past. He had been the head caretaker at the orphanage and had herded the girls from one place to another and led their group exercises. When the police arrived, April had seen him get into his fancy, gray four-wheel-drive and shoot up a dirt road into the hills. Now, he was sitting in a dirty outdoor café eating the second half of a sandwich and a bowl of soup. May and April exchanged a look. April held her belly and looked at her sister with a gentle, pleading countenance. They approached him with their heads down.

The man immediately recognized the batch of girls to which the sisters belonged. He'd taken an enormous financial loss when the sixty-four girls scattered into the city.

"It's okay," he said to the waiter, by way of stopping him from ejecting the girls outside of the plastic chain that marked the edge of the dining area. "Two grilled cheeses and soda."

After that, the man said nothing and preferred to simply read as he chewed. The girls said nothing, either. The understanding of the arrangement was implicit by both parties.

They were quiet, also, as they rode on the comfortable leather seats of the man's car. Without a word, they seemed to understand that this was the quiet ending to their lifelong journey to find their parents.

The people who raised clones on farms had invented a new kind of abandonment. For an orphan, there is hope simply in the knowledge that Mom and Dad are out there somewhere. Even when reunion is an absolute impossibility, the imagined personas of one's parents could form an illuminating presence in a child's life. For May and April, even this was denied. They'd had a mother in a detached, biological way, but at no time had they ever had a mom. It was the possibility of this profound absence that always stoked the fires of their denial. The illusory journey was not to find their parents, but simply to cling to the belief that they'd ever had them.

The orphanage was in an old factory. There were broken sewing machines in the corners and giant racks of empty spools that stretched to the ceiling. A herd of little girls (two different kinds) milled about playing with toys and chasing each other. Some older girls, maybe thirteen years old, were sitting in chairs in the corner looking through magazines. May caught the expression on one of the girl's faces and realized that she knew. All the older girls knew. It was like Santa Claus; at a certain age, the facts were just too hard to ignore.

•••

Ament needed money. He'd spent it all on vodka. He remembered, almost as an afterthought, that the army must owe him back pay. The fifty dollars a week they gave him was not his full pay, it was simply a spending allowance deducted from the total salary. He had no idea what his pay actually was. The secession occurred when he was twelve. He started fighting at seventeen, and in the intervening time he'd had so little use for money that the fifty dollars a week was more than enough. He lived in army housing, ate army food, and blew his allowance buying drinks and women at an army strip club once every week or two.

They owed him $297,675. The private doing the accounting was as surprised as Ament. "Holy crap," he said, and checked his figures. Five hundred dollars a week minus $50 for the allowance and $100 for food and lodging came out to $350 a week. At fifty-two weeks a year, for eighteen years, two months and one week, that equaled $330,750. At the special-active duty flat tax of 10 percent his pay totaled $297,675. The kid shook his head. "I don't think I've ever seen a rich infantryman before. Did you want to transfer that to a private account?"

"Can I write checks through the army?"

"You bet. We'll even start giving you interest. How does 3 percent sound?"

"All right. Can I have some money now?"

"Just tell me what you need."

•••

Clone farming was illegal, but like prostitution and gambling, it was an institution that lived in an uneasy harmony with the law. The right people got money and the farms were generally tolerated except when politics or the tide of public outrage forced a brief period of intolerance. It was not difficult to find characters who worked within this community, but establishing contacts seemed like a daunting task to Ament. His years in the army included zero undercover work, and there was no aspect of his personality that didn't reek of the military. He knew, however, that none of that mattered anymore because the roll of bills in his pocket was an ally more powerful than the weapon he'd shouldered for eighteen years. If he couldn't earn the confidence of the criminal underworld, then he would buy it.

He paid his way through the dripping trash-juice of the city, buying drinks and whores for the sleaziest people he could find. The story he was developing was that he'd been ripped off by two grapes with scars on their wrists, and now that he was retired he wanted to find them. The story didn't seem plausible as it rolled off his lips, but what did that matter to the men he was dealing with?

Eight hundred dollars later he caught a break. He'd met a pimp who wore a brown leather shirt and long, braided black hair. After several nights of providing the slender man with strange and exotic things to smoke, they were chummy enough for Ament to see the back room of the club he frequented. Ament explained (as casually as possible) his predicament with the larcenous grapes and wondered out loud how to find them. The man looked around for a Russian catalogue from which one could select grapes from other countries. As the helpful pimp sat on a couch and slowly picked through a pile of magazines on his lap, a girl of seventeen entered the room with a black rubber halter-top and miniskirt. She looked cautiously at Ament, not sure how to interpret the huge man's astonished glance. Beneath her pimples and taut skin, Ament could see instantly that she was May's genetic twin, though they must have been farmed about eight years apart. One hundred more dollars bought him a name.

•••

Adam Marovan was a calm and businesslike person who made Ament very uncomfortable. He had a full beard of thick black hair and a quiet scholarly manner. In short, he seemed like what he purported to be: a caretaker of lost children. From the first glance, he seemed to see right through the soldier. From Adam's perspective, the giant man who strolled up to the gate and started waving money was so obviously lying that it was almost laughable. Mr. Marovan couldn't be sure exactly what the man was after, but guessed he might be an academy cop looking to make trouble. Alternatively, he supposed, the man might work for a rival farm.

"Sir," said Adam, "I don't know anything about the girls you're looking for. This orphanage accepts all children and, yes, some of them are clones, but I don't have any girls fitting that description."

"Let me just look around then; it won't take a minute."

"Really, I can't. I'm sorry if that's an inconvenience to you, but this is a private facility and we don't allow access to the public. Like I said, some of the children are clones, and as you probably know, there are people who take a very negative view of clones. For the safety of the children, it's our policy to prohibit access to the public."

Ament held out the fist of bills once more. "Five minutes. That's all I'm asking. I promise you it will be the most money you've ever made in five minutes." The bearded man shook his head with an apologetic face that held a hint of embarrassment at the crude spectacle the man was making of himself.

Nearly defeated, Ament decided to try a different tack. "I know this is a farm," he said weakly.

Adam Marovan wasn't shaken by the remark, and even gained a hint of surprised indignation. "Sir, I don't know what you're implying, or what sort of business you're in, but we certainly don't need any of it around here."

Ament was at a loss. He had absolutely no idea how to deal with the situation. He stood there, searching for words and not finding any. Just when he was about to walk away, the man with the beard lost some of his nerve and pressed an intercom button next to the door behind him. He called two armed guards, who stepped outside with submachine guns slung from their shoulders. One of them approached Ament and asked in a polite tone, "Sir, can we show you to the gate?"

It was like beating a shark in a game of chess and then challenging it to a swimming race. This was a situation that Ament understood. Now that violence was involved, his brain had something to work with. As the two guards moved toward him to usher him out, Ament calmly pocketed the money he'd tried to use as a bribe and then grabbed their guns—one in each hand. The movement wasn't especially fast, but it was smooth and absent-minded, and by the time the men reacted, their guns were locked in his fists. When they pulled the triggers, the levers that protruded from the action jammed against his flesh. He ripped the guns away from them like a man pulling weeds, and he crushed the weapon in his right hand against the face of one guard. Hopping into the air, he drew up his knee, and as his weight came down, he shot a thrusting kick with his heel into the ribs of the other one, launching him across the gravel into the wall of the building. He looped the straps of the guns over his shoulder and approached Adam Marovan, who was trying to punch the door code into the keypad, but seemed to have forgotten it in the excitement.

Ament grabbed him by the collar and picked him up into the air. Adam's brain whirled as he tried to decide what information he could risk telling the monstrous man. It was obvious he had to tell him something, but he couldn't afford to lose his whole operation again. It was another miscalculation by the head caretaker. Ament didn't want information; he was just looking for something to open the door with.

The crack of the metal door being torn from its hinges echoed through the factory, and when the girls looked up, they saw the bearded man's limp body skidding across the enameled concrete floor.

The instant that Ament saw the girls, it suddenly occurred to him that he had absolutely no idea what he planned to do when he found them. He stood holding his machine guns, looking out over the room of astonished and mostly identical faces. It was very quiet. Only May and April, who'd been expecting this very thing, jumped up and down. May rushed to the giant and embraced the trunk of his leg, while April poked at the bearded man with her foot. In the back of the room, personnel were scurrying down a metal staircase and fleeing out the back door. Ament made no effort to stop them, but he removed a phone from his pocket and called the police. He guessed it was the only reasonable thing to do. He hoped that it was a clone farm, or he was in serious trouble.

It took all night to sort out the mess. Nobody was dead, though Adam Marovan's spine was shattered in a number of places. Some of the farm's doctors and administrators were apprehended and some weren't. The girls were carted off to various institutions; though, of course, May and April stuck to the giant like warts. There was also a substantial media contingent. Ament hoped that the press might help some of the girls find homes. The cameramen patiently took footage of incubators and lab equipment being carted off by the police.

One reporter, a brown-haired woman in a white T-shirt and brown vest, was especially helpful to Ament. By the

end of her interview, he felt that she was explaining the
situation to him and not the other way around. To Ament,
all the events that unfolded since his broken leg were a
disjointed, irrational mess. In her skilled hands, it became
the simple story of a soldier whose life is saved by a
grape, and how he repays the favor. Ament liked this
story quite a bit. The idea that his actions were motivated
by simple gratitude was more easily understood than
the confusing and powerful paternal feelings that somehow sprang fully grown from a life that had previously
been filled only with the toilsome routine of combat.

Leslie (the reporter) urged him to pick up May and
April for a still photo after the interview. He had no idea
how to do that. After some thought, he hefted them
like two bags of groceries and tried his best to smile as
the girls clung to him in thrilled fear of their altitude.
Leslie clicked the picture that would appear on the Net
the next day, and Ament set them down feeling a bit
frightened about what he was getting himself into.

• • •

As Ament climbed the stairs, he tried to peer around
the steamer trunk he was carrying. He was always
looking at his feet, scared he might step on May or April.
He set the trunk in the corner of his bedroom and
returned to the main floor. He needed to buy more stuff.
The small private room he'd had in the barracks was
decorated sparsely, and there was little chance those
ornaments would fill a house, especially after he discarded the pictures and calendars containing depictions
of women that were inappropriate for children.

He looked out the large window at the shrubby hillside and houses below. It wasn't so different from the

terrain he'd been prowling his whole professional life. They were a safe distance from the front, but as an airplane rolled across the sky in the distance, he found himself mentally tracking and targeting it. The noise of a football game dragged him away from the view, and he pulled a beer from the fridge before joining May and April. They were sitting on the carpet, watching the TV that was also on the carpet. Leslie had helped him to pick out the large TV, which so far was the only furniture he had. She'd been very helpful during his transition, and for a single woman, she seemed able to fill Ament's head with an astonishing volume of information on how to enroll the girls in school, where to get them medical checkups, and other items of that ilk. She also helped to convince him of the wisdom in returning to the army as an instructor. His enormous supply of money didn't seem so big after some simple calculations involving house payments, school, food, clothing, etc., and he'd be eligible for a pension in three years.

Ament noticed who the girls were watching. Nathan Wood caught a ball in the gut, but it popped free as he was drilled from behind. As the kicking team trotted onto the field, he unsnapped his chin strap on the way to the sidelines.

Ament had aggressively avoided the whole topic of the girls' unusual upbringing. He dug at the carpet with his thumb.

"May," he said. "Do you know that's not your real daddy?" He began to wish he'd consulted Leslie first, as the words felt coarse in his mouth, and he braced for the worst.

"Yeah," May said smiling. "I know."

HELLO
AND GOODBYE

Written by
Michele Letica

Illustrated by
Amanda Anderson Gannon

About the Author

Michele has hunted water buffalo in South Africa, sipped a Pepsi in Red Square and celebrated Chinese New Year in Singapore. Besides her travels, her life is reasonably dull. She will undoubtedly live with lots of cats and possibly a horse when she's in her eighties. Michigan will always be home.

Doctor Samir Patel wiped condensed sweat off his palms and onto the slick fabric of his new pants as the wall before him evaporated and he stepped through. The numbness in his fingertips still lingered, though the technician had said it would only last a day. It had been two.

Inside, a curtain of sharp, misshapen colors stopped him. It was like looking through crackled safety glass.

The wall behind him reappeared and the veil of distortion dissolved. A room reminiscent of a suite at the Fairmont, his favorite hotel in San Francisco, was revealed. A queen-size bed sat on the left, a small, floral-patterned couch on the right, and behind them through an enormous window stretched a storm-blue bay dotted with islands and surrounded by rising golden hills. The only things missing were bridges and buildings.

Samir felt a pang of longing as he wished he could see the city once more—knowing that it, and everything like it, had been deconstructed long ago. The earth was whole again. He told himself he should be happy with that, but somehow he wasn't.

"Sorry to leave you standing there so long, Samir." Wilhelm, the man he'd been awakened to help, appeared in the archway behind the couch—an archway that hadn't existed moments before. A little disconcerted, Dr. Patel studied the cool gray eyes and aging, but still well muscled, body. "I was skimming over your history," Wilhelm said, as he came within an arm's length of Dr. Patel and stopped. "Green Peace. Save Humanity. Interesting as well as enlightening." His head dipped forward and back in a gentle nod.

"Not too disappointed, I hope," Dr. Patel replied, mimicking the gesture.

"Is that humility speaking, Samir," Wilhelm said, "or the psychologist attempting to gain my trust?"

"Both, possibly." Samir couldn't help but smile as he pointed to the couch. "Might we sit down, please? My body hasn't quite recovered, I'm afraid."

Wilhelm nodded, then went and sat on the end of the bed with a grunt. "The long sleep does that. From what I've seen of the few they've awakened."

Samir knew it was meant to shock and it did. The contract between the sleepers, most of humanity, and those left to regrow the earth specified the awakenings would begin once the earth was stabilized enough to support humanity again. The images Samir had seen yesterday said that had happened decades ago, if not longer. He merely assumed he was part of a later group.

"They didn't tell you," Wilhelm stated. "You are one of the few. A chosen."

The patient was merely acting out emotional stress, Samir told himself. Whatever was happening, whatever had happened, they would surely tell him once the crisis was over. For now, he had to gain control of the conversation.

"Is that why you attacked humanity?" he asked, leaning forward.

Wilhelm relaxed on the bed. "I've decided to set them free," he said.

"You have destroyed humanity's ability to reproduce," Samir said. "How does that set them free?"

"By bringing down the gods of earth and returning them to their natural state." He touched a small bracelet around his left wrist. Images Samir had already seen appeared in the window. "I'm sure they boasted. Showed you the great triumph so many were sacrificed for." The image changed to a high angled view of what looked to be a small town plucked from Samir's child-hood imaginings of life in America. The perspective swooped down to a row of twenty bungalows with large front porches, many with swings or rockers on them. A few were occupied by middle-aged people looking out onto a street where a half-dozen children rode bicycles.

"It's lovely," Samir said.

"I'm glad you approve." Wilhelm sat up on the bed. "They still allow towns on the surface . . . for the children's sake. But only in small numbers. All offices and manufacturing—what little of it is left—are under-ground. As we are now." The picture changed, showing rooms similar to the ones Samir had visited: soft-white walls with images of the outside mutating across their planes. People moved slowly about inside the rooms, obviously at work. It stopped at one with five people sitting in heavily padded chairs. All wore matching clear safety glasses. "What do you see?"

"Well . . ." Samir shrugged. Looking closer, he saw silver filigree webbing the individuals' hands. He forced a guess. "People working at computers . . . Wilhelm, why are you showing me all this? Does it matter to you what I think?" Samir hoped it did.

Wilhelm shrugged again. "I'd like someone to understand," he replied. "Especially you."

Samir smiled. "Why me?" he asked.

"You," Wilhelm said, color rising on his pale cheeks, "you herded others into a decision none could

Illustrated by Amanda Anderson Gannon

comprehend. You've brought us to this; you should see what you've done."

Samir clicked off signs of PPD (paranoid personality disorder) in his mind. Sudden anger. Use of the terms "you" and "us." The call to take down the gods. He showed significant indicators of a pervasive distrust and suspicion of others. Samir would have liked to know if there had been any suicide attempts. He would have to find that out later.

"Explain to me, Wilhelm," Samir said in a calming voice. "What is it you need me to understand?"

"What they've done!" Wilhelm shoved off the bed, took a few paces, then stopped and faced the window, breathing heavily. His finger stabbed at the image. "Look at that."

Samir blinked as he studied it. "I wish to understand, Wilhelm," he said, finally. "But you must explain your problem."

"It's not my problem," he said suddenly, hovering over Samir. "It's theirs-yours-humanity's." He turned toward the window again. "Don't you understand? You've been asleep for three hundred years, but you can still recognize the technology at a glance." He shook his head. "My actions mean nothing. Humanity is already doomed."

Their gazes locked and Samir tried to smile again.

"It can't be all that bad," he said. "The frenzied development of computers couldn't continue forever. Besides, there were other concerns. Changes in technology usually follow need. And the need was to heal the earth." Wilhelm turned away, worrying Samir. They had told him Wilhelm wasn't a physical threat. He hoped they were right. "What about the doors?" He stood and walked to where Wilhelm had entered the room. The wall looked solid till he stared at it awhile. "To me, they seem to dissolve and appear by magic." He thought he saw a faint outline, just a lightening of the area where the door should be. He stepped toward it and the wall vanished, leading him into a smaller room. He gloated a bit at this small accomplishment while looking around. The room contained a slim bed and fat dresser, all in black lacquer. On top of the dresser sat a pair of safety glasses.

As Samir wondered about the second bed, Wilhelm's voice called him back into the other room.

"As you said, technology follows need." Wilhelm was again on the large bed. The stark blue of his tight-fitting shirt clashed with the vivid gold and orange of the coverlet. His eyes were fixed on the screen once more, where great herds of kudu, cape buffalo and zebra flocked around a watering hole. "For breeding purposes," Wilhelm said, "barriers were needed to separate the various species while keeping them confined and out of restricted habitat. Conventional fencing systems were inadequate or simply too cumbersome for the job and so field barriers were eventually created. The door system you are so impressed with is a crossover."

"Could it be," Samir said, "that you are too accustomed to the technology around you? That you fail to appreciate it?"

"No," Wilhelm said.

Samir watched the animals and waited. The abundance and variety of animal life became more apparent as he studied the images. He was amazed that someone could be dissatisfied with such beauty.

Maybe selfishness had prevented more awakenings. He couldn't blame them for wanting to enjoy it alone for a while.

Wilhelm blocked Samir's view. "The barriers were created before I was born. They were one of the last significant accomplishments since the Great Sleep of 2049." Once again, he stabbed at his bracelet. Schematics and diagrams flashed across the window. They made little sense to Samir. "Look at these . . . these pathetic attempts they call change. They're barely improvements of existing devices. Many are worse than the original designs." The images switched more rapidly, corresponding with Wilhelm's increased agitation.

Samir gently pulled Wilhelm's hand away from the band and the window settled on a white-on-blue schematic.

"Wilhelm," he said, "I can't understand anything if I'm not certain of one point." He waited for a nod. "Can you really destroy the gamete storage facility?"

Wilhelm stared at a gilt-framed picture on the wall behind the bed. A tear streaked his cheek as he nodded.

•••

Samir's advisor and guide, Eunseon, met him in the hall.

"Why did you leave?" she demanded. "You couldn't have cured him that quickly."

"Obviously not," Samir said, amazed anyone could think of curing mental illness as if it were a rash. He rubbed grit from his eyes, uncertain of what to tell her. He could have told her Wilhelm had dismissed him, but didn't.

Samir stepped past a pair of guards and into the lift. They rode in silence as the sudden thud of a sleepless night weighted him down. He shook it off with a few deep breaths as they entered another hall.

Samir could sense Eunseon's anxiety, feel her need to ask questions, but ignored it. He had his own anxiety to face. Wilhelm had perceived Samir's exhaustion and used it to end the session, thereby hiding Wilhelm's own fear and insecurity.

This left Samir with the dilemma of what to tell the council and how to get their permission to continue his efforts.

If only Samir knew the importance the gamete facility held for Wilhelm. He might then decipher the motivating factors. And with that, Samir might dissuade Wilhelm from releasing the virus on the control systems.

If he were given the chance.

Eunseon stayed back as they entered the boardroom and Samir was motioned forward to stand amidst the Board's arced table. Thirteen faces stared at him, studied him just as Wilhelm had. Expectations were palpable.

Samir shook his head, and there was a round of soft gasps and disapproving grunts that prevented explanation.

"It is over then," said the Board's Chair, a woman with strong Central African features and a curt, judicial bearing that hadn't eased since Samir's brief exposure to her this morning.

"I told you all, loyalty wasn't enough," said a muscular Asian man. "We should have gotten someone better qualified. Someone less a preacher and more—"

"As I said before, Qing-Nian," the woman replied, "he had a reputation as a fine psychologist."

"A zealot with radical underpinnings was more like it!" The new voice came from a lanky woman, whose age and race could not be set, though her warm-chestnut skin spoke of a tropical region.

Feeling like a ghost at a funeral, Samir studied the tiny placards shimmering softly in front of each person: Chair of Wildlife Habitat; Administrator for Human Health and Well-Being; Dean of Geologic Survey and Reconstruction. His eyes became irritated before finishing all thirteen.

It was an odd sort of nongovernment that ran the planet. Set up temporarily to oversee deconstruction and healing till the time of the awakenings, the Board seemed to have mutated into a permanent body while the elected government had disappeared.

During breakfast, Eunseon had told him the positions could only be held for five years—to avoid a despotic-style regime.

With such a small populace, Samir thought, it couldn't help but become despotic. The universal clique to end all cliques.

This scenario, and other similar ones, had shown in the generated forecasts done by the statisticians and futurists. And preventative steps had been taken. But control was never absolute and the risks had been accepted.

Tired of the bickering, Samir spoke in the voice he'd found worked best when lecturing. Since it was a small room, he toned it down to more of a radio or television level.

"This does not mean I cannot obtain the codes or stop him from using them," he said, "merely that more time is required." He tried to waylay more skepticism. "As I attempted to explain this morning, there are no miracle therapies."

Qing-Nian, the man who'd attacked Samir's qualifications, waved a dismissive hand. "Next he'll call it an art and say we all must learn to finger-paint." He leaned forward. "Chair," he said, "I say we dismiss this mistake and move on to our alternatives immediately."

Samir worried about what those alternatives might entail. Eunseon mentioned him being a real sleeper this time. What had they sent before?

He hated himself for what he was about to say, but it appeared the only way he would get another chance at helping Wilhelm. "You might consider drug therapy," he said, "which could . . . if used properly . . . ease the patient's, Wilhelm's, anxieties and thus allow a remedy. There are a number of antianxiety drugs that I might suggest." It wasn't the most ethical suggestion. But he doubted they knew the difference between a psychologist and a psychiatrist, or they would have wakened the latter—their wishing for the most expedient solution would have called for that. Or a professional interrogator.

The idea went over well.

"Tell your advisor what is required," the Chair said, as she surveyed the others' faces. "We shall allow Samir one more day, if it is agreed."

As the others nodded, Samir took the moment to ask, "It would help greatly if I could have a profile of Wilhelm's behavior prior to this incident. Could someone tell me if he had periods of depression? Any suicide attempts? Was there violence by him or by others towards him?"

Frowning, the Chair conferred with the woman next to her before speaking. "There was one instance of violence." Nervous movement echoed throughout the room. She waited for quiet. "Some time ago, there was an outbreak of smallpox in one of the schools. Many children died, since vaccinations are limited to endemic diseases. We suspect Wilhelm was the source of the outbreak."

Samir was astounded no one had thought this information pertinent before. The Chair's posture became straight and hard.

"Is there any further information that could enlighten me to his current intentions?" Samir asked. The Chair remained still. ". . . behavior toward family, loved ones, coworkers . . . threats or further acts of violence?" She began talking with the woman next to her once more. "Does he have pets? . . . Was he abusive to them? . . . Has he ever disemboweled a cat?"

The rest of the Board began talking amongst themselves and Samir knew they were going to adjourn without helping him.

He changed direction, hoping for at least one more answer.

"One last question," he said, trying to keep them in their seats. "What if Wilhelm destroys the facility?" The discussions ceased. "Surely a populace of one hundred thousand is large enough to maintain itself through natural breeding. And if not . . ." An air of disgust and disbelief permeated the room. ". . . and if not, then you could easily increase the rate of awakenings." Disgust turned to hostility as he forced out the next words in a rush. "If you'll excuse me, what is the current rate of awakenings? An approximate number per month or year would be sufficient."

Attention in the room turned to the Chair.

"Is there truly a point to your talking with Wilhelm tomorrow, Samir?" she asked.

He tried not to look annoyed. "Yes," he said, "very much so. But . . ."

She nodded solemnly, then rose, as did the others, and the boardroom quickly emptied. Frustrated, Samir forced himself to follow Eunseon from the room, wondering who was more in need of therapy, the Board or Wilhelm.

Handing him a stylus and mylar pad, Eunseon said, "Write down the drug and required dosage and I'll check our stores for it or a reasonable equivalent. I'll specify delivery in a concealed hypodermic. All you'll have to do is get close enough to touch him. It only takes moments."

The lift took them to his sleeping quarters as Samir did what Eunseon asked, knowing he shouldn't, in good conscience, administer the drug without at least knowing Wilhelm's past medical history.

They probably wouldn't give him that information either. Governments in any form never seemed to change. Their love of secrecy was limitless.

"How is human reproduction handled?" Samir asked. Eunseon tried to ignore him, but he pressed. "If I'm to help Wilhelm, to turn his mind from destroying the gamete facility, then I have to know its significance."

Taking back the pad, Eunseon studied it in silence.

"I know that many sleepers had sperm and eggs harvested to protect them from damage during the sleep. And to be used to maintain racial diversity among the waking populace." He stepped in front of Eunseon to force her attention on him. "But there's something more, isn't there? Tell me. I promise I only want to help."

She stared down at him as he wiped sweat from his palms.

"Not merely some sleepers," she said. "All were harvested then sterilized."

Samir's jaw clenched as the implications became apparent.

Eunseon's face softened. "I guess it would be a bit of a shock," she said, "but it's done to everyone, even me.

Reproduction is strictly controlled now. Children are harvested soon after puberty, then sterilized."

Unable to speak, Samir felt the emptiness of Eunseon's absence before realizing it and the fact that he was firmly clutching his privates. He removed his hand after another check, then cursed himself for failing to ask Eunseon more questions when he had had the opportunity.

Needing information, Samir searched the walls of his cell-like room for any type of control that might activate a screen. But he found nothing. The screens must all be controlled with bracelets, the small, leathery bands that everyone seemed to wear. Auxiliary controls were probably superfluous and, of course, no one had seen fit to give him a bracelet. He searched the nightstand next to his bed, hoping to find glasses and gloves for computer access. It was empty.

He slumped down on the bed, then sprawled backward to stare at the harsh white ceiling.

Dealing with Wilhelm tomorrow loomed ahead of him, but he was unable to concentrate on how to handle it. Nor could he think of the children Wilhelm had murdered or why the Board had hidden the information.

Maybe he was afraid of the answers. Whatever the reason, Samir found himself fumbling for memories of the sterilization procedure, though there could be none. No memories. Sleepers' minds were static, frozen in darkness. There could be no memory, no dreams. For sleepers never slept.

He scratched an itching scalp and felt the numbness still in his fingertips. Shutting his eyes, he hoped his first dreams in three hundred years were pleasant.

• • •

Samir stared at the window, watching as a slip of water wound through a dry, wide riverbed filled with long grass and grazing water buffalo. The image was familiar, though it could be many places. He hoped it was India.

Wilhelm lounged on the bed—feet dangling over the edge, head resting on an outstretched arm. He wore a forest green one-piece that flowed over his hard body like the water in the image.

They had barely said more than a greeting since Samir's arrival. Both lost in thought; Wilhelm looking as miserable as Samir felt. Samir wondered if the man had slept poorly, then asked aloud.

"As well as you, it appears," Wilhelm said. "Are they pushing you hard . . . the Board?"

"They're worried," Samir said, his hand closing over the small patchlike hypodermic hidden in his palm. "I can't blame them for it. Can you?"

"No," Wilhelm shook his head softly. "I guess one can't. Though they brought it on themselves."

Samir avoided the natural accusation.

"Wilhelm . . ." Samir pulled on the sleeve of the shirt he'd slept in. "Wilhelm, why is the facility so important to you? With the current population, I estimate there to be at least fifteen thousand fertile children. Enough to keep humanity viable, though not as diverse." He looked up. "What do you hope to accomplish?"

Wilhelm rolled onto his back, rubbing the shoulder he'd been lying on. "You missed a great deal by going in early," he said, "a great deal."

Again, questions without answers.

"I wanted to show people they need not be afraid," Samir said to keep the conversation going. "Anything but first would have been hypocritical."

"How righteous of you," Wilhelm said. "You, who had no children to leave behind."

Glass temples. Samir stared at the window once more. No, he might not have children of his own, but he had more than two dozen nieces and nephews. He tried not to think of them lying in cold-storage bins waiting for their turn to live again.

Wilhelm groaned as he sat up, still rubbing the arm that had fallen asleep. "It's the Sabarmati River," he said and jutted his chin toward the window, "near Ahmadabad, I believe."

Samir stared in disbelief. Ahmadabad was an industrialized city, a wasteland like ninety percent of India. The years of blight and famine, the nuclear exchanges with Pakistan, the destructive mass of humanity that engulfed every inch of the country, had seen to that.

The last time he'd seen the Sabarmati, it was a length of mud bounded by crumbling shacks and dilapidated factories. The only bright spot he'd ever seen was when an eddy would fill with the bright colors of marigolds thrown in prayer.

The sudden joy overwhelmed Samir as he blinked back tears.

"It's everything I'd hoped." Samir walked over to the window and touched the image. Though it looked like glass, his hand passed through to the wall. "How can you hate them for doing this? It's perfect." He turned toward Wilhelm. "I left as soon as I could attend university in America . . . hoping it would be different there. Better."

He paced the room. He had wanted to be a chemist. Had wanted to develop a cost-efficient transgenic product that would stop the bacterial blights that had destroyed India's rice crops. But without the talent, he had been forced to change studies. In the next year, the 560 million tons of rice grain produced around the world per year had dwindled to a mere 180 million tons and over one-third of the world was starving. He took a deep breath to calm himself and stepped toward Wilhelm.

"I wanted to help humanity survive," he said aloud. "I used psychology and Green Peace, later television along with a lecture series. And when the world's leading intellectuals formed Save Humanity, I used my celebrity to help them reach out to the masses." He tugged on his shirt cuffs to calm himself, then met Wilhelm's steady gaze. "It worked. We actually saved the planet and humanity. Why are you working against everything now? Why are you hurting the people who accomplished all this?"

"At what cost?" Wilhelm's cold eyes forced Samir to step back. "Is it still worth it to you at a few million lives? How about ten billion?"

"What are you talking about?" Wilhelm had mentioned children. "Are you thinking of the gametes or of the children you . . . hurt?"

Wilhelm turned away. "Children . . . gametes . . ." He hunched against the wall. "I'm talking about the sleepers. The billions of people who died because the Board allowed . . . ALLOWED their cooling facilities to break down. To fall into such disrepair that the bodies rotted on their pallets." His head swung from side to side. "You worry about gametes. About the children I killed." He shoved away from the wall. "Yes, I killed them, the fertile ones." He laughed, quickly and tonelessly. "Thousands of them. It was so easily done. Just a little smallpox here, E. coli there—young children are so vulnerable these days. But what of the Board?" He nodded to the window. "I'd show you what they accomplished, but they've wiped the records. No pictures. No proof. No guilt." His stare came as an accusation. "I suppose they showed you pictures of my crimes? Corridors of dead children. Hospital beds. Funerals."

Samir stared at the picture above the bed: a picturesque scene of rolling green meadows. He wanted to step through the picture, wanted to hide himself in the lush grasses. The silence told him Wilhelm was waiting.

"I am alive," Samir said, his voice struggling to leave his throat. "If so many are dead, then why not me?" Samir closed his eyes to the sharp stab of laughter at his back.

"Your celebrity earned you a reprieve. All the great minds, the talents. All the higher-ups were eventually moved to one facility. The one kept operational."

Samir thought of Eli, his favorite niece. She had volunteered to go with him in the first wave. Only for his sister's sake had he begged her to wait. He wondered what age she had made it to before sleeping, before they had killed her.

He stopped himself from thinking. Told himself Wilhelm was lying, was manipulating him to get at the Board. Like ice cubes dropped in a water glass, Samir saw how Wilhelm had worked on him. The room similar to his favorite hotel. The pictures of his hometown. What else had Wilhelm done, used against him?

Anger rose and was swallowed as he thought of the Board. Their lack of information. Reluctance to answer questions.

Samir found himself sitting on the bed not knowing who, if anyone, to believe. Everything could be a lie, or truth. He looked around the room feeling lost. Betrayed and lost as to what to do about it.

"You think I'm a monster," Wilhelm said. "Possibly. Probably. I don't know anymore. I've been killing so long, individual lives have little meaning for me. But I still care for humanity. Believe that. You have to believe that."

Samir buried his head in his hands, nearly injecting himself with the hypodermic before remembering its existence. "I don't know if I can," he said.

There was a weight on the bed as Wilhelm sat down. Samir couldn't look at him. He kept his face hidden. His numb fingertips searching for sensation. He wondered if their saving him had been an afterthought.

"I was born about seventy years after you and the first group went under," Wilhelm said. "Did you think they would all follow you peacefully?" His voice sounded pained. "It wasn't a pretty time. Half a billion refused the sleep. Those who couldn't be taken at gunpoint were left where they died. By the time I was old enough to know what was going on, most of the wars were over. But outside the system, there were still several thousand feral humans left—small bands of individuals who hid themselves in dense forests and jungle areas. The Board had mercenaries to care for them—people like me, who thought the planet was worth a few lives."

Samir shook his head and stared at the floor. "But you can't be over two hundred years old."

"Why not?" he said. "You are."

"Only because—" Samir chewed on his lip—a habit he'd stopped as a child. "They froze you. Against your will."

"I asked, begged for it. It seemed the only way out besides suicide." He answered Samir's next question. "They thawed me during the Conception Revolt when a small group was demanding free access to their personal gametes. I was put in charge of the security force to help protect the gamete storage facility. That was over forty years ago."

"And that's why you can override the facility's systems." Samir laughed. It was more nerves than humor. "They trusted me enough to change your mind but not enough to tell me who you were." He sunk lower onto his elbows. Was he to help murderers stop a murderer? And where did he, himself, stand in the hierarchy of guilt? As Wilhelm said, Samir had led the way. "When will you release the virus?" Dumbly spoofing his own growing paranoia, he asked, "They can't hear us in here, can they?"

"No," Wilhelm said, "my rooms are completely protected. That's why they haven't killed me yet. Though they've tried." He lifted his wrist and pointed to the bracelet. "If you look closely, there's an alphanumeric keypad. I have a control code." He grinned. "As you do, they think I'm waiting to release the virus. I'm not." His grin wavered as his eyes glassed over, worrying Samir. Whatever it was passed quickly. "It's already in the system, waiting. Every day I enter a code to prevent it from dispersing."

Samir patted Wilhelm's thigh with the hypodermic, then pushed to his feet and walked away from the bed. The action was quick and nearly thoughtless.

Wilhelm kept talking.

"I'm sure they haven't broken my codes," Wilhelm said. "Or they wouldn't have sent you."

"So why not forget the code?" Samir asked, suddenly afraid of what he'd just done. "What are you waiting for?"

Toward his back, Wilhelm's voice sounded weak, unsure of itself. "I'm waiting for them to awaken the surviving sleepers." It gained strength. "To free the gametes. To allow humanity to revert to its feral nature. To allow it to survive!" The strength was gone with a grunt. "I'm waiting for them to apologize for what they've done to me," he said, "what they've put me through."

Samir finally understood. Turning to ask Wilhelm how long he would keep this up, Samir found the man clutching his arm, chest heaving silently.

"Oh, no." Samir lunged for the bed. Falling onto his knees he helped Wilhelm lie down. "What's wrong?" he asked, already guessing the truth. "You need help. Call someone. Please."

Wilhelm fumbled with the bracelet as he tried to speak and failed. His hand clamped over Samir's wrist as a wash of cooler air came into the room.

Samir turned toward the door.

"He needs a doctor," he said to Eunseon. She looked at Wilhelm but didn't move. The guards rushed past her, yanking Samir away. "He's going to die if you don't get someone here. Now!" No one moved. "If that happens, a virus will destroy the gametes. It's already in the system, waiting. Only Wilhelm can stop it."

Eunseon's fingers danced over her bracelet as she ordered the guards away, and Samir scrambled back, leaning over Wilhelm to check his pulse and breathing. Wilhelm spoke against his ear.

Forceful hands pulled Samir away and he stood by Eunseon while the medics went to work. As they tried to bring Wilhelm back to life, Samir wondered if anyone had tried saving the sleepers in their forgotten warehouses. Had they known what was happening to them? Had any reached consciousness just enough? Ancient tombs in which people had been buried alive came to mind. He wiped the horror from his mind as the medics pushed away from the couch.

Watching them collect their equipment, Eunseon asked, "What did he say?"

Samir stared at her, confused.

"What did he say?" she repeated. "He whispered something to you. I'd like to know, as I'm sure the Board will."

He plucked at his shirt cuffs, trying to hide the leather band around his wrist. A flicker of movement caught his eye, and he looked up to watch a water buffalo lift its head and gaze quietly into the distance before returning to its feeding.

No more cages, he thought as he peeled off the hypodermic and tossed it on the floor.

"Well?" she said, looking down at him.

"Goodbye," Samir told her. "He said goodbye."

T.E.A. AND KOUMISS

Written by
Steven C. Raine

Illustrated by
Andy B. Clarkson

About the Author

Steven Raine is a twenty-seven-year-old university student based in Adelaide, South Australia. He tends to write mostly hardish SF stories with astronomical or unusual backgrounds. He has had two stories published in an anthology called Tesselations, and the New Mexico–based Hadrosaur Tales will publish another soon, which will probably render him ineligible for further entries. He has also published a number of nonfiction pieces, based on his interest in astronomy. Steven has recently returned to Australia from a six-month scholarship at Okayama University Japan.

eat.

Stickiness.

The stench of an almost overflowing chamber pot. Not the nicest of introductions to the then Russian capital of Kiev in A.D. 1217. "I always thought that the medieval time was romantic," Elena said, her face wrinkled in disgust.

"Ah, the wonderful romantic Dark Ages when the majority's idea of good hygiene was to empty your sewage into your neighbor's backyard rather than your own," I commented wryly.

"What are we going to do?" Elena asked.

"Change history, assassinate someone, burn some books."

"Really, who?"

I wanted to say *Assassinate you, Elena,* but she probably would have thought I meant it literally. "A bloke called Vladimir."

"A Russian king or prince?"

"Noo." I sighed, weary at her continual state of incomprehension. "Not from Russia, from Nabotakov-Nine." Now her eyes really opened, her eyebrows virtually vanishing into her straw-colored hair, the blue irises of her eyes expanding like a puddle of that stuff people put in toilets that makes the water blue.

"Look, we're here to correct history . . . to stop the Meddlers intervening and changing it to suit their whims. Vladimir zipped back in time to change the past. With his background, our psych reckons with 90 percent probability that his goal will be to make medieval Russia supreme through guiding the Great Prince here. By giving him technical help and historical advice, the Russians may be able to take over Europe and eventually the world. If he succeeds, we may not exist at all."

"Really? Then what are we doing here? Now? I mean in the past? I mean . . . you know, existing. If we succeeded, he didn't, so we exist and he can't succeed. So what are we doing now-here?" Elena reached out to her right hand with her left, tapped her palm with her fingers, her cover-girl face reflecting her uncomprehending mind.

I was wishing I didn't have to work with her, but I knew she was invaluable. *Idiot savant.* I knew my contempt would be read by her. Telepaths are irritating that way. *Damn it all, teleps are irritating in every way.*

"Do you want me to stop thinking?"

Shit, perfect example.

"No, I'd rather you started!" I snapped back, knowing I couldn't keep my thoughts to myself. There could be no such thing now. I couldn't hide my private comments, my annoyance, my temper. Manners were as pointless as re-engineering the first Elena clone.

How did it happen this way and how the hell does it work? I wondered. *Isn't it typical that the one proven telepath ever created in the whole of history, by some freakish and still unfathomable accident, had to be, by Murphy's Law, also a genetically engineered sex kitten?*

"Don't be mad, I can't help being me," her voice small and whiny as ever. *Looking to me as a big sister.* Not only had the sex-crazed bastards who made her been content to make her a caricature of every *Playboy* centerfold, they had to make her psychologically unthreatening, compelled to adore others and look up to nearly everyone.

I hugged her as though reassuring a child. *After all, her mental age was probably somewhere in the mid-teens.* Finally, I pulled free while she continued to stare at me. "Sorry, Germaine, I'm afraid I've done lots of kinky things in my time, but time-traveling was never one of them," she said.

I couldn't help wincing.

"Who is this Murphy and his law you keep thinking of, anyway?"

I sighed yet again. "Lionel Murphy was an Australian High Court Judge who ended up going barking mad," I replied absently with an ironic smile. She was even more perplexed, surprisingly. I'd thought she couldn't get much worse. *In fairness,* I reflected, *probably no one outside of Oz has heard of him either.* "Never mind. Let's find Vladimir."

She paused, looking round the room with staring eyes and wrinkled nose. "There're hundreds of people here. How can I find . . . ?"

Arghh! The stupid bastards who designed her would have to give her what they thought—or hoped—was the typical blonde's memory, wouldn't they? "Vladimir's mind is fundamentally different. It's a twenty-ninth century mind with concepts and ideas beyond any of these lot," I said, pointing out the window. "Just scan for somebody thinking 'What the fuck have I let myself in for?' and you'll probably detect him in no time." Her eyes were already blank, her mind elsewhere—correction, even more elsewhere. I recognized teleptrance and, with an exasperated snort, stopped to examine the room.

Illustrated by Andy B. Clarkson

I checked the bodies at my feet, a thickset man with smallpox scars and soiled clothes and a semiclad; plump and gaudy woman. In the first quarter-second after materializing, our time machine had blasted the nearby surrounds with an anesthetic gas. Consequently, these rightful occupants of this room would be out for at least an hour. They lay where they'd fallen, breathing stertorously. "You don't look like you were anyone important, anyway," I addressed the prone forms wryly.

How much harm has Vladimir done already? I wondered. The anarchic space settlement of Nabotakov-Nine had always been a stronghold of Meddlers. Ever since their construction in independent solar orbit, they'd dabbled in the politics and societies of all other worlds from Freedom-Fifteen through to Earth itself. But now they had gone beyond the pale. Manufacture and usage of an interference-permissive timezipper is illegal in every statute book in the system. *This time the System Government would close them down for sure. That is, if the Sys-Gov still existed.*

"Got him!" Elena's cry of triumph interrupted my musings.

About time. *Usually a telep would click onto their target within seconds, ten at the most. Elena had taken at least a minute.* "Where? What's he doing?"

"Far away from here. Talking to a bloke called Temujin."

"Genghis Khan! He's planning to help the Mongols?"

"No. I said 'Temujin,' not whoever Kan!"

"Genghis Khan. It's a title, meaning Ruler of the Universe or something like that. Temujin became Genghis Khan."

"Oh. Because of Vladimir?" I squeezed my recorder furiously wishing it were Elena's neck. Then I took it out and studied it quickly. Next year, Genghis would turn his attention from flattening China to crushing Europe as well. If it hadn't been for Temujin's death and the in-fighting after the demise of Genghis's successor, Ogodei, they may well have succeeded in conquering all Asia—including the European peninsula. As it was, the Mongols ruled the largest land empire in history from China through to Russia, including just about everything up to Vienna.

"And they were nomadic hunter-gatherers!" I spoke aloud, annoyed now at the obviousness of it all. The Nabotakovites, like all good spacers, loved to think of the environmental consequences. If the Mongols (and their descendants, the Yuan Dynasty and Mughals) maintained their nomadic lifestyle, they would be a great improvement, ecologically speaking, over the festering cities which would create the modern world—if they succeeded. With their tent- or yurt-based cities constantly moving and their penchant for depopulation via massacre of resistant cities, they would radically improve the European ecosystem.

At quite a cost in human rights . . . I grimaced, remem-bering images of pyramids of skulls rotting where unimportant little towns like Moscow had been stamped out.

"Urgg!" Elena was in my arms, already scared half to death by this mental picture.

"It's all right." I spoke softly, trying to pry her from my imaginary security. My thoughts couldn't lie to her like my voice, though. I knew we were both expendable. The Sys-Gov had many more Elena clones, and although I was at least biologically unique, there was no shortage of espionage-cum-assassination agents back (or should that be forward?) at home.

I readied the zipper for return to the Temporal Enforcement Agency (T.E.A.) headquarters. "Come on. Let's put these two in the timezipper for hypnotic interview and post-disturbance return and get out of Kiev and into Karakorum," I instructed her, hoping to stop us both from shaking in our boots.

• • •

After dropping off the bodies and a quick debrief, we were dispatched again to the right location at hopefully the right time . . . about five hours before we'd arrived in Kiev. Vladimir should be due to arrive in about three or four hours' time according to Elena's vague mindfeel. When he came, we'd arrest him and take him back before any damage was done. Failing that, we'd terminate him as inconspicuously as possible. At least, that was the plan.

The anesthetic gas had knocked out three Mongol warriors. Karakorum smelled, if anything, worse than Kiev. Rancid butter and goat's cheese, adding to the stench of bodily wastes, combined with the thick aroma of cattle, camels and the favorite Tartar beverage, koumiss—made from fermented mare's milk.

I examined the timezipper suspiciously. Tents are notoriously obnoxious to materialize in. It's always harder when your walls can flap around in the breeze. Fortunately, we'd zipped into the center of the yurt. Unfortunately, the tent pole had been knocked askew. Our timezipper was holding the roof up—but it must have been shaken when we materialized. God only knew what would happen when we left.

"Trouble already?" Elena asked.

I had just started to nod when the tent flap burst open and I changed my noncommittal grunt to a scream. Several heavily armed men burst into the room. Their heavy arms were lasers and zappers. These soldiers all had grenades in their belts too. I'd already given a quick shriek of fright; now it was time to follow up with another screech—this time of indignation. These troops wore a very familiar, if out of place, uniform.

"What the hell are you doing?!"

"Back up! You ordered us!"

"What? No, I didn't!"

"Well, you will— Shut up!" One of the troops grabbed Elena, who was still screaming, and covered her mouth with his hand. "Ow!" he yelled, and uncovered her mouth. He stared at the bite marks in his glove; she shut up at last.

"We were ordered here urgently. Mongols and Vladimir's Nabotakovites were attacking you." I looked up to see myself walk through the door. I was covered with unpleasant red stains.

"Damn," the other me said.

"Fuck," I answered my self's dismay.

A horde of screams and a sudden volley of arrows interrupted our reunification. Our back-up fell like flies. I saw myself duck—my other self, that is. The arrows that missed her hit me. Exactly matching some of the bloodstains on her—that is, the later me.

As our surviving troops returned fire, I screamed in agony. An arrow had nicked my arm, sending out a spray of blood from the top of my shoulder. Then pain blasted through my leg, where another arrow had grazed past, missing my knee by only centimeters. I was temporarily blinded by a flash of light that left my forehead stinging.

Elena was screaming again. "Help me!"

"Don't shoot—you'll change history!" I yelled at one of our soldiers.

"Screw that!" he said, then he paused. Obeying orders, he lowered his gun, then pulled a grenade from his belt instead, preparing to throw it. Before he could do so, he collapsed with a gasp, hit by a flurry of arrows. As he dropped to the ground, the grenade flew from his fingers and rolled outside the yurt. It detonated. The result was a loud bang followed by a huge mess.

"Help me! Hel—!" Elena's cries were cut off. I glanced around to see her legs kicking furiously as they disappeared into a neighboring yurt.

"Get reinforcements now!" one of our surviving troops screamed.

I had a horrible feeling I knew what would come next.

"Wait!" There was the hiss of arrows as well as the incongruous fizzing hum of lasers. I saw the officer fall who'd ordered back-up. A zapper's blue pulse sparked out, taking him in the face. His eyes popped out of their sockets. Quite literally. I saw our back-up's timezipper shimmer out of camouflage and begin dematerializing. I thought of jumping for it and then cursed. I knew I'd never make it. The last of our re-reinforcements had been slaughtered. There was only one way out.

Dodging a spear, I threw myself against my timezipper. "Ouch!" *Would you believe it?* I'd cracked my head on the bloody thing; and as if that weren't enough, also barked my shins on the timezipper's frame. I was glad they'd made the zipper's controls so distinctive. I knew them by feel. A very useful, even essential, feature when your transport is, to all intents and purposes, invisible. The dematerialize lever had never felt so good. I slammed it down hard, content in the knowledge that the default time setting was minutes after I'd left.

As the shimmering form of a Mongol spear emerged through the super-foam window, I arrived home. Slowed by the temporal journey, the spear only fell to the floor of our zipperhangar's reception bay with a thud. It lay there pointing at me, as if disconsolate in its failure to kill. I could sympathize.

But not for long. A vaguely familiar soldier grabbed me. "Come on!"

"What . . . oh, shit, no!" I was dragged rapidly toward a very familiar timezipper. "Not again!" The Rapid Response squad stood there, ready to go.

"Wait! Jesus! Wait!"

"No time! Sergeant Menakay's just returned—he's told us enough! We need your expertise there-then. Now!"

"Hey—what's the rush? We can . . ." I saw the cozy confines of the zipperhangar shimmer out of reality. A horrifying sight, considering that our inevitable defeat might make that whole reality deactualize. ". . . always come back in time later," I finished wearily, literally knowing it was destined not to be. *Don't you just hate prophecy?*

"Go! Go! Go!" The squad vanished as I reached for their sleeves, backpacks and, finally, ankles to try and stop them. I missed, not even slowing them. *I knew it. I really did just know it. Damn Rapid Response team. If they were a bit less rapid and more responsive . . . they would still have been alive five minutes from then-now.*

I wiped my eyes and felt the blood ooze over my face. I was well and truly covered in unpleasant bloodstains, just like someone I knew better than myself.

In a daze, I stood and walked out of the yurt. Typically, it had developed a distinct and revealing lean as our back-up timezipper had emerged right in the middle, knocking skew-whiff the central supporting pole.

Now, there is something I can change, something I must do to survive this. I know . . . What is it again? I heard shouts and screams coming from the yurt next door. I walked in, my face contorted from the pain of what were luckily fairly superficial, if bloody, wounds. I entered the yurt to see myself standing frozen, with my mouth wide open and eyes bulging. I saw Elena being restrained and sinking her teeth into her captor.

". . . ordered here urgently. Mongols and Vladimir's Nabotakovites were attacking you," the leader of the RR team was saying. I stared into my own eyes. Behind me, there was a sudden scream as the Mongols prepared to attack. That sound almost overwhelmed the faint crackling of the Nabotakovite's timezippers materializing.

"Damn," I said.

"Fuck," I heard myself reply.

I threw myself to the ground, a microsecond before the volley of arrows that had already hit me last time around. *At least they wouldn't get me twice.* I rolled under my original timezipper. Elena's eyes widened as she spotted me. She raised a hand to her mouth. The soldier behind her stopped examining her teeth marks like a single-minded dentist, and started examining the arrow sticking from his breastbone. He didn't give it much more than a cursory inspection before dropping to the ground without a chance to diagnose that rather obvious medical problem.

Now I remembered exactly what I should have done. *I should have waited at the back-up timezipper and used that to return and report what was going to/had already happened. Isn't hindsight wonderful?*

Too late. The area was chock-full of Mongol warriors, Nabotakovite Meddlers with superior firepower and the rapidly dying Rapid Response team. I whispered obscenities savagely. Elena was screaming as I watched her being taken away again—or, rather, taken away that first time—from a different angle. I cursed louder, knowing that my swearing wouldn't be heard until my other self had escaped. *Escaped in this very timezipper, which I couldn't control from underneath! Shit.*

I rolled out and saw my own legs jump over me. Heard my earlier yelp of pain. I hadn't known I sounded that bad. I tried to jump up and get aboard. Then I recalled the spear and, for the first time all day, got something right. I ducked, felt it pass overhead, shimmering and crackling as it did so. I fell forward into the space where the zipper had been. I hadn't seen myself coming or going. I put my arms straight out before me and felt the heavy weight of a hairy, hot and sweaty Mongol warrior on my back. It was over and we'd hardly begun.

●●●

After capture, I'd been stripped, searched and enslaved. Elena had been taken by Genghis Khan, according to all the accounts I was hearing in Mongol— so crude it was almost unintelligible—for specific recreational purposes. I was also going to be awarded to someone as their prize. As one of the spoils of conquest, I wasn't expecting much.

I'd been placed in one of the yurts, guarded by two strong, not to mention brutally armed, Mongols. That didn't worry me. As a T.E.A. agent, my training included the harshest martial arts syllabus, studying under all the well-known masters of history and quite a few of the less well known. It was having no-when and no-where to flee that was the real cage. I'd been treated well so far, but was anticipating my captor's arrival about as much as I looked forward to my funeral. After what seemed like half the night, my new owner walked in. He was a thin man, beardless and scrawny and he should have been in my gunsights.

"Vladimir! I never thought I'd be glad to see you. No, wait, I did think I'd be glad to see you—but that was to put you under arrest."

"Under arrest or under the ground? I imagined assassination was more your policy. Still, it's nice to meet whoever you are under happier circumstances then." Vladimir looked more like an awkward teenager than a madman out to eradicate our very existence. Still, Vlad's black robe and hat, with their semialgebraic symbols, looked the part, even if he didn't.

"My name's Germaine."

"Germane to what?"

"Nothing, just Germaine." He *ahhed* and nodded, his prominent Adam's apple bobbing. I snorted with almost—but not quite—disgust.

"Where did you get your costume? Fancy-dress shop?"

He laughed, nervous but genuine. "Da. Merlin costume, only two hundred N-roubles."

"You won't get away with it."

"Why not? Temujin has never seen the shop, never been to the future. How's he to know?"

"Not the clobber, this whole thing. The future is set. If you change it, you cease to be."

"Ahh, cease to be what? The old grandfather paradox? Has it ever been tested?"

"How could it be? If it can't happen, it can't happen."

"Well, it's happening now-here."

"We'll stop you. The T.E.A. will just send more of us back before this particular mammoth stuff-up and get you before you've done any of this."

Vladimir grinned, then showed me the chronoshield. Uncovering a large black case that resembled a laptop computer, he opened it to reveal a minuscule neutrino-tachyon-converter and computer readout. It appeared to be doing exactly what Vlad told me—creating an unbreakable shell of chronon particle static around this-when. I should have known, since this was still happening without further attempts at intervention.

"Face it, Germaine, your T.E.A. spies have lost."

Vlad's face was passionate, but I no longer dreaded rape. His eyes blazed as he outlined his dream: a tolerant, multicultural khanate, stretching from the Pacific to the Atlantic, preventing European wars, protecting the environment; spreading west to the Americas and south to Australia. World government by the year 1700? A Mongol on the moon by 1600, even 1500? "I will make sure it happens, Germaine, I promise you."

I knew for sure now Vladimir wouldn't kill me. He just didn't have it in him. Make me vanish into nonexistence, yes. Murder me here-then, never. My elation was short-lived. If Vlad wouldn't kill me, almost everybody else in Karakorum could, and with sadistic pleasure at that. Everybody except one. *Elena, where are you? Please be all right; be yourself, be stupid and sexy, but please, Deity, be okay.* I thought quickly, then sucked in my breath. Thinking of Elena had given me an idea.

If I can seduce Vlad, get him vulnerable and use that to get influence over him, I might have a chance to do something. It was a plan born of desperation and lack of alternatives, but it was all I could think of.

Vlad was now on his own, cut off by the chronoshield from visitors on either side. While not as perfect as Elena with her inbuilt sauciness, I wasn't—I hoped—devoid of all the feminine charms. Anyway, Vlad surely must be desperate for a modern woman. After all, the Mongol females I'd seen had all the sex appeal of their horses. To the Mongols, our clean, regularly washed bodies were like those of goddesses. The hordes, known to those they slaughtered as the "scourge of heaven," believed the exact opposite of the "cleanliness is next to godliness" saying—and stank of it.

Before I could begin my half-hearted flirtation, I was saved by the bell, or, in this case, the gong, as a Mongol warrior banged on the Tartar equivalent of a doorbell, asking admission. With a suspicious look, Vlad left me and went to see what the soldier wanted. It turned out to be an audience with the Great Khan himself.

Escorted by more well-armed, malodorous Mongol guards, Vladimir led me to the grand central yurt, Genghis's palace. Temujin was sitting on a richly embroidered cushion in a sumptuously decorated throne. He was a squat, tough-looking figure despite his opulent silk robes. He was youthful, with a straggly fuzzy beard and the bowed legs of a man who spends more time on horseback than on foot. But what really interested me was the satiated, overly contented look in his eyes and the fact that a very exhausted, but also soppily happy, Elena sat at his right hand.

A red carpet brocaded with fine designs was unrolled for us with ceremonial pomp. Unfortunately, as it was unrolled, a rather squashed and finely dressed corpse flopped out to lie at my feet like a repugnant doll broken in a fit of temper. Obviously, the carpet had just been used by one of the Khan's loyal soldiers to stomp out the life of an enemy nobleman. It was an interesting confirmation of the old story that this customary form of execution had been practiced by the khanate to avoid spilling royal blood.

The servant unrolling the carpet paled and sank to his knees, terrified of Genghis Khan's lethal wrath. The mighty man himself merely coughed. "My apologies, I'd forgotten about that." His words were directed at Elena, whose cheeks had gone green at the sight of the crushed but clean carcass. At an imperial gesture, the body was removed, and we were ushered along to the end of the carpet to prostrate ourselves before the Khan of Khans.

"Magician Vladimir, you have aided me well and I am indeed pleased by your assistance against these other enemy sorcerers." Vladimir gave a weak smile, knowing there had to be more to this audience than just flattery. He was right, and we were both in for a big surprise.

"I shall double your prizes in exchange for her, but I shall claim that concubine of yours." I saw Elena smile broadly at me, and Vlad's face fell at this decree. Elena had been a step ahead of me and had used her influence to arrange our reunion. I privately thanked the gods for my fortune, while trying simultaneously to translate the Khan's archaic Mongolian and look as sultry and desirable as possible.

"O Great Khan, do not do this, I beseech you. She is a tricky Magus and a warrior. If you take her for yourself, you will surely be betrayed and destroyed by her."

That, I thought to myself with elation, *is not the sort of thing you tell the founder of the greatest land empire in history.*

Temujin's face reddened and Vlad cringed; I waited, tensed up with my fingers crossed. *Who will he believe?* Then the Khan settled back into his throne, his eyes sharp but the expression on his face shifting to amusement.

"You sought to trick me, didn't you, my lusty Magi?"

"Khan, believe me, I desire only to serve you . . ."

"Then serve me now by giving over this greatest of concubines." *Eh? Greatest of what?* Much as I liked compliments, I was getting a gnawing suspicion of trouble ahead.

"Khan, you cannot trust this slave; its mind and will are unbreakable. . . ." Vladimir continued his faint but unmistakable opposition. *If the Khan asked me—and, oh, how I wished he would—I'd say Vlad was asking for the nasty kind of red carpet treatment.*

"None have stronger wills than mine and I shall break all who oppose my rule." *Such tolerance—how very democratic. Just what you wanted, isn't it, Vlad?* I thought sarcastically. "I shall be magnanimous with you only so far."

Aww, I felt quite disappointed. *If the Khan would just be a little more despotic, he could save us an awful lot of trouble.*

". . . but then, my *loyal* Magi, having loved this slave girl, I can understand your reasons. She has been the best of all my lovers; yet herself confesses she is but the merest moonlit shadow of her master—and you know well who that master of desires is."

As the Khan's eyes, together with everyone else's, turned to focus on me, I realized that I had been far too hasty in my gratitude to Elena. I was now firmly back to wishing to throttle her.

"Vladimir, my splendid Magi, you shall have three other concubines in her place and a quarter of the spoils of the next city we crush; and in exchange I will have this master sorceress's body, as I have had her student's. It is my command."

There was no reply from Vladimir; none was needed. I was lifted from my prostration and hustled away.

•••

While the Khan carried on with the day's business, deciding which cities to attack, I was placed in the care of the Khan's slave master. I was taken to a yurt of my own, shared only with another concubine, whose familiar face creased in a deep frown as she teleped my murderous fantasies of revenge on the one who'd got me into this mess.

"Sorry, Germaine. It was the only way I could think of to meet you."

"You're sorry! You realize I'm going to have to outdo you in the only area where you have a natural superiority over me."

Elena's sapphire blue eyes widened along with her troublesome hole of a mouth.

"Telepathy?"

"No, your only other natural—or, rather, engineered—talent."

She paused for a good five seconds before the realization struck. "Oh. *That.*"

"Yes, *that*. You were genetically engineered for it, I'm not. Do you have any idea what he's likely to do to me once he discovers I'm not as good as you've cracked me up to be?" By the way she was clutching her head and making little gagging noises, I guessed she did—at least from what she could see in my mind.

Genghis chose that moment to enter the yurt. His eyes were burning with desire and he was already half naked. It was probably just as well, since one less than sanitary custom of the Mongols was to wear the same clothes without washing—ever. Elena's eyes stared into mine; Genghis was watching me too, with an ominous twinkle in his eye. Puzzled at the strange noises Elena had just been making, Temujin, son of Yesugei, Khan of all Khans, made a strange face at her.

Then he grabbed my arm and pulled me to his hairy chest. Now it was my turn to try and conceal my retching. The smell was unbelievable. This guy had BO on an imperial scale; a nauseating glance showed he had lice to match. Bile filled my mouth; I was just about to be sick all over a man whose pastime was razing cities to the ground and whose idea of an insult was to surrender too slowly. Elena saved us both from an unpleasant fate by throwing her arms around Temujin and pulling him away insistently.

"Wait! Oh, Temmie, my beloved, wait . . . she'll kill you."

Thanks a lot, Ellie, I thought, tensing myself in readiness for my imminent demise.

Elena kissed Temujin right on the mouth just as he was about to order my execution. I thought it was the bravest thing she'd ever done.

"Please, let me explain . . ." Elena said, as Temujin pushed her back. "Germaine is so skilled at the art of love she drives men to an ecstasy that bursts the hearts of those not experienced with it."

Genghis Khan looked puzzled and—it had to be admitted—slightly silly.

"I'll show you. Last night I only used the very lowest level of my art," Elena continued. *Careful, careful,* I thought, *this is one bloke you don't want to upset.* "You remember how good it was?"

Temujin smiled, showing yellow teeth and evidence of salivation. I felt an intense burst of pity followed by admiration. If Elena did it with him, as it seemed, she'd indeed endured the nearly unendurable. *Even if she had been designed for it and allowing for powerful aphrodisiac qualities.*

"Well, that was with my skills being used only as much as I felt you could stand. If you take Germaine straightaway, her skills are so superb that you will surely die in her arms, no matter how easy she goes on you!" Temujin cast me a wondering look. With my looks, I felt I'd been miscast. I tried to glance down demurely, without wetting myself with either laughter or terror.

Elena was whispering in Temujin's ear. "Here, I'll introduce you to the next stage. You should recover, but it may knock you out for a bit." Their faces met and I peeked out with my peripheral vision and saw Temujin's face go red. They were clasped together so tightly I seriously feared for Elena's rib cage. Their eyes shone brighter and brighter, their bodies were so hot they nearly smoked. Then Temujin's eyes rolled up in their sockets and he fell back to the carpeted floor of the yurt like a corpse. Elena breathed in, a long gasping sigh.

"Wow! Now that's what I call a knockout kiss."

"Gahh! With his breath, if it had gone on much longer I'd have been the one knocked out," Elena confessed, her well-endowed chest moving in and out like a concertina. I wondered how she'd managed earlier, then feeling faintly nauseous decided to let it rest, something they clearly hadn't managed.

"Thanks. For that effort, I could just about kiss you myself."

"Er, no, thanks all the same," Elena replied with a smile.

I looked down at Temujin's sprawled body and a horrible thought struck me.

"Is he dead? If you've changed history by killing Genghis Khan . . ." The implications didn't bear thinking about. *No Mongol hordes, no Yuan dynasty, no Mughals, thus no Taj Mahal. What would happen to Marco Polo if there were no Kublai Khan? What would happen to Coleridge's poem? To Russian and East European history?* The whole future flashed before my eyes—or was it now the past? *Was there now going to be a present?* I sunk to the soft floor of the yurt and began to hyperventilate.

Then I heard Elena's voice. "He'll live. I just telepathically stimulated his pleasure center to the point where he lost consciousness." Elena put her arm around me, helping me up.

"Come on! He'll wake up shortly."

"Shit. How shortly's shortly?"

"I don't know, I've never done this on purpose before."

"On purpose? . . ."

Elena ignored my last question and hustled me toward the door.

"Mongol guard," I reminded her, hustling her back to the center of the yurt. I gestured to climb the central pole—where the hole in the center of the yurt allowed the smoke from the fires lit inside to escape.

"No! I can't climb that, I hate heights," Elena hissed and tried to hustle me back to the door. "Look, can't we cut through the wall or something?"

"No, with our luck all we'd do is poke a guard in the bum with the sword." Elena was about to laugh or protest further, I didn't care which. I put my hand over her mouth and picked her up, swinging her in the air toward the pole. She grabbed it half a second before I fell over. I blocked her way down. Symmetrically enough, she blocked my way up. I tried to push her upward. Elena clung on with all her might. Finally, I climbed around the other side and Elena reluctantly inched after me, both eyes firmly shut.

The yurt was definitely wobbling. Reaching the top, we gazed down along the roof while somewhere below us two tough and smelly Mongol guards guarded their hopefully still-unconscious Khan. The good news was they were upwind of us. The bad news was that I could smell them.

"This way," I whispered to Elena, pointing in the downwind direction. "Copy me," I murmured, then dropped in a sort of half-aimed barrel roll. The roof sagged, but didn't quite collapse, as I rolled with a soft rustling, whirring noise along to the edge, then went over. I landed nimbly with knees bent, and had just regained my balance when Elena landed heavily on my back with a short shriek.

As I picked myself off the ground, and kept Elena silent by the most unsubtle of choke holds, I heard several voices raised in wonderment. I hoped they just thought their leader had been shaking his yurt in the throes of his passion. I feared otherwise. "Quiet—this way," I hissed, still struggling to catch my breath, as we ran to Vladimir's yurt and our only chance of returning.

As we carefully moved around the back of his yurt, two stout Mongolian guards with very un-Mongolian machine guns emerged from behind us. With the subtle ramming of the barrels into our backs, they conveyed the news that Vladimir had stayed up late and was expecting us. Grabbing our arms, they frog-marched us into Vlad's yurt.

Vladimir's scrawny body was positioned firmly on his primitive timezipper, so firmly indeed that the only thing he held more tightly was the chronoshield.

"That's a bit quick for one so well skilled at providing pleasure, isn't it? Well, maybe he'll return you to me now, even if that means I get you in piece-by-piece installments," he leered. "First, though, I want to know exactly what you've done to him. Oh, and·by the way, which kneecap would you like me to shoot out first if I don't believe you?"

"Neither. We haven't harmed him; even you can guess why not," I volunteered and Vlad nodded.

"Noninterference in history. All right. So what did you do?"

"I kissed him," answered Elena.

"Go on."

"That's really all there was." Elena pouted flirtatiously.

"You expect me to believe he let you free after a single kiss?"

"It's true!" I yelled, just as Vlad started to gesture to the guard to blow her leg off. "Honestly! You haven't seen anyone kiss the way she does."

"Oh, what's so special about it?" Vlad inquired, and Elena twisted around in her bonds to demonstrate on her guard. That particular fiercesome scourge of heaven relaxed, letting her go, then held her tightly again, becoming responsive in a way far different from Vlad's expectation.

My guard swung around to point his new toy at his mate with agonized indecision, then glanced at me briefly as if hoping for similar treatment. All he got was an excruciating kick in the balls and his gun torn from his hands. As I tried to aim my newly acquired weapon at Vlad, he slammed into me, screaming, "Guards!" We both fell to the floor, but I was first up.

Vlad grabbed the gun in one hand and the chronoshield in the other. I did the same in mirror image fashion. Then I let go of the chronoshield and dropped to one knee. With one hand, I wrenched the gun away, sent it flying out of reach. Using my other hand, I drove my fist hard into Vladimir's groin. He folded up on the floor, both hands to his family jewels, as I seized the chronoshield.

I hit its off button and leapt into his timezipper. By the time I'd entered our coordinates, Vlad had caught his breath and as I finished typing, he gripped my shoulders and yanked me backward. I was clutching the lever and pulled *dematerialize,* as we both cracked our heads on the back of the zipper. As we crackled out of view, I was aware of a familiar noise behind me. It sounded like materializing timezippers and they looked like ours.

•••

Over a thousand years later, but in the space of only half a second, Vlad's timezipper materialized in our zipperhangar. I was wrestling with Vlad and starting to lose. He was on my back, scratching my face and pulling my hair as we fought for the controls. Then I knocked the dematerialize button, and we crackled out of time-space, back to the last setting—the T.E.A. zipperhangar two seconds earlier.

As we fought, the lever was knocked again. I struggled to prevent Vlad entering new coordinates, pushing him away with my feet as he shoved and writhed toward his goal. Every time I moved, we went back in time to half a second ago. Each time, the desperate brawl continued and I suffered more under his fanatical strength.

Despite my training, I was in an awkward position, unable to get the space to deliver a telling blow and not in a suitable position to perform any effective lock or choke. Vladimir had his hands around my neck, choking me as I held the lever down and attempted to drive my elbows into his body. It wasn't working. A yellow tinge crept over my blurring vision, my head felt faint and I knew I was facing defeat. I slumped back, releasing the lever, feeling the sweat which saturated my body, sting and sizzle in my grazes.

Then, with my last reserves of energy, I twisted, corkscrewing around, and slid from Vlad's grip. For an instant, I was staring into his eyes just millimeters away, before I whipped both hands up and slammed Vladimir's head heavily backward against the back of the timezipper. There was a horrendous blare of alarms as I saw Vlad's zipper crackle into and out of existence repeatedly, each one displaced slightly by the spatial exclusion principle. In each, the pair of us, minus real time, were fighting, brawling and bumping levers to set us both back to where the whole debacle had begun.

I gasped, coughing for air to fill my pained lungs. I was lightheaded, exhausted, without any strength whatsoever. Vlad was out cold. For about five seconds. Then he opened his eyes and with a howl of rage threw himself at me and the controls behind me. I was helpless, totally spent, as Vlad made his last attack with the war cry "ARRgghh . . . !" (thump) "Ouhhhh . . . " and plunged past his intended target to crunch onto the zipperhangar floor. *Turns out, he was pretty stuffed too*, I thought, groaning in relief as T.E.A. guards sprinted over to grab Vlad and drag him away. Friendly, familiar faces surrounded me and lifted me from the zipper.

"What happened? Where-when's Elena? Where's the RR squad?" The babble surrounded me like a wet blanket. I staggered to my feet, wiped my grazed and bleeding forehead and started to walk for the door.

"Wait! Germaine, come back here!"

"I've got three weeks' paid leave owing. I'm taking every day of that, starting from now. We can go back to 1217 in three weeks' time. I've had enough of this caper for a lifetime. I deserve a holiday," I told them and shut the door. The last thing I heard was one of the staff whingeing, "Lifetime? She can't take that much off!"

●●●

In Karakorum, the day after the disappearance of the magicians, Genghis Khan assembled his finest generals. While Temujin had lain unconscious from Elena's knockout kiss, the magician foes of Vladimir had magically appeared and taken the two sorceress-concubines and the other Magi back to wherever they'd been before. Finding which land that was and getting vengeance was Temujin's new most burning goal.

Genghis Khan looked around at the faces of his war-hardened old generals, Subotei, Mukhali and Jebe; he stared at his sons: Jochi the quarrelsome, the eldest; Ogodei; Chagatai; and Tolui, the youngest. For their sake, and his, the story of his humiliation at the hands—or more accurately, the lips—of these sorceresses had to be stomped on, hidden and buried. There could be no mention of it in any of the chronicles.

Still, the idea of finding the Land of the Magi and winning such women now drove him onward with more power and drive than Temujin would ever have believed possible. He had thought long and hard about how to accomplish the task. He needed information, but how could he get it without making himself look an idiot?

"I've decided we need to invent a legend about these Magi we seek. Let's make up some tale of a girl whose kiss can wake the dead . . . or better yet, make it a prince whose embrace can wake the world's most beautiful woman, who's been dead—or in a sleeplike death—for many years. Set this among people living in a far-off land, whose skin is pure and white, whose hair is golden and whose lips are red.

"The land from whence these Magi came must lie toward the furthest West. Mukhali, I'm leaving you here to complete our victory over the Sung Empire while I lead the greatest force we've ever assembled beyond the Merv oasis and the deserts and vast open plains. We must force this land of Magi to submit." *And I must hold her in my arms again and learn to blissfully endure the next levels of her skill until I have enjoyed her finest powers,* Temujin added to himself.

Shortly afterward, the Mongol hordes set outward for the West to make history . . . again.

AN IDIOT RODE TO MAJRA

Written by
J. Simon

Illustrated by
Dwayne Harris

About the Author

Jeremy Simon was born in Madison, Wisconsin, in 1973 and has lived there ever since. He graduated from the University of Wisconsin in 1996 with a degree in mathematics and computer science and now works as a computer programmer. Mr. Simon has been a fan and author of science fiction since childhood.

About the Illustrator

*Dwayne Harris has done the illustration for
the story that follows.*

In distant Sa'bahr, divinely inspired lunatics spend their lives inscribing every story ever told upon the backs of giant tortoises. The tortoises spend their lives weeping, for they cannot read the wondrous tales written upon their own backs. Here there are stories of monsters and heroes, gods and djinn— even my own humble tale, and the tale of my people.

Serzhen alone of all the lands was created by the Devil. It is harsh, it is desert. It is a lie. There is beauty for those who seek, and comfort. We work, we play, we make good lives for ourselves. We tell our tales, and they are lies. We sing our songs, and they deceive. So it must be, for the Devil works his mischief by sprinkling small truths upon the tongues of those who think themselves wise. We must speak falsely, that he be lulled into complacence.

And there on the back of a tortoise is written the story of Serzhen, of its conquest and occupation by the Majeri, of my own conscription—and even, perhaps, of my heart's fondest desire.

So it is told, and so it must be. . . .

• • •

The full heat of the midday sun smiled down upon dusty lanes empty of nearly all Serzheni. Time for those not of addled mind to rest inside, to sup and close their eyes and hear the elders speak. The occupying Majeri, of course, were much in evidence—soldiers and officials, traders and caravansers, wives and whores. We paid them little heed and demanded none in return.

Father and Sar Efrem walked together, taking care to speak of anything but my suit for Efrem's daughter Eyla. I walked a step behind, as was proper, and did not speak. It was compliment enough that such an important man had chosen to consider my suit—nothing good could come of breaking custom. And so I walked behind, allowing my anxieties to slip from my mind, and dreamed. Of cool nights under the semsemmel trees, of falling petals and of her touch—a trysting forbidden in word, true, but Serzhen is a land of veiled meanings, is it not? And when Eyla decided that I should plead for her hand, I admit that I could find no untruth to speak. I promised, simply, that I would.

"A fine day for a walk," Efrem murmured, placing his hand on Father's arm. We slowed, waiting as a trio of Majeri soldiers approached behind the lead of a gray-faced official. The soldiers grimaced even in their light armor, feathers and lacquered plates clicking in music incongruous to such prisons; sweat poured down faces unaccustomed to the full ardor of a more impassioned sun. The lone official hid his discomfort well, though his uniform was as elaborate as theirs. I recognized him by his three white plumes as the scribe who had copied out Serzhen's contract of surrender—such as it had been, with no blood shed on either side. He came to a halt in front of us, flipping open a small book hanging on a chain from his belt.

"'Thou shalt clothe the beggar, and feed him; and see to his every need.'" He snapped the book shut, cool eyes appraising. "'Thou shalt clothe the beggar.' All residents of occupied Serzhen are to wear proper garb at all times, males included. The next time I see a bare back, I'll grant a few stripes to adorn it."

Sar Efrem placed fist to forehead, bowing slightly. "Would that we were blessed by your god," he said. "Would that Serzhen could partake of the divine grace of fair Majra, where truth flows like water from the tongues of all who speak . . ."

"Golden Majra," Father said, "whose citizens love justice and despise iniquity. Peaceful Majra, land of tall smiling men and pleasantly plump women, of docile babies and intelligent children . . ."

"Blessed Majra," Efrem agreed. "Never have there been such wise magistrates, such honorable merchants, such fetching whores . . ."

"Every swindler an honest swindler, every thug a lover of his fellow man. Every beggar an avid student of philosophy . . ."

"Celestial Majra," Efrem replied gravely, "where life itself has been answered and lays writ within a little book. Or so it is told . . ."

". . . and so it must be."

The scribe consulted a page of notes, glancing keenly at me. I placed my thumb in my ear. "Savages," he murmured, unimpressed. "You will tell me where to find Aris, the apothecary's son."

Father did not speak. Sar Efrem did not speak. I took it upon myself to break with custom, choosing my words with care.

"I fear to say that I have not seen his face in many a day—"

"That's him." The scribe's book snapped shut. He exchanged a knowing glance with the oldest of the

Illustrated by Dwayne Harris

soldiers, explaining to the one who seemed confused: "The filthy devils would rather be caught in an obvious lie than tell even the simplest truth. Winning their souls for God isn't going to be easy."

"—but I very much approve of your quest for knowledge," I concluded, "and hope the answer you seek is soon found within one of your books."

"In distant Majra," Father said to Efrem, "they have a grand machine made entirely of gold, a machine whose every gear is as large as the finest horse. It is a knowledge machine, its engines containing a thousand holy books—some written by gods, some predating the present universe, some having generated spontaneously from the Primal Everything. A thousand eyeballs made of crystal and glass and silver peer at the books, each set upon one of a thousand golden eyestalks, and perceive all that is and ever may be—"

"That will do." The scribe's tone was patient, unworried —as if dealing with a disobedient animal. He opened his little book: "'Lies pave the clearest path to the Devil's door.' 'Let him speak clearly, and mark each word.'" The book snapped shut, his eyes moving between us. "No lies. No stories. Answers, clear and correct, when asked. You are Aris?"

I placed fist to forehead and bowed slightly. The scribe nodded.

"And you know your letters, your basic figuring and numbers."

I placed my thumb in my ear, gazing levelly at him.

"As it were." He marked a check in his book, feathered plumes bobbing with the movement of his head. "You are conscripted for archival and research duties," he said, not looking up. "Report to me in the archives tomorrow morning, one hour after sunrise precisely—

garbed decently, of course. You will be paid. There will be opportunity for advancement." He glanced up. "There are many ways for a studious young man to find his way to the academies of Majra itself."

I bobbed my head in an abbreviated bow, eyes never leaving his. "Of course, I cannot protest this compulsory betterment of myself. Your pity warms my heart of hearts."

The scribe marked another check. "'Be thou humble and ever earnest.' A day's pay lost to irreverence. You will try to do better."

I said nothing, and the scribe, after completing his notes, led his grimly sweating men along their way. Father, Efrem and I resumed our walk in silence.

"The apothecary will do better without your bungling to slow me down," Father said, but softly. Efrem—the father of my Eyla—merely examined me with a speculative eye, and that was a great and many times worse.

• • •

We sat in the shade—Father, Efrem and I—sipping a light wine bought just for this occasion. A wine I'd spent two weeks laboring under Sar Daran to buy. Mother's finest outdoor hangings moved in the breeze, their stitched birds and tigers no longer so wondrous now that it was Sar Efrem they had to impress. A quiet murmur occasionally reached us from the other side of the house, where the women had gathered to commit politics and share their own stories.

Sar Efrem sipped his wine, gazing thoughtfully at a threadbare tapestry. "In distant Padresch," he said, "wondrously intelligent serpents speak all the tongues of man and forever seek to convince lovely young

women to lay with them." He leaned back, watching
Father nod his agreement. "Some women even seek such
company, and ask their fathers to arrange marriage. The
serpent clever enough to win a woman's heart must also
possess wisdom enough to avoid her father's snare—
such creatures being greatly prized by certain foreigners
who would cage and keep them. So it is told, and so it
must be."

Father's eyes didn't waver from Efrem's. "You would
not know who betrayed my son's name to the Majeri?"

The wealthy Sar drained his cup of its expensive
wine and gestured for another. Smiling. "I revile the cur
who would place such an obstacle—such a test—before
young Aris. May the betrayer feel the cold sting of
shame for what he has done."

I filled his cup. Father considered the swaying tapes-
tries, the clear sky. Minutes passed.

"In distant Marak," he said, "there once came a
mighty djinni who burned like a thousand threads of
flame made one. The djinni prized knowledge above all
else, and decreed that each morning the wisest man
remaining in the village should be brought to him, to be
branded and shackled in collar and chain." He drank,
sipping slowly so as to conserve the wine. "The greatest
merchant in all Marak, horrified by the sight of the
brand, swore before the gods themselves that his young
daughter should never marry any but a free man." The
corners of his mouth twitched upward. "Each day,
another man was marked, though his life changed little.
Each day, the daughter grew taller and more beautiful,
and found herself courted by the wisest, the kindest, the
most generous, of men—but all of them bore the djinni's
brand. By the time she came of age, alas, there was none
left for her but a small and slightly lame boar. So it is
told, and so it must be."

"As well it might," Efrem allowed, running a finger around the rim of his cup, "but in distant Azherya, where the stones themselves sing of gods long dead and heroes not yet born . . ."

I sat at their feet and listened. I heard tales of sultans and kings, of djinn and artificers, of lions and rocs. Almost, I could forget that my possible fates did battle in their words. Almost. Instead, I tried to imagine what my first day inside a windowless Majeri fortress would be like, substituting a lesser anxiety for the greater.

The sun moved, and midday passed in the swapping of tales.

• • •

The archives were dark and close, humid and stifling. I sat at the scribe's side, sweating into a stiff collar and researching answers under his supervision. The present supplicant was a young Majeri woman, her face flushed and beaded with perspiration under an elaborate bonnet. She approached, wordlessly placing a crumpled strip of paper on our desk. I recognized it—a Majeri soldier had paid his money and posed the question only two hours previously—but read it anyway: "'. . . and obedience is the wife's lot, that she should hear and respond . . .'"

"How wise the man who rules his wife by Law," I murmured, sliding the paper back toward her. "In distant Majra, or so I've heard, the holy books overrun with passages on when it is right to castrate one's husband."

The scribe glared at me, but our supplicant merely shook her head, puzzled. "No. I want something to stop his drinking. And make him give the money to me."

I closed my eyes. The dull click of coins on wood told me I had no choice but to obey.

"In distant Elegia, winged men fly over seas of . . ."

She sat in a small, hard chair, hands folded in her lap. Waiting. I sighed and got to work on her problem.

The charts were simple, leaving no room for interpretation or choice. I entered her query into the grid, converting it to a logical shorthand: "husband/wine/cease + wife/money/receive." I began to draw out the word charts, pausing as the scribe leaned over to correct a line I'd intentionally misplaced.

"You could apply yourself," he said, tapping quill against paper. "You could study in Majra itself, come back a knowledgeable and cultured man, ready to lead your people from barbarism—"

"Generous Majra," I agreed, "where each bird is given a suit made of skin, that it might return to its brethren and feel shame at their ungrounded ways. . . ."

"—you could learn the ways of knowledge, of truth—"

"I used to believe there were as many truths as men," I said piously. "But I wish to learn your truth, now, to see as you see, think as you think, know as you know. But tell me, brother, how then shall we tell ourselves apart?"

"You will be serious!" he snapped, his hand slapping down on the desk. He glared at me. "There is truth and there is falsehood. Even you can see that. Even you can understand. In Majra, you would learn what is true."

"Would that I could," I replied wistfully. "For what greater burden is there than responsibility for one's own soul?"

The scribe hesitated, uncertain whether the words were meant in mockery. I completed the final query-grid and began to search through the three vast index books that rested on our table. One would reveal the chapter and verse pertinent to the query at hand; another, the system of mathematical logic necessary to derive anything not explicitly stated; the third, whatever additional references might be required. I wrote down chapter and book, reversing two of the numerals. The scribe corrected me.

I went to retrieve the book in question. The cellar was hot and uncomfortable, ranks of mold-touched books marching patiently off into the darkness. I counted off numbers and found the one I needed. Hefting it to my shoulder, I carried it back to the querant's chamber so the scribe could watch over my shoulder as I searched.

It took only minutes to find the indicated verse— ". . . rest not while thou canst eat and drink, for never again wilst thou carouse . . ."—and unroll a strip of paper under the scribe's watchful eye. As I dipped quill in ink, however, an older man appeared at the chamber door. I recognized him as the Majeri arms master, a former soldier plagued by many an ill-healed battle wound. His questions were always profound, concerning age and sickness, purpose and pain. The scribe hastily left my side to take the old man's money, speaking earnestly to him.

It was all the opportunity I needed. My quill skated smoothly across the paper, writing—". . . in temperance doth find surcease, and profit not of thy ill habits . . ."

I gave it to the woman, who seemed pleased, but I didn't feel better for what I'd done. I sat behind the desk, sweat dripping slowly into my collar, and tried to understand.

• • •

Falling evening, the cold and deepening chill of desert night. Shadowy forms under the semsemmel trees, and Eyla there, waiting for me. She gazed up at me, petals in her hair—"I love you."

I stroked her cheek, smiling. "Is that a lie, or did the Devil place a truth upon your tongue?"

Her hand brushed against mine—fleeting, caressing. She turned her back to me and I turned mine to her. Thus could we speak freely—under cover of dark, each pretending to be alone and unheard. A deception, of course, but what less could Serzhen author?

"My father has heard that more young men might be taken to Majra," she said. I did not need to see her face: The sad clarity in her voice was picture enough. "He regrets what he has done. You may be taken."

"I would return."

Silence fell. We refused to speak the unspeakable. For me, to ask how long she would wait—a month, a season, a year? And for her, to ask whether I might return speaking Truth and holding my life as a book on a chain. The wind blew, and petals fell. Night birds crossed an ashen sky.

"A woman came to me seeking answers," I said. "And a man, her husband. They each came several times. I fell asleep that afternoon and had a dream."

Tactfully, Eyla said nothing. To my detriment and shame, I sleep soundly and do not dream. I have never had an inspirational vision, so must attempt to explore my forebodings by making up my own.

"In this dream," I said, "the wife and her husband came to me in the archives. They gave me coins and I gave them the nails they desired in some cases, nails of my own devising in others. I threw two great books on the floor and two gnarled, tortured trees sprouted up, each precisely like the other." Eyla's back moved against mine—sensual, firm, comforting. I gazed at a night sky profoundly afflicted with stars. "The woman placed her husband upon one of the twisted trees and he placed her on the other. They took up nails and began striking them into the other's flesh, forcibly binding each other to the tortured wood, forcing each other to conform to its shape. It was they who struck the blows, but the blood was on my hands."

"So it is told . . ."

". . . and so it must be."

Again there was silence. My hand found Eyla's. Waiting. Thinking.

"You are too clever. They will take you to Majra."

"I am too clever. They will not take me to Majra."

We turned to face each other. I spoke sweet lies, and she twined hungrily into my embrace.

• • •

The sun was two hours into the sky before I arrived at the archives building. It had been a long morning of travel between homes and shops, telling my tale and sharing my oblique requests. Eyla, it seemed, had succeeded in her own task: Sar Efrem met me on the steps, his voice betraying a mix of anxiety and anticipation.

"A fine day, my friend. One might almost call it uneventful."

"What else could it be?" I scanned the courtyard. To an unknowing eye, the merchants and buyers seemed no different than those of any other day. Only one familiar with Serzheni families would spot the familiar faces—Efrem's brothers and cousins, his sons and nephews. My own uncles and cousins and, of course, Father, cloaked in a trader's caftan and pretending to hawk silver. Finally, there were Eyla and all her five sisters dressed as herder's boys, standing around as if trading untoward stories—though, knowing Eyla, they probably were.

"I seem to have misplaced a large number of coins," Efrem said mournfully. "If you see any of the Majeri soldiers that I lent them to, perhaps you will think of me. Such men are susceptible to bribery, I've heard, and mustn't be trusted."

"Were I to find the cur who betrayed me to the Majeri," I said, "I might almost forgive him." Clasping hands with Efrem, I left him there on the steps and entered the archives.

The scribe looked up when I reached the query room, his eyes pale and unwavering. He started to reach for his little book, then stilled, simply staring at me. "You're late."

"In distant Saithan, a greedy lord once decided that he would rather not pay taxes on his land—" The scribe began an angry retort, but I raised my voice, speaking over him. "—so he called all his men and vassals to come with picks and shovels and take all his land away. They dug for fifty days and fifty nights until his entire estate had sunk to the bottom of a pit more than three miles deep, resting on the back of Ajhemza herself—" The scribe brandished his book, face turning red, but I shouted out the finish: "—and so, as seen by those at the bottom of that pit, the sun has not yet risen and I am perfectly on time!"

I inhaled, ready to embark on as many stories as necessary to keep the scribe occupied, but the day's first supplicant delivered me by coming through the door, eyes wide with alarm. It was the soldier's wife, no doubt fresh from the residential barracks.

"I've come to get my new answer," she said breathlessly.

The scribe frowned, glancing at me. "If you wish to pay . . ."

She shook her head mutely. "That's not what the soldiers said. The mistake in the books has been fixed, so—"

"Hello?" called the old arms master, sticking his balding head through the door. "I've come for my new answers. All of them."

The scribe hurried to comfort his best customer, leaving the soldier's wife to me. I escorted her to the desk with a cordial smile.

"Are you ready for your answer?" She nodded mutely. I made a great show of opening one of the huge index books and examining it. "Your new answer is . . . hmm . . . 'spin, spin, little fork, dancing in the salted pork.'" I wrote the nonsense phrase on a slip of paper, pressed it into her limp hand and pushed the startled woman toward the door.

Efrem's coins were earning their weight: Three more querists had already arrived, alarmed by what they'd heard and clamoring for their corrected answers. While the scribe remained occupied with the arms master, I pulled the others aside one by one and wrote out whatever replies came to mind. Six more querists came through the door, desperate to have their shaken lives set aright. The scribe rose, his face a brilliant red, and began to scream for the guards.

I scrawled a hasty answer—". . . but only if the hate desires of copious wish and fishes' sires . . ."—then stood and began my own bellowing to counter his. A small contingent of guards appeared at the door, finding themselves unable to enter for the sheer press of Majeri citizens demanding their new answers. Between the scribe's shouting and my own, it must have been nearly impossible for them to tell exactly what was happening.

The soldiers—nearly the entirety of the small contingent assigned to the normally tranquil archives building—waded hesitantly into the fray. I happily fought on the side of chaos, arguing and shouting and prodding, helping new querists press into the seething mass of bodies, alternately denying and agreeing with everything the scribe said.

A robed figure appeared at the door, gesturing broadly with one hand. I fell silent, fighting my way back to the desk so I could scrawl a note to the scribe. It took particular effort to keep it simple enough for him to understand: "All is not lost. Bargain with me and your superiors needn't learn what has happened."

Without my opposition, the roomful of confused, milling querists was gradually herded out into the hall. I merged with them, following along until I was able to split away and head down into the cellar.

A broad smile touched my lips. Efrem's family and my own had done everything I'd asked, and more. During the grand distraction in the query room, every single Majeri holy book in all Serzhen had managed, quite simply, to vanish.

• • •

The sky, painted red and orange, darkened gradually into evening. A surging tide of laughing, drinking

Serzheni surrounded the great communal cook-pots, adding whatever they had to give—meat, spices, tubers, semsemmel blossoms. The occasional Majeri soldier wandered past with suspicious eyes. Three white plumes bobbed and danced, marking the scribe's location with ridiculous clarity. I decided to sup first, and only then permit him to find me.

Eyla wasn't available, of course, since she was able to read and write, so I sought out my parents' company. To my considerable astonishment, I found them and several others of our family clustered around none other than the drunkard Majeri soldier and his harried wife.

". . . if you do have the books," she said plaintively, "just give us our answers. Please?"

"Ah," Father replied heartily, "but in distant Ezeria, small gods ride in people's pockets and demand that tribute be paid in crumbs and droplets. Those who ride in the pockets of the less faithful become small and mean, and demand greater and greater amounts of food and drink. Their bellies grow great, their tempers foul. Some leave their pockets and seek a believer, while others perform small miracles to win back their worshipers' faith . . ."

"Their *worshipers?*" Mother asked sharply. "Better to think upon distant Felendia—"

A hand closed upon my shoulder. Turning, I found myself gazing into the scribe's pale eyes.

"I could have you hung."

"A man would do well to remember that a rope has two ends," I said, smiling sardonically. "I imagine your superiors will be most interested to hear your explanation of how you lost the holy books—a forgiving empire, golden Majra. What need fear a scribe who has allowed this ultimate sacrilege to take place?" I raised a finger, holding him silent: "But I've heard it said that your books will be returned to you, every one, within three days."

He stared at me, fingering the tiny book hanging from its chain at his waist. "They'll be returned?"

"Every one. In three days, or so I've heard."

The scribe's eyes narrowed. "Tomorrow morning," he said. "And you'll go to the academies of Majra. To learn or to rot—it makes no difference to me."

"The books will be returned in two days," I said. "And I will remain in Serzhen."

"Tomorrow afternoon, and you will go to Majra." His grip tightened on my shoulder, forestalling further haggling. "It will be as I say, or I will call up the garrison—regardless of the cost to myself—and we will have blood. The books will be returned and you will go to Majra."

It was in his eyes: He would not back down. Odd how the Majeri tell their purest, most terrible truths at the times when lies would be most welcome.

I thought of Eyla, of semsemmel blossoms, of Father and his apothecary. Of Serzhen and what I would be leaving behind.

Then I thought of golden Majra, of the scribe and of a thousand men exactly like him; and though I do not dream, I saw a thousand orchards of gnarled trees each identical to the next, and a thousand bins of rusted nails waiting to be struck home.

"I have long wished to see distant Majra," I finally said, bowing low. He saw the smile on my face and hesitated.

"Tomorrow afternoon." Glaring at me one last time, the scribe turned and marched away, his triple plumes bobbing to the pulse of his step. I returned to the fire, barely noticing in my distraction that Mother was still haranguing Father and our two Majeri guests. The soldier and his wife, oddly, were speaking to each other—talking excitedly in hushed undertones—and apparently had been doing so for some time.

". . . see?" the wife murmured, gesturing excitedly. "It's a contract, and if you break your half . . ."

Shrugging, I sidled closer to get some food and listen to Mother tell her tales. Whether meant for myself or for others, her words always inspire interesting thoughts and—as often as not—lead one to make unexpected discoveries within his own mind. Tonight, I was sure, would be no exception.

• • •

The courtyard outside of the archives building was oddly hushed—Majeri soldiers to one side, Serzheni citizens to the other, and a line of citizens carrying heavy books along its center. The scribe stood atop the stairs, his three white plumes drooping slightly, staring fixedly at the oncoming volumes.

"It's too many," he murmured to himself. "That's more than were stolen!"

"As if someone had taken all your books and set a hundred men and women working night and day to transcribe copies for themselves?" I asked, smiling.

He glared at me. "Copied books are not sacrosanct. It is expressly stated—"

"And truth is not truth, regardless of the speaker?" I shook my head, letting my amusement show. "In distant Majra, so I hear, there are men called 'solicitors' who speak truth for a living. A foolish notion, surely, that men might defend themselves with words. I doubt it should ever be attempted in Serzhen."

The scribe nodded, unalarmed. "So you choose to challenge your deportation—to challenge me, rather. To face the accumulated wisdom of a man who has spent his entire life immersed in truth."

"And surely a race as barbaric as my own could never raise up anyone other than myself as solicitor," I said acidly, struggling to hide my anxiety. "I'm sure you would enjoy being buried under an unceasing tide of challenges from morning until dusk, yes? And though negotiations would be meaningless to a man of your prowess, you might wish to consider this: If you allow me to stay—"

"Seven men!" the scribe cried, clapping his hands. "Seven men for a trial . . ." He glanced at me, smirking. ". . . Majeri citizens only, by rule of Law."

I fell silent, heart sinking. Seven Majeri soldiers stepped forward, grimly confident of the decision they must reach. My own supporters placed their copied books on cloths spread over the ground, opening the volumes to random pages and studying the contents thereof. I nodded casually to the scribe, wondering whether he could see how hollow my affected confidence was.

"To begin," he stated, opening the little book at his waist, "'. . . get thee to thy source, the source of all that is good and holy.'" He closed the book, nodding significantly. ". . . to the central shrine in Majra, clearly."

Suddenly, the air shook with the shattered sound of a hundred hands turning a hundred pages, with the rasping scrape of paper against paper, paper against flesh. I left the stairs, watching friends and relatives turn page after page in desperate search. I walked amidst the storm, waiting for any sign that a counter-quote had been found. The seven soldiers idly observed the ongoing frenzy, laughing and joking amongst themselves. One stepped forth as if ready to deliver a decision.

"Wait!" I leapt forward, stabbing my finger onto an open book. The girl holding it paused, eyes widening, before having the presence of mind to shout "I'VE FOUND ONE!!!"

"Yes," I agreed, bowing my head as if to read. "'A man's home is his center, his shrine.' By all means, gentlemen," I said, startled to hear the calm conviction in my own voice. "Take me home."

The scribe reddened, cursing under his breath, and reached for his book—but then Eyla caught on and opened her own book to an appropriately random page.

"I'VE GOT SOMETHING!!!"

I strode to her side, examining a page filled with nothing but interminable and useless genealogy. "Interesting," I said. "'He who betrays the Word, be it from the tongue of serpent or man, shall never find peace in this or any life. . . .'"

The seven Majeri soldiers shifted uncomfortably, hushed conversation breaking out among them. Suddenly, it wasn't a matter of making a predetermined decision. Suddenly, they had to listen.

It was all I needed.

The scribe spoke of truth and falsehood, civility and barbarism, learning and ignorance. I answered, my improvisations always subtle enough to be credible, always weak enough not to draw undue suspicion. I kept the debate moving quickly, too quickly for the scribe to demand chapter and verse. Caught up in truth, he came forth to do battle, and I answered.

When the seven soldiers were asked to decide, five agreed that I should be allowed to stay. And so it was that Serzhen's first battle of truths was decided by lies.

• • •

Sar Efrem drank the last of Father's wine, frowning as he pondered the words he had heard. The several solicitors of Serzhen were just beginning to find their way, challenging laws and tariffs, authority and rule. The Majeri occupation, assuredly, could never be the same.

But the position, as yet, paid nothing.

Sar Efrem pondered imponderables, his wife glaring at him as if to goad him by sheer will into accepting my suit. Father and Mother waited in silence. Eyla sat at my side, her fingers nearly brushing mine. And I knew, with sudden clarity, that it was time for me to break with custom—time for me to take my place among men.

I spoke.

"In distant Ky'shar, women are given in marriage not to men but to mules," I said, "which makes for very happy mules and very sore women. The women of Ky'shar beg not to be given to the fattest and sleekest of mules, for such animals have never known harness and would balk upon hitting the first stone." Sar Efrem stared at me. Father said nothing. Mother said nothing. Eyla was as tense as drawn cord. "Rather," I said, "the discerning woman would ask to be given to a lean, strong mule who treasures her touch, for he will overcome any obstacle to please her and so bring prosperity upon their house."

I waited. Holding my breath. Unsure, suddenly, whether I'd done right. Or whether I'd lost it all.

Sar Efrem leaned forward, staring intently at me. Almost, I thought I saw him smile. He spoke:

"So it is told."

Father's breath hissed out in what might almost have been a prayer—"And so it must be."

Someone cried out, a joyous sound. Eyla's hand found mine. And the rest, I fear, has been far too happily uncomplicated to find its place upon the grand and storied tortoises of distant Sa'bahr.

LIFE ETERNAL

Written by
Bob Johnston

Illustrated by
Dwayne Harris

About the Author

Bob Johnston is thirty-seven years old,
married with three children. A native of
Glasgow, Scotland, he now lives in rural Argyll. He is an
admin. and sales clerk for a major U.K. bank. He heard about
the Writers of the Future from an ad placed in his local newspaper a couple of years ago.

She often wished on nights as perfect as this that she were still alive. But as often as she had this thought, she would catch a glimpse of him somewhere in the shadows and the despairing impermanence of her situation would chill her gut. Years before, in the early days of the deal, she had questioned whether it actually was him on the fringes of her vision. A shadow in the trees perhaps, a distant tree stump seen through twilight? Years on, though, after many sightings had led to meetings, she knew it was him. Always.

She stood at the chain-link fence, looking over the abandoned dockland area, smoking an expensive cigarette, ignoring him (off to the left and darker than the shadowed rubble he was sitting on). Her expensive car stood ticking over behind her, its headlamps casting bright light through her expensively clad legs. She sighed. In the beginning, she had been determined that the wealth which was a condition of the deal would not give him the pleasure he had hoped for. Years on, she had to admit that he had taken the measure of her to the millimeter. The despair to which she was constantly prone was usually assuaged by some bauble in the wealth that surrounded her. A hand touched her, but she had been aware of the smell of the three of them for some time. The conspiratorial whispers had carried on the gentle easterly wind a little before the smell of them had assaulted her.

Disturbing. One distinctly female, awash in a haze of alcohol, cheap perfume and unwashed menstruation. A man, cleaner, but sweating alcohol and breath like an ashtray. The third was something she had encountered before and her breath caught like fear in her throat. This was not fear, however. What have the dead to fear on this side? This was outrage.

It was the third who touched her. A light touch to terrify her out of what he took to be a deep concentration. She turned smoothly and blew his guts to mince with the expensively handmade pistol she always had expertly palmed when she left the house or the car.

She saw now that she *had* been careless. The second man was standing shadowed by the car's headlights but the woman was gone, and the smell of spent gunpowder and hot bowels gave her no chance to sniff her out. She would get to her, but first the one before her who was jabbering in a language it took her a moment to recognize as English.

She shot high to the side of the headlights, toward his voice. His headless corpse stood for a moment spraying gore from the tattered remains of its neck before crumpling heavily to the ground. Only then did it occur to her that if he had been just a centimeter smaller, the bullet which killed him would have blown out the car's windshield after its trip through his head.

The woman! She suddenly burned a little, now predatory. She holstered the pistol and swung around the open car door and . . . stopped.

What?

The woman was lying on the driver's seat. She was not hiding but dismantling the CD player. Kallie stood in disbelief, removing the pistol again before pausing as the woman continued to work on the CD with a pen-knife. Was she deaf?

Kallie palmed the pistol and silently moved back to the corpses, which she searched briefly. Both were armed. The woman clearly thought her companions had done the shooting—which left the disturbing question of what she thought they were doing now with an injured or dead lady driver.

She wasn't going to need the pistol to finish off this business. Her movements became fast, deliberate and center-of-gravity low and tight.

Her mind filled with memories of her "pack" hunting Turkish scouts through the Transylvanian Alps centuries before. One soldier had suffered a truly ghastly death after he had scouted too far into the snowbound forests that she patrolled.

"This one is for you, young scout," she whispered.

She hauled the woman out by an ankle and began to kill her with her hands.

It took a long time and she marveled for the first time in a long while over how durable the living are, how delightfully difficult to kill. She talked to the dying thief all through the wet horror of it. Talked of the outrage she could still feel at the banality of perceived evil in the world, at the trivial horrors in a world that had no conception of what horror and evil really were.

She had done this often before and knew her moments. The thief was a long way from dying but she was close to never knowing anything again. Time to finish the speaking.

"What it comes to really"—all the while tearing and pulling and scraping—"is you probably think this is horror. But where you'll be soon will make you want to come straight back to me."

Illustrated by Dwayne Harris

There could be no question of an identification when she had finished, but she paused as she stood and rubbed some liquid between thumb and finger, thinking of the recent advances in DNA research.

She returned to the corpse of her first victim and looked it over with a distaste she could not keep from her expression. This sort had always disgusted her and she flinched from that smell she could still detect through the reek of his savaged gut. Humans had scents like the woman's menstruation and the other man's sweat, but this breed smelled of something she always equated with fear and with hate. There was always a hint of sexual excitement about them mixed with this other scent. They were always trouble and they were always senselessly vicious.

She sighed. When she had been alive she had always mistakenly taken their actions as evil. Every random killing, every serial murder, every act of torture or genocide, had seemed an act of utter evil. Only now that it was too late, she knew better.

She slid into the car and pulled the door shut. The only effect her recent actions had had on her was the shocking mess she was in, and she wondered for a moment why she did these things that neither excited her nor slaked any sense of vengeance. Recently, the sheer pointlessness of everything had troubled her. For centuries, she had simply braced herself against this fact and plodded on.

He was suddenly in the passenger seat, a dark mass of handsomeness and finest aftershave. His appearance had never affected her. She had seen his true form.

"Gravenstein. Long time no speak."

"I have had nothing to say and no mischief worth making."

She reached to her inside pocket with fingers rapidly caking with dried blood and drew out her cigarette case. She offered him one, which he took, lighting it with a flicker of his deep green eyes. He did not light hers, leaving her to extract her Zippo from another pocket. He drew on the cigarette and frowned.

"If there's anything worse than American beer it's their cigarettes." He continued to smoke it though.

They drove in silence for a while before she spoke.

"You know where I'm going?"

He nodded. "Of course. Dinner with young Mr. Harrison at the Park Restaurant followed by drinks at the Fire Club and then back to your apartment for some human warmth."

She nodded. "Assuming, of course, you haven't come to take me back."

He smiled. "Now why would I do that, young Kallie? You're always so glumly ready for it all to end. What possible pleasure might I get from doing what you're always expecting?"

"And Phil?"

Gravenstein shrugged.

"Handsome, young, almost successful. Doesn't go to church as often as his mum would like, but he's not one I could drag away with any impunity. Anyway, I've seen your night out all the way through. Very nice."

She had a vague recollection of the *other side*'s strange relationship with time. It simply did not exist, and she supposed this was why Gravenstein seemed always to be about. Coming from outside of time, he could enter time wherever he pleased. Usually around her, it seemed.

"So, no torments tonight then?" she asked, uninterested one way or the other.

Kallie would either have a passionate night with Phil or she would not or Gravenstein would take her back. Regardless of his answer, she would not trust him. Contrary to many people's ideas about creatures like Gravenstein being deceptively honest, he was not. He was a foul, vindictive liar who used the truth only when it suited his attempts to confuse. The only deceptive thing about Gravenstein was this appearance he assumed. His true form was indescribably foul. Everything else was indescribably foul, but at least it was undisguised.

"None, my gem. In fact, I am here to tell you that I am going away for a time."

"Time means nothing to you, Gravenstein," Kallie said lightly. They had known one another for centuries and she knew better than to sound scornful. His rage was best avoided. She remembered fondly how in life there had always been those occasional moments when you had nothing left to lose and could just let slip your scorn. With Gravenstein (as she had painfully discovered), there was always something more to lose, no matter how low you had gone.

He shrugged and drew on his cigarette with a small grimace of distaste.

"Time means nothing in the other place. I am being sent elsewhere on this side."

"How long?"

"However long it takes."

In the distant past she had tried to "connect" with him. Tried to engage him in dialogue. His put down had been degrading and agonizing. She did not press him on details, and when she looked around he was gone, cigarette and all. She did not see him again for more than half a century.

Kallie returned to the great house she owned at the heart of the old canal docks and set about preparing for her night out. An hour later, she stood at the huge glass-less window of the main hall looking over the West End. Freshly showered, she stood with a cigarette in one hand and a glass of wine in the other. Every moment she expected Gravenstein to appear in his true form with his sick minions and whisk her back to that place. She shuddered and gulped down some wine to warm the nauseous chill that had struck her.

Against the window frame, she thought of her death. Condemned for protecting her adopted country from the relentless advance of the Turks. To this day, centuries later, it stuck in her throat that the Church had condemned her for the killing of its enemies. She could still hear the words of that half-heretic Roman bishop. He had talked of "excess" and "abomination" and had dismissed her demand to have her case passed to the Patriarch of Constantinople. And then the flames.

Gravenstein did not appear and she spent some time cleaning the car's interior before leaving on her date. She headed out from the underground car park and across the short concrete bridge spanning the square of canal that surrounded the house. She smoked constantly on the trip through the West End beyond the old wharf area and to the Park Restaurant where Phil was waiting for her in the car park.

All the way there, she had held down any sense of excitement lest Gravenstein appear, grinning like the demented bastard he was, and take her away. As Phil kissed her cheek, she relaxed for what seemed like the first time in centuries. Barring being snatched in the ladies' toilet, she was pretty safe around other people.

The night was wonderful and she sat by the great window looking out over the river and the southern quarter of the city. The wine was good and warmed her belly, making her feel strong and happy. How long could this last? she thought, and a darkness clouded her joy. Perhaps this would be her last night of happiness ever. Was this what Gravenstein wanted? She knew he would not be so deluded as to think she would relax, thinking he was gone. He had said he was going for a time. A time to Gravenstein might be five minutes. If he was on the other side, then any discussion of time was pointless. He had no sense of it or use for it. If, on the other hand, he had ever been human then it was so long ago that again time had ceased to have any meaning. Gone or not, her dilemma remained the same. Some day he would return and some day he or another would take her back.

She sipped some more wine and deliberately did not think of the other side. She would be there soon enough. Phil returned from the men's room and continued telling about where he had grown up. She had divulged little of herself and he seemed to like the sense of mystery this hinted at. Better to be mysterious than to tell him that she had been born in the back of an ox-drawn cart on the twenty-sixth of May, 1453, trundling westward from Constantinople, three days before the Turks had crushed the last stronghold of the Roman Empire into history. She did not doubt that her story would make a reasonable mini-series if she could ever be bothered to write it down. But then again, what the hell would be the point if Gravenstein were to turn up moments before she had completed some shattering ending and whisk her back?

It would be wrong to say she was not listening to Phil, but her primary thoughts were on her own predicament.

She had, though, over the centuries, acquired a knack of ingesting information without directly paying attention. At the same time, she had acquired the thoroughly useful knack of looking as if she were riveted to the spot with interest during these ingestions.

Gravenstein did not return that night, nor the following morning when she awoke and unwrapped herself from Phil to visit the toilet. She crept along the corridor, wary of every shadow and ridiculously realizing that, if he wanted, he could be anywhere he chose. She had crept along, nevertheless, afraid to be taken away before she could return and see Phil waking up. Afraid to be taken back before she had given him a final hug. God, how Gravenstein would have laughed himself sick over that one.

And so this afterlife took on a semblance of life and, as the months became years, Gravenstein made no appearances. In spite of this, she only relaxed when she forgot and this was only rarely and only for a little while after she awoke. She still thought she saw him occasionally, but it was always only a shadow.

•••

Phil stayed with her in spite of the lack of marriage, the lack of children and the strange coldness interspersed with periods of intense loving passion. As he aged, it became an obvious strain living with someone who never got older. By the time she should have been sixty years old, he could no longer delude himself that she simply knew how to use cosmetics extremely well.

Fifty-odd years after last seeing *him*, she thought she saw him again. She had gone out driving and had by chance ended up at the same dock area where she had

killed the three so long before. A complex of small
detached work units had been built in the area but the
perimeter still followed the same line as before. She stood
at the new wrought-iron gate and looked over the single-
floor units to the shipbuilding cranes in the museum
exhibit across the river. She lit a cigarette.

"Excuse me." A man's voice behind her. She turned
and looked the old man over.

"Could you lend me a cigarette?" he asked politely.

She gently sniffed the air. He was alone. She handed
her lit cigarette to him and lit herself a fresh one. The man
thanked her and turned to shuffle away, she concentrated
on his smell. Old man, clean but a little stale, urine at the
edge of the cheap aftershave. She scowled and dropped
her cigarette.

"Old man?"

He turned. "Yeah?"

"I'm a writer. Three people were killed here about
fifty years ago. Did you know any of them?"

He stepped closer to her and she could confirm that
smell. That damned smell. Weak, but there.

"A lot of people get killed about here. It's always
been a tough place."

She nodded, instinctively setting her feet a little
squarer, lowering her center of balance.

"Yes, but this was bad. The three of them looked like
they had been put through a mincer."

"Not all three," he muttered, setting himself an
arm's length from her.

"Really."

"My brother only got his belly blown out and my
cousin only lost his head," he sighed. "But my sister
suffered bad."

Kallie smiled and raised the pistol to his head. That smell of trouble was strong from him now.

"She certainly did—" Her smug monologue was cut short as he smashed the pistol from her hand and launched a foot into her groin. She hit the ground with a winded squeal and he landed on her, throwing surprisingly accurate and strong punches at her head. She could not believe it and began to lose consciousness. For centuries she had indulged her perverse sense of vengeance with absolute impunity. And yet here was some piss-stinking pensioner knocking lumps out of her.

The recollection that he was one of "them" came to her as something else happened. Just as she pulled her last grams of strength together for a counterattack, he stopped and looked up.

"Grave—" she thought she heard before her instincts took over and he was on his back having his bladder and reproductive system peeled from his body, and she was deliciously back on wet, screaming, familiar ground. As he died, she saw that this breed was different. Meaner and harder. He took a very, very long time to die and she stood soaked in him, almost exhilarated.

"Good kill," she breathed before wearily recovering the pistol and turning.

Gravenstein stood behind the gate. She wiped the blood from her eyes and he was gone. Had the old man known him and had Gravenstein distracted him? Had Gravenstein really been there?

She returned home to a shower and to Phil and by morning had forgotten the old man.

Phil died a decade later and she sat far back in the church in the guise of a distant cousin, watching the coffin being carried out by six of his employees. She did

not go to the graveside but sat listening to the music
Phil had chosen. Great soaring tunes full of beauty and
longing that finally broke down her walls, and she cried
for the first time in more than five hundred years.

"Tears, my little Kallie?" asked Gravenstein quietly,
beside her. She ignored him.

"Have you missed me?" he persisted.

"No, Gravenstein," she gulped, "how could I?
You've never been gone. Every damned day I've waited
for you, known you would be back someday."

"And here I am." He spread his arms out across
the back of the pew. She did not flinch from the one
behind her.

"Isn't there a rule about your coming into these
places?"

"No," he said lightly.

They sat silently, listening to the music, which
continued to play, until her tears subsided and she sat
feeling empty with Gravenstein's arm over her shoulder.

"So, is it time?" she finally asked.

"No, not yet. I just came to say I'm back. Thought I'd
see how Phil's death affected you."

"Like this. How does me being like this affect you?"

"Not a bit. You have always assumed that I get some
delight from your pain. Nothing could be further from
the truth. You never understood what happened to you.
For half a millennium you have hidden from the truth
of your situation. I thought Phil's death might jog something in you."

He looked straight into her eyes inquiringly. "No?"
he asked quietly.

She returned the gaze and shook her head, snuffling
childishly.

"It's true that time means nothing, but five hundred years *is* a while. I was human once and frankly you are pissing me off. Most people wake up to it eventually, but five hundred years, for heaven's sake!"

"Heaven?" she asked quietly.

He smiled.

"Now you know I don't believe in all that God and Heaven rubbish. It was just a manner of speaking."

"What of the Devil and Hell?" she asked carefully.

"I'm sure you would agree that our time together has been a whole lot more imaginative than all that sulfur and brimstone crap."

She shuddered, but found a flicker of stupid bravery.

"Who or what are you, Gravenstein?"

Her heart and guts skipped in different directions and she closed her eyes, waiting for the return to the dark and the claws and the tools. There was only silence. She opened her eyes and saw that he was walking around the small altar, examining the jeweled crucifix.

"I was human once. Like you. But so long ago that the world looked different. Different continents, different nations, different languages. Humanity really is a lot older than your foolish scientists think. I made choices while I was alive that made me what I became. So did you, little Kallie. You just don't remember. You just won't remember."

"I became nothing, Gravenstein. A thing you played with in the dark or back in the world."

He stood now with his back to the altar and looked at her, handsome and well dressed. He shook his head.

"No games, no playing, Kallie. Over half a million years I have come to understand the truth, and the bitterness of it drives me to remove the blinders from the eyes of all the dead who have followed me. I will not have you or any other deluding themselves as to the injustice of their predicaments. You made choices that brought you to me. Deserving has nothing to do with it. You walked your path through life straight to me, and since dying you have hidden in a sense of injustice to distract you from the truth—the truth you still hide from."

She looked at him blankly and he sighed, a small smile on his face.

"Phil isn't coming to me," he said carefully, and without a further word, stepped away from the altar and left the church.

That night she stood at the great glassless window sipping wine until she became at least halfway drunk. "Phil isn't coming to me." So where was Phil going? She mulled it over and over and over. Gravenstein did not believe in God or the Devil, Heaven or Hell. But then again, he was a vicious liar. So if he did believe in anything, where might Phil end up? And wherever it was, how was she to find her way to him?

She dropped her glass just as the penny dropped.

It was all irrelevant. She could only go where Gravenstein allowed. So if Phil was with him, he need only keep them apart. If Phil was in Heaven, she would never get to him. Those decisions she had made so long ago, in lands recently occupied by the Turks, now came back to haunt her and she saw the lack of deserving in it all. All through that short life in the Transylvanian Alps she had had directions open to her at every moment and she had always taken the direct route to Gravenstein's "workshop." And if there was no afterlife, then Phil was no more, while she was forced to exist forever with no hope of change or salvation or rest.

Gravenstein was behind her. A gentle, cold hand on her shoulder.

"There is no hope, Kallie. Not just for a century, nor for a million years. Forever. The universe might end, but the likes of us will just drift through the nothingness. Forever."

She turned and brushed past him to the wine bottle, which she gracelessly upended into a clean glass. She turned to him.

"Then why the workshop? All those filthy years in that place?"

He shrugged.

"You will become bitter in time. There will be other lovers for a time, but finally the hate will consume you and you'll choose your way of easing the agony it brings. Mine is to have no one under any delusions about hope. There is no hope. In the morning you will decide not to believe me again, but eventually you will."

And he was gone, leaving her to the wine cellar.

•••

Time has passed, but Kallie remains, and as Gravenstein predicted, she has become cold and vengeful. While Gravenstein corrects the delusions of the newly dead, Kallie butchers the young of the living. In the early days she sought out Gravenstein's minions, but any pleasure this brought has long since gone. It brought pain only to the minions, and there was always the suspicion that they deserved their last half-hour of horror. The children do not and the pain of their end spreads into the whole of society. She has become a poison sucking at their security and at their happiness;

but even as she claws at their little bodies, she howls in the knowledge that somewhere Gravenstein knows, and she knows what he thinks.

No matter what you do to them, little Kallie, they still have the hope which you will never ever know.

And she howls and howls as every pleasure becomes dull, and she weeps in the mess of blood and gore and wishes simply to cease.

Wishes a wish that can never become a hope.

Ever.

THE YEAR
IN THE CONTESTS

Written by
Algis Budrys

About the Author

Algis Budrys was born in Königsberg, East Prussia, on January 9, 1931. East Prussia (now the republic of Belarus) was at that time a part of Germany, but Budrys is a Lithuanian from birth, because his father, the Consul General of Lithuania, was merely stationed in East Prussia at the time. The family came to America in 1936.

Budrys became interested in science fiction at the age of six, when a landlady slipped him a copy of the New York Journal-American Sunday funnies. The paper was immediately confiscated by his parents, as being low-class trash, but it was too late. Shortly thereafter, Budrys entered PS 87 in New York. There, he was given a monthly publication called Young America, which featured stories by Carl H. Claudy, a now-forgotten juvenile science fiction author, and such serials as At the Earth's Core by Edgar Rice Burroughs. He was hopelessly lost, and by the age of nine was writing his own stories.

At the age of twenty-one, living in Great Neck, Long Island, he began selling steadily to the top magazine markets.

He sold his first novel in 1953, and eventually produced eight more novels, including Who?, Rogue Moon, Michaelmas *and* Hard Landing, *and three short-story collections. He has always done a number of things besides writing, most but not all of them related to science fiction. Notable among them was a long stretch as a critic.*

He has been, over the years, the Editor in Chief of Regency Books, Playboy Press, all the titles at Woodall's Trailer Travel *publications, and L. Ron Hubbard's Writers of the Future, where he works now. He has also been a PR man for various clients, including Peter Pan Peanut Butter, Pickle Packers International and International Trucks. His favorite client was Pickle Packers International, for which he participated in a broad variety of stunts; but his most challenging client was International Trucks, for which he crisscrossed the country for four years, from the Bridgehampton Race Track on Long Island to the sin palaces of Newport Beach.*

In 1954, he married Edna F. Duna, and is still married to her, an arrangement that suits both of them. They have four sons, now scattered over America and the world. Life is good.

lgis has worked on the Writers of the Future Contest almost since its beginning, and the Illustrators of the Future Contest as well. He considers it to be one of the most important things he has ever done. And that takes in a lot of things, including writing ten novels, of which four were Hugo and Nebula nominees, and the rest are not bad either.

The reason he considers the contests to be so important is because over the years he has seen scores of writers go from unknown novices to being such well-known names as Karen Joy Fowler, Nina Kiriki Hoffman, Dean Wesley Smith, Leonard Carpenter, David Zindell and Mary Frances Zambreno . . . and those are just from the first volume. To them can be added Robert Reed, Dave Wolverton, M. Shayne Bell, Martha Soukup, J. R. Dunn, Eric Heideman, Bruce Holland Rogers, David Ira Cleary, Pete D. Manison, Nancy Farmer, Mary A. Turzillo, Jo Beverley, R. Garcia y Robertson, Astrid Julian and literally dozens of others. There have been over two hundred winners in the writers' contest—which adds up to more than 250 novels and countless shorter works. Much the same could be said about the illustrators.

It's a major legacy for L. Ron Hubbard, and it's not done yet. Ron had a clear vision of what would happen—clearer, broader and more insightful than anyone else's—and Budrys is just happy to be an adjunct to it. That includes bringing in Dave Wolverton, who went from being a major success in the contest to becoming a judge, and then Coordinating Judge for several years before the press of Dave's increasingly many projects brought Budrys back.

So, here are the names of this year's winners and finalists in the L. Ron Hubbard Writers of the Future Contest:

First Quarter

1. J. Simon
   An Idiot Rode to Majra

2. Janet Barron
   Black Box

3. Marguerite Devers Green
   A Familiar Solution

Second Quarter

1. A. C. Bray
   The Plague

2. Everett S. Jacobs
   Time out of Mind

3. Tim Myers
   Brother Jubal in the Womb of Silence

Third Quarter

1. David Lowe
   Marketplace of Souls

2. Eric M. Witchey
   Dreams and Bones

3. Kelly David McCullough
   The Sharp End

Fourth Quarter

1. Meredith Simmons
   Magpie

2. Anna D. Allen
   Ten Gallons a Whore

3. Greg Siewert
   God Loves the Infantry

Finalists

Philip Lees
Lucretia's Nose

Steven C. Raine
T.E.A. and Koumiss

Bob Johnston
Life Eternal

Robert B. Schofield
Interrupt Vector

Tony Daley
El Presidente Munsie

Michele Letica
Hello and Goodbye

And here are this year's illustrators:

Carlo Arellano
Andy B. Clarkson
Barry Cote
Ane M. Galego
Amanda Anderson Gannon

Dwayne Harris
Andy Justiniano
Lee White
Yanko Yankov

Our congratulations to them all. May they flourish and prosper!

CONTEST RULES

1. No entry fee is required and all rights in the story remain the property of the author. All types of science fiction, fantasy and horror with fantastic elements are welcome.

2. All entries must be original works, in English. Plagiarism, which includes the use of third-party poetry, song lyrics, characters or another person's universe, without written permission, will result in disqualification. Excessive violence or sex, determined by the judges, will result in disqualification. Entries may not have been previously published in professional media.

3. To be eligible, entries must be works of prose, up to 17,000 words in length. We regret we cannot consider poetry or works intended for children.

4. The contest is open only to those who have not had professionally published a novel or short novel, or more than one novelette, or more than three short stories, in any medium. Professional publication is deemed to be payment, and at least 5,000 copies or 5,000 hits.

5. Entries must be typewritten or a computer printout in black ink on white paper, double spaced, with numbered pages. All other formats will be disqualified. Each entry must have a cover page with the title of the work, the author's name, address and telephone number, and an approximate word count. Every subsequent page must carry the title and a page number, but the author's name must be deleted to facilitate fair judging.

6. Manuscripts will be returned after judging if the author has provided return postage and a self-addressed envelope. All other manuscripts will be destroyed.

7. There shall be three cash prizes in each quarter: a First Prize of $1,000, a Second Prize of $750, and a Third Prize of $500, in U.S. dollars or the recipient's local equivalent amount. In addition, at the end of the year the four First Price winners will have their entries rejudged, and a Grand Prize winner shall be determined and will receive an additional $4,000. All winners will also receive trophies or certificates.

8. The contest has four quarters, beginning on October 1, January 1, April 1 and July 1. The year will end on September 30. To be eligible for judging in its quarter, an entry must be postmarked no later than midnight on the last day of the quarter.

9. Each entrant may submit only one manuscript per quarter. Winners are ineligible to make further entries in the contest.

10. All entries for each quarter are final. No revisions are accepted.

11. Entries will be judged by professional authors. The decisions of the judges are entirely their own, and are final.

12. Winners in each quarter will be individually notified of the results by mail.

13. This contest is void where prohibited by law.

NEW ILLUSTRATORS!

L. Ron Hubbard's

Illustrators of the Future Contest

OPEN TO NEW SCIENCE FICTION
AND FANTASY ARTISTS WORLDWIDE

No entry fee is required.
Entrants retain all publication rights.

ALL JUDGING BY
PROFESSIONAL ARTISTS ONLY

$1,500 IN PRIZES EACH QUARTER
QUARTERLY WINNERS COMPETE FOR
$4,000 ADDITIONAL ANNUAL PRIZE

Don't Delay! Send Your Entry to
L. Ron Hubbard's
Illustrators of the Future Contest
P.O. Box 3190
Los Angeles, CA 90078

CONTEST RULES

1. The contest is open to entrants from all nations. (However, entrants should provide themselves with some means for written communication in English.) All themes of science fiction and fantasy illustrations are welcome: every entry is judged on its own merits only. No entry fee is required, and all rights in the entries remain the property of the artists.

2. By submitting work to the contest, the entrant agrees to abide by all contest rules.

3. The contest is open to those who have not previously published more than three black-and-white story illustrations, or more than one process-color painting, in media distributed nationally to the general public, such as magazines or books sold at newsstands, or books sold in stores merchandising to the general public. The submitted entry shall not have been previously published in professional media as exampled above.

If you are not sure of your eligibility, write to the contest address with details, enclosing a business-size self-addressed envelope with return postage. The Contest Administration will reply with a determination.

Winners in previous quarters are not eligible to make further entries.

4. Only one entry per quarter is permitted. The entry must be original to the entrant. Plagiarism, infringement of the rights of others, or other violations of the contest rules will result in disqualification.

5. An entry shall consist of three illustrations done by the entrant in a black-and-white medium. Each must represent a theme different from the other two.

6. ENTRIES SHOULD NOT BE THE ORIGINAL DRAWINGS, but should be large black-and-white photocopies of a quality satisfactory to the entrant. Entries must be submitted unfolded and flat, in an envelope no larger than 9 inches by 12 inches.

All entries must be accompanied by a self-addressed return envelope of the appropriate size, with correct U.S. postage affixed. (Non-U.S. entrants should enclose international postal reply coupons.) If the entrant does not want the photocopies returned, the entry should be clearly marked DISPOSABLE COPIES: DO NOT RETURN.

A business-size self-addressed envelope with correct postage should be included so that judging results can be returned to the entrant.

7. To facilitate anonymous judging, each of the three photocopies must be accompanied by a removable cover sheet bearing the artist's name, address and telephone number, and an identifying title for that work. The photocopy of the work should carry the same identifying title, and the artist's signature should be deleted from the photocopy.

The Contest Administration will remove and file the cover sheets, and forward only the anonymous entry to the judges.

8. To be eligible for a quarterly judging, an entry must be postmarked no later than the last day of the quarter.

Late entries will be included in the following quarter, and the Contest Administration will so notify the entrant.

9. There will be three co-winners in each quarter. Each winner will receive an outright cash grant of U.S. $500, and a certificate of merit. Such winners also receive eligibility to compete for the annual Grand Prize of an additional outright cash grant of $4,000 together with the annual Grand Prize trophy.

10. Competition for the Grand Prize is designed to acquaint the entrant with customary practices in the field of professional illustrating. It will be conducted in the following manner:

Each winner in each quarter will be furnished a specification sheet giving details on the size and kind of black-and-white illustration work required for the Grand Prize competition. Requirements will be of the sort customarily stated by professional publishing companies.

These specifications will be furnished to the entrant by the Contest Administration, using Return Receipt Requested mail or its equivalent.

Also furnished will be a copy of a science fiction or fantasy story, to be illustrated by the entrant. This story will have been selected for that purpose by the Coordinating Judge of the contest. Thereafter, the entrant will work toward completing the assigned illustration.

In order to retain eligibility for the Grand Prize, each entrant shall, within thirty (30) days of receipt of the said story assignment, send to the contest address the entrant's black-and-white page illustration of the assigned story in accordance with the specification sheet.

The entrant's finished illustration shall be in the form of camera-ready art prepared in accordance with the specification sheet and securely packed, shipped at the entrant's own risk. The contest will exercise due care in handling all submissions as received.

The said illustration will then be judged in competition for the Grand Prize on the following basis only:

Each Grand Prize judge's personal opinion on the extent to which it makes the judge want to read the story it illustrates.

11. The contest shall contain four quarters each year, beginning on October 1 and going on to January 1, April 1 and July 1, with the year ending at midnight on September 30. Entrants in each quarter will be individually notified of the quarter's judging results by mail. The winning entrants' participation in the contest shall continue until the results of the Grand Prize judging have been announced.

Information regarding subsequent contests may be obtained by sending a self-addressed business-size envelope, with postage, to the contest address.

12. The Grand Prize winner shall be announced at the L. Ron Hubbard Awards Event to be held in the year subsequent to the year of the particular contest.

13. Entries will be judged by professional artists only. Each quarterly judging and the Grand Prize judging may have different panels of judges. The decisions of the judges are entirely their own, and are final.

14. This contest is void where prohibited by law.

Mission Earth

BY

L. RON HUBBARD

"A superbly imaginative, intricately plotted invasion of Earth."

— Chicago Tribune

An entertaining narrative told from the eyes of alien invaders, *Mission Earth* is filled with captivating suspense and action.

Heller, Royal Combat Engineer, has been sent on a desperate mission to halt the self-destruction of Earth—wholly unaware that a secret branch of his own government (the Coordinated Information Apparatus) has dispatched its own agent—whose sole purpose is to sabotage Heller at all costs, as part of its own clandestine operation.

With a cast of unpredictable characters, biting satire and interesting and imaginative plot twists, the two protagonists struggle against incredible odds in this intergalactic game where the future of Earth teeters in the balance.